THE LEAVISES ON FICTION

THE LEAVISES
ON FICTION
An Historic Partnership

P. J. M. Robertson

First published 1981 by
THE MACMILLAN PRESS LTD
London and Basingstoke
Companies and representatives
throughout the world

ISBN 0 333 27886 0

Printed in Hong Kong

For Rosalind, Lucy and Flora

It's my wife (who's very different from me—hence our lifelong collaboration is historic) who's the authority on prose fiction. She's both critic and scholar. I think that, on the novel, she has no rival in the world.

F. R. Leavis, letter to the author,
29 January 1975

Contents

Preface

People with (and even without) a serious interest in literature and the modern world do not lack for words in speaking or writing about F. R. Leavis. The man, his beliefs and judgements have been an intensely live issue for half this century, and the steady run these days of commemorative articles and books seems likely to keep them alive. So far, agreement that Leavis is worth discussion prevails over argument about what is most important in his work—his criticism of poetry, or of the novel, or of culture and society. And all commentators seem agreed merely to allude to Q. D. Leavis, though occasionally one notes and deplores, but does nothing to put right, the general neglect of her contribution.

I see the criticism of the novel as central in Leavis—growing out of his criticism of poetry and sustaining his critique of twentieth-century civilisation. I should prefer to say, 'central in the Leavises'. What the acknowledgement in *The Great Tradition* intimates, *Dickens the Novelist* confirms, and the tribute to Mrs Leavis (which I print as an epigraph) seals: the Leavises' criticism of fiction has been a partnership, with the author of *Fiction and the Reading Public* by no means the junior partner. In fact, as influence on Leavis in his work on fiction Mrs Leavis seems hardly less important than Henry James or D. H. Lawrence, though she undoubtedly learned from him, and from them, too.

Before the Leavises, good criticism of fiction had been provided largely by eminent novelists—James, Conrad, Lawrence, Woolf—though sometimes it was to be found in the pages of Victorian essayists such as Leslie Stephen (much admired by the Leavises). It had, however, a piecemeal look, the novelists not surprisingly writing to their own idea of the novel—especially James, whose late preoccupation with form seemed to license, through Lubbock's influential *The Craft of Fiction*, theorising about form as the authentic criticism of fiction. For the Leavises, aesthetic considerations necessarily involve moral ones: more than a skilled craftsman or stylist or wordsmith, the really important novelist is a transmitter of human values. Hence a theory of the novel must be grounded in evaluation, otherwise a real masterpiece remains undistinguished from artful counterfeit. Maps were needed on the novel, showing sharper contours than marked hitherto by the literary surveyor. So the Leavises set to to chart and evaluate the mainstream of the English novel, having at the same time the practical and laudable aim of providing an essential reading-list for university students and intelligent general readers, not just for initiates.

Theirs was a collaborative effort made in two phases. The first spanned the years of *Scrutiny*, 1932–53. Mrs Leavis, at first more scholar than critic, carried out the reconnaissance work in *Fiction and the Reading Public* and *Scrutiny*; Leavis, the practised critic with a well-honed analytical method from evaluating English poetry, followed with the strategic discriminations in *The Great Tradition*. In this period, the Leavises mainly agreed with T. S. Eliot in affirming writers who exhibit the 'classical' virtues of order and discipline.

With *D. H. Lawrence: Novelist* Leavis completed the first phase and began the second. He linked Lawrence with George Eliot in the puritan tradition, but also found that Lawrence's affirmation of individual creativity was a 'romantic' strength and made him a saner, braver and greater writer than T. S. Eliot, whose classicism and Anglo-Catholicism seemed now negatively establishmentarian. By finely discriminating between the strengths and weaknesses of these opposed geniuses Leavis realised himself (in the full sense of that term well used by him) as a critic and thinker independent of, and perhaps equal to, them.

From the early 1960s and sparked by interest in Lawrence's romantic strengths, the Leavises embarked on a further reassessment of the impact of the Romantic movement on English fiction, Mrs Leavis revaluing the major nineteenth-century women novelists, including Jane Austen, and Leavis revaluing Blake and Dickens. This culminated in *Dickens the Novelist*, where they combined to confirm Dickens as the supreme English novelist and Lawrence's most important precursor. In this phase the Leavises assimilate romantic virtues with classical ones, rather than esteem one set over the other: they expand rather than alter their criteria.

Leavis's essay on *Hard Times* in 1947 has a pivotal importance. For it he coined the phrase 'the novel as dramatic poem', to signify that the most important novels are best understood not as linear prose narratives of character and plot, but as dramatic prose-poems having metaphoric power and complexity of organisation akin to a Shakespeare play. The discovery crowned the Leavises' efforts to approximate criticism of the novel with criticism of poetry, and shaped all their later work. Leavis possessed the key to Lawrence's difficult masterpieces (which had baffled him earlier), Mrs Leavis became fully a critic as well as a scholar of the novel, and together they vindicated this approach in using it to judge Dickens 'the Shakespeare of the novel'.

The Leavises have kept evaluative criticism—criticism in its original sense—in the centre of the critical map, through blending the strengths of the two leading schools: the analytical precision of the formalist and the sociological depth and breadth of the historical critic. Mrs Leavis shows more of the historical critic's interest in the genesis of a literary work and more of the formalist's interest in technique than does Leavis, and as a result emerges the more complete scholar and critic of the novel. But Leavis's analysis of novels that 'affirm life' makes his criticism unique and compellingly central. *Dickens the Novelist* is the Leavises' best work on the novel, since their distinctive strengths have matured and harmonise in it.

I have tried to be objective in this study, hoping to avoid the two attitudes typically adopted towards the Leavises, modish obsequiousness and modish dissent. In doing so I hope I haven't fallen into a third type, bloodless neutrality. The method of study chosen aims at objectivity: to examine the works, mainly in chronological order, without resort to biography—in adaptation of Lawrence's dictum about trusting the tale rather than the artist. Perhaps there are losses as well as gains in this approach. Certainly, I should remark that the warm courtesy shown to me by both Dr and Mrs Leavis in the two or three letters I have received from them suggests that longer contact would have made disinterestedness very much harder.

The study was completed in substantially its present form in March 1977, when Dr Leavis was still living. I have made some revisions since, and added a reaction to Mrs Leavis's latest work, her perspective on Melville's 1853–6 phase.

Since these paragraphs were written, a number of Leavis and Leavis-related studies have been published, of varying focus and merit. In *The Moment of 'Scrutiny'* (London: New Left Books, 1979) Francis Mulhern systematically examines from a Marxist point of view the impact of *Scrutiny* on the cultural and intellectual life of

England. *The Leavises, the 'Social', and the Left* (Swansea: Brynmill, 1977) by Garry Watson conducts a tireless, if somewhat mannered, pursuit of the literary-academic Barnacles, Gowans and Stilt-stalkings of the past half century. R. P. Bilan makes a lengthy tracing of Leavis's criteria through his *oeuvre* in *The Literary Criticism of F. R. Leavis* (Cambridge: Cambridge University Press, 1979), and Edward Greenwood has usefully summarised Leavis's achievement in *F. R. Leavis* (London: Longmans, 1978) for the British Council's 'Writers and their Works' series. In his *F. R. Leavis* (London: Chatto and Windus, 1980) William Walsh makes some welcome amends for the general neglect of Mrs Leavis's achievement as a critic of fiction, granting a chapter to her in guise of 'the Principal Collaborator'. But his advocacy of her achievement falls short, as if to speak boldly for it were to subtract from Leavis. Thus Mrs Leavis's major Dickens criticism is pushed off into a chapter on Leavis, and the opportunity missed for a decisive judgement in her behalf. Evidently unaware of the irony, Walsh says that Mrs Leavis's criticism, 'perhaps under the huge wing of her husband's reputation, has not had its proper recognition' (p. 118). It needs saying and showing, boldly, that Mrs Leavis has strong wings of her own.

Of particular interest is the study by an American critic, Robert Boyers's *F. R. Leavis: Judgment and the Discipline of Thought* (Columbia, Miss.: University of Missouri Press, 1978). As well as writing perceptively on Mrs Leavis and Edith Wharton, Boyers testingly examines the kind of criticism practised by Leavis, which he calls 'judicial'. No mild follower or apologist, Boyers emerges with an independent-minded vindication of the Leavisian emphasis on language, especially in literature, as the transmitter of human and spiritual continuities and values. A welcome vindication in these days when language and literature seem to be at the mercy of the new 'scientists' of the word.

Within a few days of checking and returning the proofs of this book, came the sad news of Mrs Leavis's death, but also the glad news that she was active to the end with two articles, one for the *New Universities Quarterly* and the other for *English Studies*. From the sound of them they give fresh evidence of her major stature as scholar-critic.

Sackville, New Brunswick   P. J. M. R.
6 April 1981

Acknowledgements

I am indebted to Dr F. R. Leavis, not least for kind permission to quote from his doctoral thesis written in 1924 for the English School at the University of Cambridge. I wish to thank the Canada Council for its generous financial assistance, and also Lauriat Lane, Jr, Marjorie Chapman and others at the University of New Brunswick for wise help, Mark Spilka of Brown University, and above all my dear wife.

The author and publishers wish to thank the following who have kindly given permission for the use of copyright material:

Basil Blackwell, Publisher, Ltd, for the extracts from '*The Affirmation Is of Life*: the Later Criticism of F. R. Leavis', by Roger Poole, in the *Universities Quarterly* (winter 1974).

Cambridge University Press, for the extracts from *Scrutiny* and *A Selection from 'Scrutiny'* by F. R. Leavis.

Chatto and Windus Ltd, for the extracts from *Fiction and the Reading Public* by Q. D. Leavis; *Lectures in America* by F. R. Leavis and Q. D. Leavis; and *Poetry and Morality: Studies on the Criticism of Matthew Arnold, T. S. Eliot and F. R. Leavis* by Vincent Buckley.

Chatto and Windus Ltd and Oxford University Press, for the extracts from *Thought, Words and Creativity* by F. R. Leavis.

Chatto and Windus Ltd and Alfred A. Knopf, for the extracts from *D. H. Lawrence: Novelist* by F. R. Leavis.

Chatto and Windus Ltd and Pantheon Books (a division of Random House Inc.), for the extracts from *Dickens the Novelist* by F. R. Leavis and Q. D. Leavis.

Chatto and Windus Ltd and New York University Press, for the extracts from *The Great Tradition: George Eliot, Henry James, Joseph Conrad*, © 1952 by F. R. Leavis, and *The Common Pursuit*, © 1960 by F. R. Leavis.

Grosset and Dunlap Inc., for the extracts from *Writer and Critic* by Georg Lukács.

Lawrence and Wishart Ltd, for the extracts from *Towards Standards of Criticism* by F. R. Leavis.

Macdonald and Jane's Publishers Ltd, for the extracts from the introductions by Q. D. Leavis to *Sense and Sensibility* and *Mansfield Park* by Jane Austen.

Prentice-Hall Inc., for the extracts from *D. H. Lawrence: A Collection of Critical Essays* by Mark Spilka.

The University of Louisville, Kentucky, for the extracts from 'The Dickens Forum', by R. Giddings, in *Dickens Newsletter* (June 1975).

Every effort has been made to trace all the copyright-holders, but if any have been inadvertently overlooked the publishers will be pleased to make the necessary arrangement at the first opportunity.

Note on the Texts and Notes

Though the editions of the Leavis texts used in this book are fully documented in the Bibliography, it may be helpful to note at the outset that their publisher is in every case Chatto and Windus Ltd, London, with the exception of

New Bearings in English Poetry (1932; Harmondsworth: Penguin, 1963)
For Continuity (Cambridge: Minority Press, 1933)
Revaluation (1936; Harmondsworth: Penguin, 1964)
The Great Tradition (1948; Harmondsworth: Penguin, 1962)
The Common Pursuit (1952; Harmondsworth: Penguin, 1962)
D. H. Lawrence: Novelist (1955; Harmondsworth: Penguin, 1964)

Parenthetic page references are appended to quotations wherever possible and consistent with clarity.

In the notes, book publication details are limited to the date of publication of the edition actually cited, and the place of publication, where not London. For fuller details, see the Select Bibliography.

1 Introduction: the Leavises and Criticism of the Novel

In 1924 F. R. Leavis completed one of the earliest doctoral dissertations for the English School at Cambridge. Entitled 'The Relationship of Journalism to Literature: Studied in the Rise and Earlier
Development of the Press in England', it deals in effect with the
rise of modern prose and includes long sections on Addison, Defoe
and Swift, as well as notes on Fielding, Sterne and others. Between
1927 and 1931 Leavis published a number of brief review articles
chiefly for the *Cambridge Review*, and in 1930 two long essays: *Mass
Civilization and Minority Culture* and his first critique of D. H.
Lawrence. In 1929 he married Q. D. Leavis, who was then at work
on her own dissertation at Cambridge, which she published in 1932
as *Fiction and the Reading Public*. The dissertations of husband and
wife dovetail at many points: for instance, both contain chapters on
the growth of a reading public and both are concerned overall with
the development of English prose. The year 1932 also saw the birth
of *Scrutiny*, the influential critical quarterly of which the Leavises
were the mainstays till it ceased publication in 1953. So began a
literary partnership which lasted till Leavis died in 1978 and which
produced some of the best-known criticism of the novel.

The spirit of challenge which informs all their work is a con-
spicuous feature of the Leavises' contribution to literary studies in
general and particularly to criticism of the novel. Whatever misgivings the reader of their work may have, it will be conceded that few,
if any, have stimulated interest in the study of English literature
and discussion of its value more than they. Such works as *Fiction
and the Reading Public*, *The Great Tradition* and *Dickens the Novelist* are
significant not least for being controversial. They promote debate.

The promotion of debate is a valuable achievement. But if the
Leavises' work is memorable for the stir it causes, the tone of their

1

dialectics and the polemical stance they adopt sometimes have the effect of drawing the reader's attention away from the criticism to the Leavises themselves. When this happens, criticism as personal judgement quickly sounds like criticism by impress of personality, and its value becomes blurred. Thus, in assessing their contribution we have always to consider carefully the style, attitude, and tone of their writings. Because they persistently quarrel with fellow critics and use language emotively and evocatively, they have tended to provoke emotional responses from readers of their criticism, often to their own disadvantage. As a result, their audience is commonly divided into two camps: the sympathisers, labelled 'Leavisites', and the dissenters, some of whom genuinely dissent and others of whom do so merely to avoid being labelled sympathisers. Meanwhile very few literary observers have tried objectively to assess the strengths of the criticism while unemotionally taking stock of its undeniable weaknesses.[1] This cannot be a profitable situation, when the Leavises have important things to say.

It continues to be an emotive situation so long as literature on the Leavises remains fixed by loyalties and biased one way or another. For a long time, commentary on the Leavises consisted mainly of brief review articles. And considerations of space in these, together with the Leavises' forceful challenges, seemed to constrain the reviewer to be himself a combatant and snatch up his own weapons as on a point of honour, instead of remaining collected and detached. Till recently, the few extended studies of F. R. Leavis's writings focused primarily on his criticism of poetry or on his writings on education, society, and culture, leaving that on the novel, though at the centre of his writings, and though especially intriguing since *Dickens the Novelist*, inadequately treated. And meanwhile no extended study at all as yet exists of Q. D. Leavis, though her work has been almost entirely on the novel, and though it strikingly parallels and complements her husband's.

The capacity to provoke debate links the Leavises with a great precursor, Dr Johnson, with whom they share other qualities. The following observations of and about Johnson apply exactly to the Leavises: 'When he commenced the *Rambler*, Johnson, in disclaiming the pursuit of novel truth, acutely remarked that "men more frequently require to be reminded than informed" ', and 'What interests us in Johnson is the spectacle of a man who, in a time (like our own) of rapidly shifting values, strove never to lose sight of fundamentals.'[2] Like Johnson in his day, the Leavises have in our day committed themselves to reminding rather than informing readers of the fundamental truth that literature is an expression of human experience, and consequently that literary values cannot be divorced from human values, that literary judgements entail human ones. They are, like Johnson, rootedly anti-theorist. Just as Johnson rejected the doctrine of the unities in favour of a common-sense appeal to human experience as the basis of his judgements,[3] so have the Leavises pertinaciously avoided the proliferating systems, doctrines, and theories of twentieth-century criticism in favour of a common-sense appeal to human normality as the basis of their judgements. Only, Johnson lived in a much more homogeneous society and could count much more easily on an accepted norm of human behaviour and on a 'common reader' who knew what the norm was. The Leavises have not had this advantage in the fragmented society of the twentieth century, and so have been forced to make their appeal far more vociferously than Johnson. When, for instance, Leavis insists that 'a real literary interest is an interest in man, society and civilization, and its boundaries cannot be drawn',[4] he expounds a truth to which Johnson would have immediately assented, yet Johnson would have found it too obvious to need stating. The Leavises, addressing a very different age, have found themselves having to insist on such truths with a force for which they are not easily forgiven.

I. A. Richards supplies a reminder of what the Johnsonian critic faces in the twentieth century. 'To set up as a critic is to set up as a judge of values', he says, and continues,

> The expert in matters of taste is in an awkward position when he differs from the majority. He is forced to say in effect, 'I am better than you. My taste is more refined, my nature more cultured, you will do well to become more like me than you are.' It is not his fault that he has to be arrogant.[5]

The Leavises appreciated the truth of this statement from the start. When they began teaching and writing, the literary–academic climate did not favour what they stood for. Neither the university nor the world of literary journalism welcomed Leavis's efforts to give new value to the function of literary criticism by combining the roles of teacher and critic, and making criticism a university discipline. The university looked down on criticism as a poor relation of scholarship and as a close cousin of dilettantism. A critical interest in Joyce was even taken for moral laxity, Leavis wryly recalls.[6] The world of letters outside the university was equally suspicious and hostile, seeing Leavis and *Scrutiny* as another highbrow movement to intellectualise literature for an élite.[7]

Thus the pressures against the Leavises have been from the start intense. The modern cultural environment, as Leavis explained in *Mass Civilization and Minority Culture* and in *Culture and Environment*, provokes unusually keen polemics on the part of the critic who is in good faith concerned about it. And so to accuse Leavis of bad manners is often of dubious profit, since he usually knows when he is being ungracious and is usually careful to give his reasons. 'Even at the cost of indecorum', he says, 'you must do all that can be done to discourage illusions.'[8] We find plenty of indecorum in the Leavises' criticism of the novel, some of it excusable on these grounds, some of it not.

While Mrs Leavis has written almost exclusively on the novel, Leavis's criticism of the novel has become the core of his *oeuvre*. As a critic of our age, Leavis has turned more and more to novelists rather than to poets to argue his case for literary studies as a humane education, and to find clues as to how the individual can nourish human sympathy in the conduct of life in society today. His interest in Dickens and Lawrence bears this out most strikingly. Leavis appeals more to novelists than to poets for several reasons: since the beginning of the nineteenth century, novelists have portrayed individual lives in their social interaction more effectively and more frequently than poets; the outstanding novelists have been the most effective critics of the Industrial Age, which continues now in its technological phase; and they have written greater poetry than the poets writing in the same period.

Thus Leavis's writings on the novel in *For Continuity*, *The Great Tradition*, *D. H. Lawrence: Novelist*, '*Anna Karenina*' and *Dickens the Novelist* mark with progressive intensity his search to justify the human and humane values he puts on the study of literature today. His primary concern is with the human relevance of the great novel to life as it is lived now.

Little Dorrit confronts the technologico-Benthamite world with a conception of man and society to which it is utterly blank, the blankness being a manifestation of its desperate sickness.[9]

[Dickens is] a vindicator of the spirit, such as we sorely need.[10]

His criticism of poetry has in comparison a subsidiary importance, because with the exception of T. S. Eliot and Blake he finds no poets of the modern age to match Dickens, Lawrence and the novelists of the 'great tradition'. And this is because 'in the nineteenth century and later the strength—the poetic and creative strength—of the English language goes into prose fiction. In comparison the formal poetry is a marginal affair.'[11]

But it is hard to believe that Leavis could have made such a statement so confidently had he not been so thoroughly a critic of poetry before he turned his attention fully on the novel. More significantly, he made this observation as a result of a sequence of highly successful experiments with the revolutionary notion that some of the most important novels have the same kind of poetic complexity and organisation as Shakespeare's plays. With the concept of 'the novel as dramatic poem' Leavis encouraged readers to see beyond the fact that the novel is a relatively recent literary genre written in prose to the perception that in its best examples it has evolved directly from Shakespeare's dramatic poetry. For him, as for Mrs Leavis, Shakespeare becomes the touchstone for criticism of the novel, and the great novelists are the 'natural successors' of Shakespeare.[12] Leavis's concept of 'the novel as dramatic poem' and his insistence that the great novelists have with the great poets human centrality, distinguish him in the pioneering movement in twentieth-century criticism to gain serious recognition of the novel as a major genre of art. In addition, he has contributed to criticism of the novel the distinctive analytic method and critical idiom that he formulated for himself from his criticism of poetry. Such evaluative terms as 'realisation' and 'concreteness' had certainly been used by other writers before Leavis with reference to the novel and other art forms, but Leavis adopted them as key criteria and deployed them with a force all his own.

In other words, Leavis's criticism of poetry, which includes his early appreciations of Shakespeare, provided the foundation for his own and for Mrs Leavis's criticism of the novel. But it took them many years to justify the affinity between a great novel and great poetry, and not least because current opinion did not favour the affinity.

When the Leavises began to publish their thinking on the novel in the early 1930s, they found a great deal of serious aesthetic interest in the novel. But few, apart from the disciples and successors of James, valued the novel equally with poetry. Attitudes to the

novel suffered too much from the influence of the Bradleyan attitude to drama, so that it was widely felt that the novelist, like the
dramatist, was principally a creator of interesting characters.[13]
This state of affairs had troubled all the sensitive novelists—from
James to Virginia Woolf—who practised the novel as a serious art.
For their part, the Leavises felt with the editors of the *Calendar of
Modern Letters* that a merely aesthetic approach did not reach the
root of the problem. The technical critic might explain how a novel
is constructed, but he could not, or would not, account either for
the total impact of a novel, or for the fact that some novels may be
technically brilliant but lifeless.[14] And because he did not satis-
factorily explain what gives a novel its life, the Leavises felt that the
technical critic ignored a fundamental truth that literature has
value in so far as it communicates insights into human nature and
human experience. Consequently for them criticism of the novel
had not adequately begun the necessary pre-theoretical work of
evaluation.[15] And to do so it needed to establish standards of judgement and a suitably economical method for analysing so large a
structure as the novel.

Lamenting the scarcity of guidance in these matters, the
Leavises none the less pointed to Henry James, I. A. Richards,
C. H. Rickword and Vernon Lee for many helpful hints. From
James and Richards they drew encouragement for positing moral
criteria as the basis for judging the novel. In Richards and Lee they
found help as to method and approach. And Richards and
Rickword encouraged them to see certain kinds of novel as poems
in prose.

Looking for a sound critical basis for evaluation, Mrs Leavis
specified the passage in James's 'The Art of Fiction' (1884) where
he discusses the closeness of the 'moral sense' to the 'artistic sense'
in a good novel; and she quotes approvingly James's 'very obvious
truth that the deepest quality of a work of art will always be the
quality of the mind of the producer. . . . No good novel ever proceeded from a superficial mind.'[16] A year later (in 1933) Leavis
referred to James more generally but with little enthusiasm:

Where is a critic to find help with 'principles' in criticizing fiction, the head under which the bulk of the output demanding attention will come? With little more than a few hints from Henry
James—from the prefaces and *Notes on Novelists*—he will have to
do everything for himself.[17]

Yet 'The Art of Fiction' bulges with ideas that look like pure Leavis:

> A novel is in its broadest definition a personal, a direct impression of life: that, to begin with, constitutes its value, which is greater or less according to the intensity of the impression. . . .
>
> It is equally excellent and inconclusive to say that one must write from experience. . . . What kind of experience is intended, and where does it begin and end? Experience is never limited, and it is never complete; it is an immense sensibility. . . .
>
> One can speak best from one's own taste, and I may therefore venture to say that the air of reality (solidity of specification) seems to me to be the supreme virtue of a novel—the merit on which all its other merits (including that conscious moral purpose of which Mr Besant speaks) helplessly and submissively depend. . . . It is here in very truth that the [novelist] competes with life. . . .
>
> A novel is a living thing, all one and continuous, like any other organism, and in proportion as it lives will it be found, that in each of the parts there is something of each of the other parts.[18]

The intensity with which a novel corresponds to life and its air of reality, the limitlessness of experience and so the limitlessness of the novel's scope, the dynamic connectedness of a novel's organisation—all these are basic tenets in Leavis's criticism of the novel, as a glance at almost any page of *The Great Tradition* will reveal. Even James's phraseology and his parenthetical style uncannily anticipate Leavis. And, of course, *The Great Tradition* includes James.

However, James's essay stays on the level of theoretical argument. Leavis organised such hints and others into an efficient method for evaluating fiction practically. Leavis's lack of enthusiasm may also reflect, too conveniently perhaps, his and his wife's disenchantment with the later James. They felt that in the prefaces and the late novels James departed from the truths he enunciated in 'The Art of Fiction' and became too intent on 'composition' at the expense of 'life'. And they deplored Percy Lubbock's canonisation of the late James in his influential *The Craft of Fiction* (1921). But at several points in *The Great Tradition*, particularly in the section on George Eliot, Leavis also acknowledged James's many excellences as a critic of the novel. And he pays a solid tribute in the essay 'James as Critic'.[19]

As to dealing economically with the novel's length, Mrs Leavis advised that the soundest method would be 'to reinforce a general impression by analysis of significant passages on the lines of Vernon Lee's *The Handling of Words*', though less pedantically. [20] Leavis adopts this method everywhere in his criticism. For an analytical method the Leavises derived most help from I. A. Richards's notes on poetry analysis in *Principles of Literary Criticism* (1924). But, whereas Mrs Leavis seemed to vacillate and equivocate about Richards's usefulness for criticism of the novel, [21] Leavis, fresh from publishing his first criticism of poetry in *New Bearings*, took a lively interest in Richards's discussion of 'rhythm':

> It suggests what the critical analysis of a Shakespeare play would be. If one adds that it suggests what would be the critical analysis of a novel, no one will now suppose that novel and play are thus assimilated because they both contain characters. [22]

In the same essay Leavis praised C. H. Rickword for explicitly linking fiction with poetry in his 'Note on Fiction':

> This bringing together of fiction and poetry is the more richly suggestive because of the further assimilation it instigates. The differences between a lyric, a Shakespeare play, and a novel, for some purposes essential, are in no danger of being forgotten; what needs insisting on is the community. [23]

These hints from Richards and Rickword, [24] together with G. Wilson-Knight's anti-Bradleyan view that Shakespeare's plays are richly-wrought symbolic poems, [25] eventually germinated in the idea of 'the novel as dramatic poem', which the Leavises used for all their major criticism of the novel from the essay on *Hard Times* in 1947 to *Dickens the Novelist* in 1970.

In sum, as a critic of poetry and the novel Leavis owed much to Richards. Again, many of his key evaluative terms, such as 'concreteness', 'realisation', 'poise', 'sincerity' and 'impersonality' are traceable back to Richards. But Richards, like James, was more theorist than critic, and it was Leavis who put the theory into practice, first with poetry in *New Bearings* (1932) and *Revaluation* (1936), and then with the novel. In addition, both these books and *The Great Tradition* (1948) readily reflect Leavis's sizeable debt to T. S. Eliot in the 'classical' rigour with which he took his bearings on the literature of the past in the light of the literature of the present, and *vice versa*. But he was soon to break from Eliot and from a strictly classical reading of literature when he fully realised the significance of D. H. Lawrence.

At this point it is of paramount importance to remember that the Leavises are teachers as well as critics, and that their criticism is the product of their teaching of, primarily, undergraduate students. No doubt the same is true of very many critics. But the Leavises back their common-sense appeal to human experience as the basis of literary judgement with an equally common-sense attitude to the students they teach, and to the time that undergraduates have at their disposal. They know that not all their students will pursue an academic career. They know too that three years is a desperately short time for anyone to derive real value from the study of so vast a subject as literature.[26] Consequently they have devoted themselves to the Arnoldian endeavour of starting their students off with the best that is thought and known in literature.

Leavis crystallised this attitude in the early pamphlet *How to Teach Reading* (1932), which he reprinted significantly in *Education and the University*. Agreeing with Ezra Pound, for whom he designed the pamphlet, he sees that the great concern of the teacher–critic is 'to save the student from the usual laborious dissipation, to put him in the way of the concentrated reading that will truly educate him by giving him, as it were, the essential structure of literary experience'.[27] For Leavis it should be the essential structure of one's own literature first. *New Bearings*, *Revaluation*, *The Great Tradition* and *D. H. Lawrence: Novelist* execute this idea. Mrs Leavis shared this view and helped decisively in the formation of *The Great Tradition*.

Such an attitude helps to explain why Leavis has no large theoretical statement such as Northrop Frye's *Anatomy of Criticism* or Wayne Booth's *The Rhetoric of Fiction* to his name. It is hard to imagine his either finding or justifying the time needed to work one out. The Arnoldian tasks pressed more urgently and took all his time.

Conceivably he might have written a comprehensive statement of his theory of literature after his book on Lawrence, when he had drawn up his first chart of the essential structure of English literature in poetry and the novel. And interestingly, he remarked in a footnote in the revised edition of *Education and the University*: 'I hope to bring out before long in collaboration with Q. D. Leavis a

book that deals with the grounds and methods of the critical study
of novels' (p. 126). But instead he found that changing times[28]
forced him to continue the practical work of revaluation, of revising
the map of significance. Eliot remarked at the outset of Leavis's
career that 'every generation must make its own appraisal of the
poetry of the past'.[29] Leavis lived long enough to appraise the novel
twice: once in *The Great Tradition*, and again in *Dickens the Novelist*.
And, significantly, he continued to be an active teacher long after
most people would think of retirement. It should be added that in
light of the preceding observations the Leavises' notorious anti-
academicism is not just a demonstration of anti-Establishment
pique, but derives too from a sincere desire to keep great literature as accessible to intelligent readers outside as to those inside
the post-graduate seminar and the research booths of academic
libraries.

A further note on 'influence' may help to explain why Leavis's
famous attack on Eliot in *D. H. Lawrence: Novelist* was no mere freak
of temper as many have thought, but sprang from a much more
honourable source. That book dramatises a crisis of allegiance in
Leavis. He found himself having to decide which of the two
twentieth-century writers he most admired was the more right
about life and art, Eliot or Lawrence. It was a kind of spiritual
crisis involving Leavis's identity and independence as thinker and
critic. He found that he was forced to discriminate between the key
but contrary beliefs he prized in both writers. Like Eliot, Leavis
had a 'classical' education, believed in criticism as a rigorous
'classical' discipline, and accordingly he at first followed Eliot in
distrusting Lawrence's 'romanticism' (see the essay on Lawrence
in *For Continuity*). However, Leavis like Lawrence was by tempera-
ment nonconformist and carved his own path in the world, as
Scrutiny illustrates; and so he came with Lawrence to value creativity as the expression of strong individuality: in other words, as
the romantic imagination does.

Therefore, the questions of how to strike a positive balance between these two writers, and of how to become master of himself as
critic and thinker independent of them, lie at the centre of Leavis's
criticism and energise it. He valued the best in both Eliot and
Lawrence too well merely to take sides. Rather, Leavis's criticism
dramatises an intellectual voyage in quest of a personal philosophy
of life and art steered between two powerful opposites. And he
reached port in *English Literature in Our Time*, a book substantially in

homage to Eliot but which includes an essay making Lawrence his 'necessary opposite'.

To understand that Leavis's criticism is a keen struggle to find his bearings *vis-à-vis* Lawrence and Eliot is to understand better its uncompromising nature and the characteristic force and urgency of his manner. Since Eliot and Lawrence are indisputably major forces in twentieth-century literature and thought, Leavis's preoc-cupation with them is another example of his concern with essential importance. This large question remains as yet scarcely touched. Martin Green has recently made an exciting beginning with it in *The von Richthofen Sisters* (1974).

The more or less chronological scheme of chapters followed here seems to me the best way of doing justice to the Leavises' criticism, which I see as a continuous process of valuing and revaluing great imaginative literature as a complex recreation of human normality. That basically is what Leavis means when he says that great literature affirms life.

The example of Shakespeare lies behind this conviction. And to understand the importance of Shakespeare to the Leavises we should note very particularly some perceptive early pieces Leavis wrote on Shakespeare and tragedy. Several of these—'Tragedy and the "Medium"', 'Diabolic Intellect and the Noble Hero', '*Measure for Measure*', 'The Criticism of Shakespeare's Late Plays'—he later collected in *The Common Pursuit*. There is, too, a key discussion of Shakespeare's dramatic poetry (in *Macbeth*) in *Education and the University*.

2 Q. D. Leavis: *Fiction and the Reading Public* and *Scrutiny* (1932–47)

In the period 1932–47 Mrs Leavis conducts a reconnaissance of the field of fiction and brings discussion of tradition and importance in the English novel to the point where her husband's 'essential discriminations' in *The Great Tradition*[1] are the natural consequence of her work. Her work in these years is more the investigative work of the scholar with a critical interest in literature than criticism as such.

Never in her approach does Mrs Leavis become strictly the literary critic in her husband's way, since she consistently uses the methods of scholarship and retains more than a passing interest in the biographical and sociological background of literature. At this stage her work is partly scholarship, as in *Fiction and the Reading Public*, partly literary journalism, as in numerous *Scrutiny* reviews, and partly literary biography, as in her essays on Jane Austen; and in all cases she is only incidentally a critic. And yet the whole tendency of her work in this period is towards criticism, and towards Leavis's book. Significantly, her own first extensive work of criticism, the essay 'Hawthorne as Poet',[2] appeared three years after *The Great Tradition*. Meanwhile her work on Jane Austen, which begins in this early period and continues into the next, illustrates especially well the way she came to link scholarship and biography with criticism. 'A Critical Theory of Jane Austen's Writings' (*Scrutiny*, 1941–4), though tantalisingly veined with criticism, is more a piece of literary biography. But the 'Theory' looks forward to and is completed by the critical introductions Mrs Leavis provided for the Macdonald editions of *Sense and Sensibility* (1958) and *Mansfield Park* (1957). These writings together make a satisfying whole, and they in part prompt the phrase 'scholarship that functions as criticism',[3] which Leavis was to use to describe his wife's work in *Scrutiny*. But in this early period of her writing, the relationship in Mrs Leavis between the scholar by training and the critic by aspiration is not always satisfying, as can be seen in her first major work.

Fiction and the Reading Public (1932) is by turns a stimulating and frustrating book. Though ostensibly her book is neither criticism of fiction nor a primer for the critic, Mrs Leavis has included enough criticism, and enough discussion of criteria and method for evaluating the novel for the reader to wish she had included more. For instance, when she has finished exposing the inferiority of the bestseller to the good novel by referring to the canons of good taste and good sense in eighteenth-century fiction, the reader wishes she had gone on to compare the best novels from that century with the best from the nineteenth and twentieth centuries. Instead, she has kept to her thesis and indicated only that good fiction, like poetry, is increasingly not popular in these centuries. Meanwhile, she includes valuable notes on the relation of the great novel to good poetry. And in her discussion of Bunyan and Defoe she begins to make useful distinctions between the novel as poetic art and the novel as fictional journalism. In such ways Mrs Leavis's book has seminal value, and gives new bearings for the criticism of fiction in our age, when fiction rather than poetry is the public's staple reading in imaginative literature. The phrase 'new bearings' is chosen advisedly. In examining the state of literature and literary taste in the first three decades of the twentieth century, *Fiction and the Reading Public* relates to Leavis's *The Great Tradition* much as his *New Bearings in English Poetry* (also 1932) relates to his *Revaluation*, criticism of the present leading to criticism of the past.

Mrs Leavis's book also frustrates as it stimulates. Steadfast to her thesis that literary taste signifies the state of culture, and that taste and culture have declined together since the eighteenth century, she is ruthless with any writer, novelist or critic whom she sees not conspicuously fostering the eighteenth-century virtue of decorum in living and writing about life. This attitude is bracing, the thesis challenges, and Mrs Leavis's writing sweeps the reader from point to point with tireless gusto. But there are rough patches: hyperbole of tone and claim, partial judgements, simplifications, inconsistencies and loose ends. The shifts of emphasis in her remarks about *Jane Eyre* and Virginia Woolf's novels[4] make the reader ask: What status does Mrs Leavis finally accord them? And how can Bunyan's method be both 'unlike the major eighteenth-century and Victorian novelists' and yet 'that of the best novelists' (p. 98)? How can she justify her sweeping dismissal of technical criticism in Lubbock and Forster (p. 232)? How convincing, because how partial without quotation and analysis, are her criticisms of vulgar emotionalism in Dickens and Charlotte Brontë? These and other questions can be asked because Mrs Leavis goes far enough in discussion and comparison to cause them to be asked, and to arouse in the reader expectation of answers. She has preferred instead to let the reader draw his own conclusions, which may not, of course, accord with her own intentions.

Some of the keenest frustration occurs in her commentary on the start of the Victorian age, where she pinpoints the beginning of cultural decline. Here, in the chapter 'The Disintegration of the Reading Public' (Pt. ii, Ch. 4) and in Part iii, she shows the eighteenth-century heritage of discriminating taste and decorum giving way to vulgarity and sensationalism, the age of Misses Burney, Edgeworth and Austen lapsing into the age of Lytton, Dickens and the Kingsleys. Yet here Mrs Leavis's own perceptions are insufficiently discriminating, her judgements impulsive, and her tone and attitude overbearing and sensational. And here, curiously, she forgoes her usual scrupulous practice of quoting, comparing and analysing. In attacking Victorian popular fiction, she relies instead on the vigour of her critique against the modern bestseller, and on her determination to trace this phenomenon to its source in the Victorian innovation of serialising fiction. She singles out Dickens and Charlotte Brontë as arch-progenitors of the modern bestseller. But, in substituting attitude for analysis in her judgements of them, Mrs Leavis becomes victim herself of what she especially deplores—the stock response. Hers takes the 'highbrow' or inverted form of responding to all bestsellers with disdain without further inquiry. Moreover, in fastening upon the popular and sensational elements in Dickens and Charlotte Brontë, she forgets to enquire whether they also write at a higher level.[5] And, in overlooking this possibility, she neglects to consider them as creative writers, and drastically oversimplifies her thesis about environment forming the writer. It is true that a writer is formed by his environment, and Mrs Leavis finds ample corroboration of this in her discussions of eighteenth- and twentieth-century popular fiction. But the creative writer also transcends the environment that shaped him.[6] Indeed, his very creativity helps to transform his environment—as she would later perceive and emphasise.

Mrs Leavis's judgements of Dickens and Charlotte Brontë at this time illustrate a clash of interest and method in her book. In *Fiction and the Reading Public* Mrs Leavis seeks to combine scholarship with criticism by following an impartial inquiry into the history of literary taste with a 'discussion of values' (p. xv). It is her first experiment with the question which preoccupies her in all her work: How can scholarship serve criticism? In the cases of Dickens and Charlotte Brontë the energy of her attack on the modern bestseller has blurred her powers of discrimination and damaged both her criticism and her scholarship. The criticism becomes partial, and the scholarship tenuous. In other words, she has coerced scholarship into yielding up the data she needs to press home the attack on cheapness and crudity in popular fiction. Some of the most trenchant criticism of her book was to come years later, provided by Mrs Leavis herself in *Dickens the Novelist*, and in her introduction to the Penguin English Library edition of *Jane Eyre*.

Though her discussion of criteria for evaluating the novel is piecemeal, Mrs Leavis clearly upholds the virtues of eighteenth-century writing above all. She consistently refers to eighteenth-century writers and to passages from their novels to point out the debilities of popular fiction in succeeding ages. And her point is always that even the best eighteenth-century fiction was popular. Chapter 3 of Part ii, 'The Growth of the Reading Public',[7] is more than accidentally the centre of her thesis. Here she records English culture at its ideal moment in terms of literary taste, quality of reading-matter, and homogeneity of reading public. This is the age of Pope, Addison, and Sterne, poised between 'the naïve humour and full-bodied tragic passion' of the Elizabethan drama and 'the undiscriminating surrender to bursts of laughter and storms of tears of Dickens's public' (p. 220). The Age of Reason, in other words, seems most congenial to the rational temper of the scholar in Mrs Leavis. The succeeding age, that between Jane Austen and George Eliot, provides a turbulent contrast, not suiting the temper of scholarship merely, but requiring critical adjustment.

Mrs Leavis prizes the eighteenth-century novelist because he is concerned to keep his reader facing reality. Unlike his successors in popular fiction, who cushion their readers from reality by providing 'uplift', 'daydreams' and 'castle-building' (pp. 138, 164), 'the eighteenth-century novelist', she contends, 'is continually pulling up the reader, disappointing his expectations or refusing him the luxury of day-dreaming and not infrequently douching him with cold water' (p. 128). This attitude extends into the early part of the next century with his successors, 'who did not write for the circulating library': 'Maria Edgeworth, Jane Austen, Hannah More—are concerned to destroy any comforting illusions the reader may cherish, to make the reader more aware of, more fully alive to, and therefore better fitted to cope with, the world he lives in' (p. 138). Hence some of the eighteenth-century virtues which Mrs Leavis lists are, 'the absence of romantic idealisation', 'the presence of a rational code of feeling', 'emotional decorum', 'a critical temper that produced and maintained the code of good taste and good sense', 'the ideal of a "well-regulated mind" explicitly mentioned by Maria Edgeworth and Jane Austen', 'the positive ideal of self-discipline' (pp. 129, 302).

It might be tempting to conclude from this chapter, from its predecessor, 'The Puritan Conscience', and from the subsequent onslaught on Victorian and twentieth-century popular fiction, that Mrs Leavis has only a solemn interest in the moral value of fiction. Her valuation of Sterne[8] reveals that, on the contrary, she can delight in verbal dexterity and technical ingenuity. She insists in fact that Sterne delights because his art is highly disciplined. Only an athletic reader can appreciate it. 'Sterne requires careful and persevering reading', she says, and 'to read *Tristram Shandy* is a bracing mental exercise' (pp. 134–5).

It is logical that Mrs Leavis should go on to emphasise that good novels test the adult mind, and that maturity in subject-matter and technique is a sign of a novel's importance. Moreover, in stressing realism, self-discipline, maturity, and reading for the adult mind as characteristics of good novels, she anticipates her husband's very similar postulates for 'the great tradition'. She summarises her view as follows:

> To read any of the popular poetry of the eighteenth century it is at least essential to keep awake in order to follow the sense, and above all necessary to respond as an adult. The loss in maturity and poise[9] noticeable between Pope and Shelley is paralleled by the same disparity between Sterne and Thackeray, Jane Austen and Charlotte Brontë, Smollett and Dickens.   (p. 230)

The power to challenge the reader's capacity to read, to disturb his illusions, to compel him to face reality, and a concomitant self-discipline—these, then, are qualities in a novelist which Mrs Leavis esteems, and which she uses to expose the flabbiness and immaturity of the modern bestseller and the 'undesirable attitudes' it fosters (p. 212). The first of these she also identifies as a strength in Virginia Woolf's novels. As with Sterne, the reader needs to be on his toes to appreciate her art: 'The reader not prepared to read-just himself to the technique of *Mrs Dalloway* and *To the Lighthouse* will get very little return for the energy he must lay out in wrestling with those involved periods' (p. 61). And Forster has the capacity to disturb illusions in *A Passage to India* (p. 62). With reference to Forster again and to Hardy, she also remarks that the serious novel is always written within the limits of the author's experience of life (213 and 251); a point she takes for granted with the eighteenth-century writer.

Through Virginia Woolf Mrs Leavis also reinforces her argument that after the eighteenth century the important novel is like a poem a consciously constructed work of art. From George Eliot onwards the serious novelists cultivate the novel as art,[10] and Virginia Woolf's novels 'are, in fact, highbrow art' (p. 223). Carefully structured, technically complex, and poetic in intention, they need to be approached and judged as poetry: 'The technique and the intention are poetic, and *To the Lighthouse* requires that the reader should have had a training in reading poetry' (ibid.).

She stresses that this modern development is a conscious one. Earlier works of fiction could be poetic, too, but unconsciously so. *The Pilgrim's Progress*, as Mrs Leavis discusses it, is by implication unconsciously a poetic work of art. Her comparison of Bunyan and Defoe reveals this and more. Most important for the critic of fiction is her implication that Bunyan is the first great novelist in English. She judges him to be so by the way he uses language 'by modulating . . . from the movement and language of the Bible to the movement and idiom of common speech', and by his technique of working 'on two planes at once by modulating from allegory to realism' (pp. 100–1). These abilities distinguish him as a poetic genius from Defoe, who, working only on the plane of 'matter-of-fact' realism, is nevertheless a 'journalist of genius' producing literature unawares' (pp. 97, 102–3). The distinction is no disparagement to Defoe. On the contrary, Mrs Leavis wants to give Defoe full credit for his real achievement, and to deprecate only those modern critics who make extravagant claims for his 'artistry'.[11]

Interestingly, her notes on Defoe echo her husband's earlier ones. Leavis had already devoted half a chapter to identifying Defoe's genius for journalism, in his dissertation, 'The Relationship of Journalism to Literature'. He called *Robinson Crusoe, Moll Flanders, Roxana*, and so on, 'novels' only for convenience. But he did not call them art, not only because Defoe did not so consider his fiction, but because in *Moll Flanders*, for instance, 'there is no drama of the mind to hold us; we merely learn that this happens, and then this, and then this'. '*Moll Flanders* invites this kind of criticism', he continued, 'when offered to us . . . as "memorable writing" '; as literature, that is. But, like Mrs Leavis, Leavis concluded by emphasising Defoe's genius as a journalist:

> To discriminate thus between Defoe's various works is not to disparage his achievement—an achievement that provides a most notable instance of writing that, being addressed to a particular audience at a particular moment, has found wide and diverse audiences in all succeeding times. Defoe wrote, not as an artist, but as an artisan, to serve new needs that existing literary modes took no account of. A public had arisen that knew nothing of literary standards and professed no allegiance to art.
>
> Matter that ministered to its naïf and living interests—that alone would it read. A journalist of genius saw his opportunity to make a livelihood, and, without even a formal homage to the muses, set himself to exploiting demand.[12]

But Mrs Leavis's discussion of Bunyan also contains a curious *non-sequitur* and an instance of the kind of unsupported assertion that she makes from time to time with sufficient confidence to disarm all but the wary reader. She writes,

> Unlike the major eighteenth century and Victorian novelists [Bunyan] has no sharp black and white, vice and virtue, and no cheap system of rewards and punishments. His method is that of the best novelists—to reveal men for what they are. . . . Bunyan had observed the life around him as closely as Defoe, and he was free from the necessity which made Defoe a journalist. His observation is truer and his morality is juster (that is to say, wiser)

than Richardson's, his version of the pattern of life is more satisfying than Richardson's, proceeding from a finer mind. In consequence he is a better novelist, and whereas Richardson's
interest for the reader of Dostoievsky and Henry James is almost
entirely historical, Bunyan's is intrinsic.   (pp. 98–9)

But, who, if the major eighteenth-century and Victorian novelists
are excluded, are the best novelists that Bunyan resembles? And,
though Bunyan's morality may be juster and wiser than Richardson's, how, beyond assertion, is he a better 'novelist'? Do they
practise the same art? Though what she says of Bunyan may be
true, the comparison with Richardson is forced and unfair.

Mrs Leavis's discussion of a method for criticising fiction is
similarly flawed. It begins with the notion that 'great novels are frequently doing something like good poetry' (p. 211). Here again the
value of her remarks lies in the attention she focuses on the need for
criticism to evaluate a novel in its totality. The great novel needs to
be examined for what it 'does for the reader', she says, for what
'capacities it demands from the reader', and also 'some more economical critical method' needs to be found (pp. 212, 232).
The passages in question occur in the last three to four pages of suc-
cessive chapters, 'The Novel' and 'Reading Capacity' (Pt. III,
Chs. 1 and 2), and are separated by twenty or so intervening pages.
But a comparison of the two passages reveals ambiguities and
contradictions.

Mrs Leavis makes essentially three related propositions: first,
that the critic should approach the novel as he would a poem, with
an eye on the 'total rhythm' the novelist builds up cumulatively
through the sum of the many parts of the novel; secondly, that the
critic should judge the novel, not by 'such abstractions as "plot",
"character", "setting", "theme", "action"', but by the total impression of the mind at work in the novel as conveyed by the
language the novelist uses; and, thirdly, that 'the soundest method
for the critic of the novel would be to reinforce a general impression
by analysis of significant passages on the lines of Vernon Lee's *The
Handling of Words*' (p. 233). The last two obligations Mrs Leavis has
herself exemplified to great effect everywhere in her book, save in
discussing Victorian fiction. She quotes, compares, and analyses a
variety of passages drawn from the modern bestseller, and also
from Nashe, Sterne, Richardson, Trollope (the single exception in

Victorian fiction), Forster and Virginia Woolf. And in the process
she notes carefully the relationship of idiom and use of language to
the quality of the writing in any period.[13] But these positive stimuli
for criticism of fiction are entangled in ambiguities, inconsistencies
and puzzles of her own making. It is as if she makes the process of
dealing with a novel into a mystique in the moment of trying to
clarify it. And her attitude to other critics hinders rather than helps
what she says.

Her rejection of Lubbock and Forster on the grounds that technical criticism is profitless is too peremptory. Technical abstractions such as 'plot', 'character' and so on 'are the only terms', Mrs
Leavis complains, 'that tradition has provided for the critic, with a
few more of the same kind that Mr Lubbock in *The Craft of Fiction*
and Mr Forster in *Aspects of the Novel* have tried to put into circulation' (p. 232). The implication is that their approach is back to
front: valuation logically precedes theory, otherwise there is the risk
of saying that *qua* plot '*Wuthering Heights* and *Clarissa* are as pre-
posterous as the novels of Ethel M. Dell' (ibid.). But neither Lubbock nor Forster makes or invites such equations. Moreover, it
does not take an unusually observant, sensitive or critical reader
(the kind Mrs Leavis has designed her book for) to note that the
phrase 'a few more of the same kind' is both patronising and·un-
amplified, that the overtone in 'tried' is also patronising, and 'put
into circulation' is not far off an imputation of forgery. The reader
then remarks with some irony what Mrs Leavis says a few sentences on about the novelist and the way he uses words:

> The essential technique in an art that works by using words is
> the way in which the words are used, and a method is only justi-
> fied by the use that is made of it; a bad novel is ultimately seen to
> fail not because of its method but owing to a fatal inferiority in
> the author's make-up.   (p. 233).

Then, in admiring C. P. Sanger's structural dissection of *Wuthering
Heights* (p. 238), she readily acknowledges the serviceableness of at
least some kinds of technical criticism for the evaluative critic. And
it is one thing to deplore the lack of an economical method of
evaluating the novel, but hardly good sense to do so by scorning the
conscientious efforts of fellow critics. Moreover, by so loudly dismissing Lubbock and Forster Mrs Leavis paradoxically stirs rather
than dissipates interest in their books.

Other minor ambiguities and inconsistencies emerge from a comparison of these passages. Remarking at one point that the novel's cumulative effect should be considered, because even the serious novel has 'room for bad writing' (as in *The Return of the Native*), Mrs Leavis says later that the critic should choose significant passages to back his general impression, 'because in these the novelist will be most intensely and so most perceptibly himself' (pp. 213, 234). But when is this? Mrs Leavis wants to mean by 'significant' when the novelist writes as well as he can. And yet she has just expressed dissatisfaction with Vernon Lee's practice of precisely such selectivity: 'Admirable critiques of Hardy and Henry James are followed by an examination of a passage from *Richard Yea-and-Nay*, which we are told, exhibits the same virtues as the prose of Henry James!' (p. 234).

More curious is her equivocal reference to I. A. Richards as a source of help for the critic of the novel. Possibly she has only half her mind on Richards, because Richards does not specify the novel. Yet what she says has the effect of needlessly mystifying the process of criticising fiction so that she may herself throw some light on it. She writes,

> In so far as a novel, like a poem, is made of words, much of what Mr Richards says of poetry [in *Principles of Literary Criticism*] can be adapted to apply to the novel, but even so the critic does not get much help, for there is an important difference between the way a novel and a poem takes effect.   (p. 212).

She is saying in effect, 'Richards's help is much, yet not much.' And she goes on to explain that, because the novel is 'diffused', its 'total rhythm' must be perceived for one to arrive at a convincing estimate of its value (ibid.). Yet, on looking up *Principles of Literary Criticism*, the reader finds in chapter 17, 'Rhythm and Metre', a thorough discussion of 'rhythm', including the sentence: 'The same definition of rhythm may be extended to the plastic arts and to architecture.'[14] Though Richards does not mention the novel, his 'extended' coincides without difficulty with Mrs Leavis's 'diffused'. Again, she says that Richards's help for the critic of the novel appears to be limited because 'in criticising a poem one can safely bear out one's general impression by examining particular passages' (p. 212). And yet the reader learns that 'the soundest method for the critic of the novel' is almost identical: 'to reinforce a general impression by analysis of significant passages' (p. 233).[15]

Mrs Leavis's book has value, finally, as the best sociology of literary taste written up to that time.[16] It had also a seminal importance for criticism of the novel both in the cogency of its plea for a more scientific and less impressionistic approach and in the hints which Mrs Leavis assembles from James, Richards and Lee to that end. Also, we can detect in its pages the rough contours of the map of significance Leavis was to draw up in *The Great Tradition*.

The first number of *Scrutiny* appeared the month after *Fiction and the Reading Public*, in May 1932. Mrs Leavis's numerous contributions to *Scrutiny* continue to have the sociological slant of her book. She writes notes on the socio-academic climate, reviews of modern bestsellers, articles on critics, and a few longer essays on important nineteenth- and twentieth-century novelists. The most important of these essays is the series she entitled 'A Critical Theory of Jane Austen's Writings'. But, because she added to and revalued these at a later date, I defer examination of them till a later chapter. That leaves mainly the appraisals of Gissing, Jefferies, Hardy, James and Edith Wharton. In these Mrs Leavis can be seen consolidating her ideas about what makes one novel matter more than another, and pinpointing important traditions, both English and American. They make a welcome supplement to her detailed discussion of eighteenth-century fiction in *Fiction and the Reading Public*. More importantly, they foreshadow Leavis's *The Great Tradition*.

With the exception of 'A Critical Theory', these *Scrutiny* pieces are all brief—the longest, on Edith Wharton, running to a dozen pages. Scarcely classifiable as critiques or essays in criticism, they are rather occasions that Mrs Leavis uses to provide the critic of fiction with pointers to significant novelists and important traditions. To carry conviction she relies on an economy and precision of statement and reference, instead of quotation and analysis, and a confidence in collocating novels and novelists that testify to the expert reader of fiction.

In these pieces she has also progressed in her thinking about the novel beyond the stage she had reached in *Fiction and the Reading Public*. She now measures a novelist's importance by criteria even more akin to her husband's. As in *Fiction and the Reading Public* she still considers a novelist important in so far as he seriously engages with human reality. But, in addition, he must affirm human dignity and human values in a civilisation in which these are at risk;

and he must be able to use language and develop his art so as to convey his preoccupations in new ways. For instance, Aldous Huxley has little significance on the basis of *Eyeless in Gaza*, since 'he has chosen to resort to books instead of life for his raw material'.[17] Arthur Koestler, on the other hand, has rendered 'the Moscow trials' in *Darkness at Noon* in such a way as to make 'a work of art', which connects him with Conrad.[18] Edith Wharton receives very high praise. She is called a 'serious novelist' in virtue of her realistic portrayal of American civilisation in pursuit of the dollar; of 'the chaos that followed on the establishment of a society based on money without any kind of traditions'.[19] She is even the superior of George Eliot in several respects: she writes with more 'grace' and 'economy', has 'a more flexible mind', is 'both socially and morally more experienced'. Comparison of the two leads to the question: 'What makes a great novelist?' 'Apparently not intelligence . . . or scope or a highly developed technique, though, other things being equal, they often give an advantage. But what, then, are the other things?' (p. 134). George Eliot apparently has them:

> I think it eventually becomes a question of what the novelist has to offer us, either directly or by implication, in the way of positives. . . . [Mrs Wharton] has none of that natural piety, that richness of feeling and sense of a moral order, of experience as a process of growth, in which George Eliot's local criticisms are embedded and which give the latter her large stature.   (p. 135)

'It seems to be the fault of the disintegrating and spiritually impoverished society' which Mrs Wharton analyses, Mrs Leavis concludes (p. 135). Meanwhile Edith Wharton occupies a place of importance in an American tradition of the novel. 'The American novel grew up with Henry James', Mrs Leavis says, 'and achieved a tradition with Mrs Wharton'; and her fiction 'leads up to the fiction of Scott Fitzgerald, Faulkner and Kay Boyle, among others, and without it their writings cannot be understood by the English reader' (pp. 126, 131).

She gives similar reasons for George Eliot's superiority over Hardy:

> She is the finer artist with wider capacities, the sounder thinker in her account of the relation of man to environment, people to the community and personalities to each other, the wiser

moralist, the more efficient writer, and gives us a more interesting and sensitive apprehension of character. She is equally sincere without being so simple.[20]

The judgement of Hardy shows that it is not only a matter of George Eliot's being born into a richer environment that makes her a greater novelist than Edith Wharton. She is greater because she has a richer depth of feeling and a deeper sense of a 'moral order' and of 'experience as a process of growth'. At the same time these passages have also usefully summarised the qualities Mrs Leavis looks for in the great novelist's 'sensibility' or 'character'. It is on account of 'character' that she insists in another place that 'the Jane Austen–Emily Brontë–George Eliot circle still defies addition', and 'it is in terms of deficiency in character that Mrs Woolf's degeneration and Katharine Mansfield's deficiency as artists are to be explained'.[21]

The notion that the great novelist, in addition to having character, develops the art of the novel by his own technical experimentations emerges in her discussions of Richard Jefferies and Henry James. Though his fictions are not so much novels as 'novel-like', she finds that Jefferies is in 'the central and most important tradition of English prose style'; and she enthuses about Jefferies's technical originality:

> In *The Dewy Morn* he goes further than any Victorian novelist towards the modern novel—I mean the novel that seems to have significance for us other than as a mirror of manners and morals; I should describe it as one of the few real novels between *Wuthering Heights* and *Sons and Lovers*.[22]

Mrs Leavis does not amplify the word 'real'. But her judgement has received support in a recent full-length critical study of Jefferies. In this W. J. Keith observes that *The Dewy Morn* and *Amaryllis at the Fair*, though 'more experimental' than the earlier novels, display 'enough skill and subtlety . . . to dispose of the common misapprehension that Jefferies lacked necessary qualities for a serious novelist'.[23] Keith also likens Jefferies to D. H. Lawrence.

In 1947 with his essay on *Hard Times* Leavis inaugurated the *Scrutiny* series of discussions of the novel under the head 'The Novel as Dramatic Poem'. In the same year Mrs Leavis contributed three short reviews[24] of critical works on Henry James. They reveal her close agreement with her husband at this time, not only as to which novels and stories constitute the great James,[25] but generally as to which novelists and what kind of novel form the great tradition in the English novel: the kind 'which makes use of the technique of the dramatic poem'.

> While the novels of the eighteenth and nineteenth centuries, with few exceptions, were descended from Addison and Defoe, with some admixture of a debased stage comedy, there is quite another kind of novel, created by Emily Brontë, Melville, Conrad and Henry James, among others, which makes use of the technique of the dramatic poem.... To recognize in James's novels and *nouvelles* art of the same nature as *Measure for Measure*, to see that they are in a tradition of mediaeval and Elizabethan drama transmitted through Shakespeare, Ben Jonson and Bunyan (and so Hawthorne), is to make their meaning accessible, as it never can be if they are approached on the assumption that they are the same kind of thing as the writings of Trollope and Thackeray. This is to put James's work on a plane where the highest claims can be convincingly made for it.[26]

The 'plane where the highest claims can be convincingly made' well describes the level of greatness in the novel that Leavis highlights in *The Great Tradition*.

The review 'Gissing and the English Novel' has a particularly strong bearing on Leavis's book. Gissing interests Mrs Leavis because he exemplifies, best of all in *New Grub Street*, the difficulties facing the gifted writer trying to do serious work when critical standards were a jungle and the formula bestseller was in the ascendant. In other words, Gissing makes an impressive ally for her thesis in *Fiction and the Reading Public*.[27] He is 'an example of how disastrous it may be for a writer whose talent is not of the first order to be born into a bad tradition'; and yet *New Grub Street* is in an important tradition of the novel: it is 'an important link in the line of novels from Jane Austen's to the present which an adult can read at his utmost stretch—as attentively, that is, as good poetry demands to be read'.[28] As it continues, this passage presents the challenge for criticism of the novel that Leavis takes up and answers in *The Great Tradition*.

In the nineteenth century, to take the highlights, Jane Austen, *Wuthering Heights*, *Middlemarch*, *The Egoist*, *New Grub Street* connect the best eighteenth-century tradition with the serious twentieth-century tradition that Henry James, Conrad, Lawrence, Forster, Joyce and Mrs Woolf have built up. There are inferior novels (e.g. *The Way of All Flesh*) in this tradition . . . but they are all immediately recognizable as novels, distinct from what we may more usefully call fiction. It is time the history of the English novel was rewritten from the point of view of the twentieth century (it is always seen from the point of view of the mid-nineteenth), just as has been done for the history of English poetry. The student would undoubtedly be glad to be allowed to reorganize his approach and revise the list of novels he has to accept as worth attention; it would be a matter chiefly of leaving out but also of substitution, for the list consists only of conventional values. I don't know who will dare touch off the first charge to blow up those academic values. . . . What is commonly accepted as the central tradition is most easily examined in the middling practitioner—such as Trollope or Charles Reade. . . . It is time also that we sorted out the novels which form or enrich the real tradition of the English novel . . . from all the other kinds.[29]

Mrs Leavis's list of novels and novelists that 'connect the best eighteenth-century tradition with the serious twentieth-century tradition' hardly corresponds to Leavis's 'great tradition'. But all his great novelists are represented. And significantly there is no mention of Dickens, nor of any work of his. Hence *The Great Tradition* minus Dickens—or, rather, plus *Hard Times* (at Mrs Leavis's urging, we later learn).

3 F.R. Leavis and *The Great Tradition: George Eliot, Henry James, Joseph Conrad*

In spite of its air of Johnsonian authority, *The Great Tradition* (1948) strains at its seams. The core chapters on George Eliot, James and Conrad were written first, and they reflect the earlier Leavis of 'classical' rigour, who with his wife chiefly admired Johnson, Arnold and T. S. Eliot, but who was not yet completely certain of Lawrence's greatness as a novelist. But the framing chapters—'The Great Tradition' and the 'Analytic Note' on *Hard Times*—came later, as much as seven years after the chapters on Conrad, and they show Leavis leaning enthusiastically towards the 'romantic' strengths of Lawrence, and now convinced of his greatness (p. 34).

A certain disharmony results, because Leavis has not yet integrated his criteria; and the book has unity largely through the force of Leavis's judgements and some shrewd planning. Thus in the keynote chapter Leavis challenges that the novelists in the tradition, from the 'classical' Jane Austen to the 'romantic' Lawrence, are great because they are individually great as explorers of human morality, and as innovators and masters of the English language; and this chapter links with the one on Dickens by virtue of vigorous praise of Lawrence in each, the two chapters therefore providing a kind of envelope for the central sections. But in these the Laurentian–Dickensian criteria of vitality and reverence for life are not uppermost or obvious.

Leavis will continue to try to reconcile 'classical' with 'romantic' criteria more openly in *D. H. Lawrence: Novelist*, in an explicit counterpointing of T. S. Eliot and Lawrence. This he will do to clarify the strengths and weaknesses of each so as to discover better where he himself stands in relation to them. Already he looks forward to this exercise at the close of the keynote chapter on the 'great tradition': Eliot is mildly rebuked for championing Joyce and his lesser imitators, and Lawrence is named the sole modern heir of the great novelists (pp. 34–7).

In *The Great Tradition*, then, Leavis seeks to establish an order of importance and excellence in the novel in the manner of Arnold and Eliot. In doing so he makes the common-sense appeal that literature must be judged as an expression of life seen as a complex ethical reality, like Johnson and Arnold before; and, like all these writers and Mrs Leavis, he makes self-discipline and maturity the indispensable ingredients of good writing. Consequently he agreed with his wife to put Jane Austen rather than a more obviously romantic novelist at the head of his tradition. But, paradoxically, he judged the eighteenth-century novel to be at best important histórically, but not great. As noted in the previous chapter, the Leavises, being teachers, intended this book to provide the university undergraduate (primarily) with an essential reading-list, not an exhaustive one.

However, as the Leavises were already learning, the novel above all literary forms resists a too rigorously 'classical' schematisation. The critique of *Hard Times*, appended at the last moment, includes caveats about preconceptions regarding the English novel (pp. 249 and 266) which reverberate ironically through *The Great Tradition*. Leavis would have done well to have heeded the implications of Lawrence's words: 'If you try to nail anything down, in the novel, either it kills the novel, or the novel gets up and walks away with the nail.'[1] Leavis did go on to remove nails from his conception of the novel as a result of growing confidence in the notion of 'the novel as dramatic poem', begun with *Hard Times*, expanded with Lawrence, and crowned in the return with Mrs Leavis to Dickens.

But meanwhile *The Great Tradition* had upon its appearance the great Johnsonian virtue of stirring debate on the novel. Johnson hoped in the *Preface to Shakespeare* that 'what I have here not dogmatically but deliberately written, may recal [*sic*] the principles of the drama to a new examination'.[2] Whatever the limitations of his book, and however readers choose to describe the manner of his writing,[3] Leavis recalled readers to a new examination of the novel.

He begins his book with a handsome tribute to his wife: 'My sense of my immeasurable indebtedness, in every page of this book, to my wife cannot be adequately expressed' (p. 7). The previous chapter has adumbrated the nature of the debt. The period of genesis of *The Great Tradition*, 1941–7,[4] also reveals how closely husband and wife were working on the novel. In 1941 Mrs Leavis began 'A Critical Theory of Jane Austen's Writings', in effect the chapter on Jane Austen that Leavis chose not to provide in *The Great Tradition*, while Leavis wrote his critique of Conrad. Mrs Leavis concluded 'A Critical Theory' in 1944; Leavis followed with George Eliot in 1945–6. In 1947 both are assessing James, Mrs Leavis contributing three review articles (see p. 148 n. 24), and Leavis adding two more.[5] Also in 1947 comes Leavis's essay on *Hard Times*, and in 1948 come his essays on *The Europeans* and *The Portrait of a Lady*.

Why did not Mrs Leavis undertake the task of revaluing the English novel? *Fiction and the Reading Public* and her work in *Scrutiny* show her well qualified to have done so, academically and polemically. Several reasons are likely. Leavis was the better known as a critic, and so the better placed tactically. And no doubt Mrs Leavis must have been especially preoccupied with domestic considerations at this time. After 'A Critical Theory' in 1944, her output slackens, and her next major statement on fiction comes seven years later, with her 1951 essay on Hawthorne. More important, by 1936 Leavis had completed his revaluation of English poetry and, having established his criteria of significance, critical idiom, and analytical method, was now ready to tackle the novel. Nine years later he summarised his critical principles in 'Notes in the Analysis of Poetry', a triad of essays having key importance for understanding how he works as a critic.[6]

Significantly, two-thirds of the 'Notes' were completed just before he began his revaluation of George Eliot. A comparison of the first essay in 'Notes' with the critique of George Eliot shows clearly how Leavis sees that the qualities which determine greatness in poetry—impersonality, maturity, and reality— equally determine greatness in the novel. So he judges that George Eliot consistently spoils even her mature novels by intruding an emotional interest in the drama she portrays. Then she writes immaturely, and idealises and sentimentalises reality, instead of realising it by dramatic means. Accordingly he stigmatises her self-idealisation in Dorothea Brooke in *Middlemarch* (p. 88ff.), and he would excise half of *Daniel Deronda*, the half concerning Deronda, for similar reasons (p. 93ff.). Later he changed his mind, realising the impertinence of tampering with a work of art.[7]

Leavis had also taken his own bearings on the contemporary novel in a number of essays and review articles. He never collected these into one volume, but most of them appeared in *For Continuity* (1933),[8] which therefore links with *The Great Tradition*, as *New Bearings in English Poetry* with *Revaluation*, though more loosely.

For Continuity has importance early in Leavis's criticism in that it shows him coming to the realisation that the critic's interests and responsibilities concur with those of the novelists he admires—in this case, Dos Passos and Lawrence. And *For Continuity* is, strategically, Leavis's first book on Lawrence. Already he shows how powerfully Lawrence's attitude to life has begun to shape his own critical thinking. He realises that the kind of awareness and concern for living humanly according to the spirit, rather than mechanically according to 'ideas', that Lawrence insists on in his writing must be made the centre of his own critical beliefs.[9] Consequently, he gives notice—indirectly here, but explicitly later[10]— that literary criticism for him cannot be restricted to merely literary, or to merely aesthetic considerations. On the contrary, the critic must concern himself with everything that shapes a society and orders its values, just as the serious novelists like Dos Passos and Lawrence do.[11] This belief is basic to *The Great Tradition*.

As in *Revaluation*, so in *The Great Tradition* Leavis declares his aim to make 'essential discriminations' (p. 9), both in the English novel at large and among the works of his great novelists. That is very different from having a narrow interest in the novel—a familiar charge against him. But it does sharply distinguish his book from Granville Hicks's of the same title.[12] Hicks's book, which Leavis must surely have read (see his references to Hicks's political writings in *For Continuity*), comprises an interpretative catalogue of all the distinguished American writers—poets as well as novelists— who resisted or recoiled from the bourgeois big-business boom in America from the Civil War to the early 1930s. By greatness Hicks means something like the energy of a writer's resistance, and by tradition the cumulative force of his writers' resistance between 1865 and 1935, whether each writer develops individually or not.

Leavis also stresses energy as a chief quality in his great novelists. 'They are all distinguished by a vital capacity for experience' (p. 17), he says; and he speaks more than once of the 'energy of vision' (pp. 29, 232) that relates Conrad to Dickens. But for Leavis, unlike Hicks, the energy must be directed toward affirming life. It is not enough that a writer devote his art to saying no to life's ugliness, however brilliantly he may do so, as Leavis feels that Dos Passos does. For him Dos Passos is a 'serious' novelist, but not a great one, since he never succeeds in indicating how life might continue to be lived humanly, according to the finer capacities and resources of the human spirit, *in spite of* the mechanical jungle of the modern world he so brilliantly depicts.[13] But Hicks judges Dos Passos to be a greater writer.

Nor can a writer be great for Leavis if he channels his energy too much into the mechanics of his art. However admirable the pursuit of beauty of form and style, an addiction to art too often masks an inner hollowness of human significance, Leavis feels, citing Flaubert, George Moore (pp. 16–17), and much of the late James. Similarly, Joyce's 'elaborate analogical structure[s]' represent a 'dead end' (p. 36), for they too signify an intensity of art for art's sake, and not for life's sake. For Leavis the noblest art deals with the stuff of human experience; the truly great writer creates a vision of life; and the energy of his vision is a moral energy. The art of the great novelist is distinguished by a 'marked moral intensity' (p. 17). Evidently life in *Ulysses* is at the mercy of art.

In emphasising life as the subject-matter of great art, Leavis does not ignore aesthetic considerations. Rather, he insists that in the great novelist or poet the subject-matter determines the form it takes, the vision defines the art that expresses it. Thus, René Wellek's seemingly disparaging remark that Leavis appears to be 'quite uninterested in questions of technique in the novel'[14] holds true only in so far as Leavis does not examine style as a rhetorician would. But Leavis is a critic, not a rhetorician. And as a critic of the novel he places a very great importance on a novelist's style and technique, well knowing that he makes his vision art by his style, by the way he uses language. Moreover the novel as art does not mean a moral essay disguised as fiction. A great novel '*enacts* its moral significance' (p. 43). A novelist is great in so far as he impersonalises a significant theme by dramatic means.

The importance that Leavis places on style and technique in relation to theme and subject matter, and to impersonality, can be seen in the astringently economical use he makes of Flaubert. He constantly invokes Flaubert when discussing 'form' in his great novelists, well knowing that Flaubert is an exemplar of 'form' and a standard by which to discuss 'form' in other novelists. He does so, then, partly as a compliment to the French master,[15] and not just to snub him, as many think. But he also sees Flaubert as a

warning for what happens when 'form' is pursued at the expense of
subject-matter, when the novelist so interests himself in his art that
he cuts himself off from his richest material: human experience,
life. Leavis feels that Flaubert does pursue 'form' at the expense of
life, and consequently that his art, impersonal though it may be, is
relatively hollow and represents a retreat from life (p. 16ff.).
However, he can use Flaubert as a kind of double yardstick, both
for valuing 'form' in itself and for valuing 'form' in relation to
subject-matter. So he argues that Conrad's mastery of 'form' is
more significant than Flaubert's because it is the vehicle of a deep
human interest.

> Conrad went to school to the French masters, and is in the tradi-
> tion of Flaubert. But he is a greater novelist than Flaubert
> because of the greater range and depth of his interest in human-
> ity and the greater intensity of his moral preoccupation: he is not
> open to the kind of criticism that James brings against *Madame
> Bovary*. *Nostromo* is a masterpiece of 'form' in senses of the term
> congenial to the discussion of Flaubert's art, but to appreciate
> Conrad's 'form' is to take stock of a process of relative valuation
> conducted by him in the face of life: what do men live by? what
> *can* men live by?—these are the questions that animate his
> theme.   (pp. 41–2)[16]

And which 'animate' his 'art', Leavis might equally well have said.
For he had in fact just asked,

> Is there any great novelist whose preoccupation with 'form' is
> not a matter of his responsibility towards a rich human interest,
> or complexity of interests, profoundly realized?—a responsibility
> involving, of its very nature, imaginative sympathy, moral dis-
> crimination, and judgement of relative human value?   (p. 40)

Again, unlike Hicks, Leavis stresses the originality of his great
writers. They are all strongly individual, each making innovations
in the art of the novel which they practise in common: 'The great
novelists . . . are all very much concerned with "form"; they are all
very original technically, having turned their genius to the working
out of their own appropriate methods and procedures' (p. 16).
Even intelligence, a quality Leavis prizes especially, will not be
enough to make a writer great if he has not worked out his own

form, as he feels is true of Scott: 'He was a great and very intelligent man; but, not having the creative writer's interest in
literature, he made no serious attempt to work out his own form
and break away from the bad tradition of the eighteenth-century
romance' (p. 14).

In contrast, Jane Austen, George Eliot, James, Conrad, and
Dickens with *Hard Times* are creative and achieved at their best a
wholly individual expression in the art of the novel. They then constitute a tradition of individuals who, by dint of making original
contributions to a common art, 'change the possibilities of the art
for practitioners and readers' (p. 10). But they constitute a tradition, too, by reason of their 'common concern . . . with essential
human issues' (p. 19), and because they devote their art to promoting awareness of these—to promoting 'awareness of the
possibilities of life' (p. 10).

Leavis finds it relatively easy to link Jane Austen, George Eliot
and Henry James on this basis. But he has more trouble with Conrad. At least, the reader finds his assimilation more puzzling.

He does not give much time to Jane Austen, preferring for
special reasons to refer the reader to his wife's essays on her in
Scrutiny. Nevertheless, he implies that, unlike Scott, Jane Austen
did break away from her eighteenth-century precursors. She
assimilated what she learned from Richardson, from Fielding and
from Fanny Burney into an art all her own, especially in *Emma*
(pp. 11–18). Consequently, she makes 'an exceptionally illuminating study of the nature of originality' (p. 13). Then, quoting
from *Felix Holt* and the *Middlemarch*, he indicates an essential affinity between George Eliot and Jane Austen in their similar use of
irony in expressing a moral interest in life (pp. 18–19). But more
important, he adds, is the difference between them in the individual use to which they put their irony. It is, then, their 'likeness'
in 'unlikeness', their expressing in individual ways a 'common
concern . . . with essential human issues' (p. 19) that links them
as great novelists in a tradition of human centrality. George Eliot
added to what she had learned from Jane Austen. The 'new impersonality' she achieved for herself in handling the 'Transome theme'
(p. 67ff.) in *Felix Holt* led on to *Middlemarch* and *Daniel Deronda*,
where, says Leavis,

> she handled with unprecedented subtlety and refinement the
> personal relations of sophisticated characters exhibiting the

'civilization' of the 'best society', and used, in so doing, an original psychological notation corresponding to the fineness of her psychological and moral insight.   (p. 25)

Yet, though Leavis insists that he has no desire to 'establish *indebtedness*' between his novelists, but rather their pre-eminence together above the more run-of-the-mill novelists, he devotes the longest section of the book, '*Daniel Deronda* and *The Portrait of a Lady*', to showing how James's masterpiece grew out of George Eliot's last and longest novel. Consequently he makes his most convincing, because most detailed, illustration of 'tradition', an illustration of indebtedness. Moreover he does so seeming to grant all the laurels to George Eliot and few to James. However, he goes on in the following chapter to stress James's originality, and so unlikeness to George Eliot. He finds that James's brilliance in 'dramatic presentation' derives from George Eliot (p. 127). But the 'creative wealth' of *The Portrait of a Lady* is 'all distinctively Jamesian', and 'Madame Merle . . . couldn't have been done by George Eliot' (p. 167). Meanwhile it is a chief point with Leavis that the strong James shows a greater affinity with Hawthorne in the American tradition, and with Jane Austen and George Eliot in the English tradition of the novel, than with Flaubert and Turgenev (p. 145). That is, he is great in the novels mostly of the middle period, *The Portrait of a Lady*, *The Bostonians*, *The Europeans* and *Washington Square*, in which he richly renders life. But the late James is too Flaubertian for Leavis's taste. With the exception of *The Awkward Age* and *What Maisie Knew*, his novels have become too much like sophisticated word-pictures and puzzles, empty of human significance, and his art in general 'synthetic' rather than truly 'poetic' (p. 185ff.).

Leavis cannot so easily place Conrad in the tradition, and this may explain why he stressed his unconcern with indebtedness. Ironically, however, he keeps citing Dickens when he draws attention to Conrad's 'energy' and 'dramatic vividness' (see pp. 28–9, 229, 232 and 246). Meanwhile, he posits Conrad's originality in his 'foreignness' (p. 26), and suggests that Conrad can be linked with the others because he mastered the English language in full awareness, like the others, of the 'moral tradition' it embodies (p. 27). Moreover he says that Conrad gained this awareness as a result of his full baptism in another strongly moral English tradition, that of the Merchant Service: 'the Merchant Service is

for him both a spiritual fact and a spiritual symbol, and the interests that made it so for him control and animate his art everywhere' (ibid.). Consequently his masterpiece, *Nostromo*, may show
a Flaubertian mastery of 'form', but its range and depth and imaginative sympathy come from Conrad's inwardness with the
English language, with English experience, and with the moral
tradition associated with these.

> Here, then, we have a master of the English language, who
> chose it for its distinctive qualities and because of the moral
> tradition associated with it, and whose concern with art—he be-
> ing like Jane Austen and George Eliot and Henry James an in-
> novator in 'form' and method—is the servant of a profoundly
> serious interest in life.   (Ibid.)

We see that by mastery of the English language Leavis means
much more than an advanced skill with figurative words and poetic
diction, as he well illustrates in criticising the weaknesses of the late
James and the early Conrad. Both in different ways tend to scene-
paint with words rather than to realise poetically, he feels. In his
late novels James's images seem too deliberated, lack the dramatic
immediacy of metaphor, and look too much like 'coloured
diagram[s]' (p. 185ff.), and the early Conrad tries to evoke
significance with clusters and repetitions of vaguely evocative ad-
jectives so that this work has only a ' "picturesque" human interest' (pp. 198ff., 210). In such cases we are made too aware of the
author's presence in his work, Leavis feels. We see James as too
consciously the symbolist, and Conrad as self-conscious artist of the
tropics. But Leavis insists that a true mastery of language shows
itself when subject-matter is communicated dramatically and
speaks for itself with the immediacy of metaphor, as in Shakespeare
and in the great novelists at their best. Such use of language Leavis
typically calls 'poetic–creative', and by it meaning is 'enacted'
rather than stated by the writer.[17] This brings us back to his key
postulate that works of art '*enact* their moral valuations'.[18] This
phrase also describes his notion of impersonality, but only partly.
For him the truly significant impersonality includes psychological
and moral depth, as in Shakespeare and in his great novelists at
their best.

Leavis, then, presents his 'great tradition' as a line of strongly
individual masters of the English language, who made the novel

into a richly poetic communication of essential human experience, and as such a major literary genre. They have a common human centrality. But they are all original in the technical innovations they have made, and in the way they have increased man's awareness of his human or spiritual potential.

> [T]he major novelists . . . count in the same way as the major poets, in the sense that they not only change the possibilities of the art for practitioners and readers, but they are significant in terms of that human awareness they promote; awareness of the possibilities of life.   (p. 10)

I say 'his "great tradition" ' mindful of the many readers and critics who have called Leavis's selectiveness narrowness, and poured cold water on his book saying that it constitutes an arbitrarily private tradition[19]—as if it were capricious or narrow to base a tradition of greatness on artistic excellence and human centrality. And as if Leavis ever thought or suggested that he has a monopoly of the writers he calls great, or that they are the only ones worth reading. In any case, it is specious to argue that merely by adding others he would make his tradition any less private. For that matter, when ever did anyone (except for the special tribe of thesis-writers) spend much time on a writer he did not care for? All critical studies of any importance or length originate in a personal or private preference. On the other hand, it is undeniable that Leavis made a bad mistake in excluding Dickens, who so patently meets his criteria. But, significantly, he has restored only Dickens of English novelists, and, so passionately does he believe in literature as the basis of a humane education, it is hard to believe that he would not restore others if he could.

Few now would question Leavis's choice of Jane Austen, George Eliot, James and Conrad as great English novelists, or deny his reasons for choosing them. Rather, later criticism has confirmed Leavis, and added to his reasons. Moreover he has been credited with largely pioneering the revival of interest in George Eliot and Conrad.[20] What remains debatable is the exclusion of the eighteenth-century novel and of a host of worthy candidates in the novel of the nineteenth and twentieth centuries. And it seems to me that the only profitable line to take to this question is to re-examine Leavis's opening chapter, where he distinguishes the few from the

many, in the spirit of Arnold's phrase: 'to see the object as in itself
it really is'.[21]

The basic aim of the chapter called 'The Great Tradition' could
not be more basic, or more full of common sense. It is to provide
an essential reading-list in the English novel. Given the vast-
ness of the field, this is what every good teacher at some time provides for his students, and every reader with a more than casual
interest in literature decides on for himself, or so Leavis reasons.
The teacher and critic's 'great concern is . . . to save the student
from the usual laborious dissipation, to put him in the way of the
concentrated reading that will truly educate him by giving him,
as it were, the essential structure of literary experience',[22] he declared almost at the outset of his career. Accordingly he wrote
New Bearings, Revaluation[23] and then *The Great Tradition*. Only,
Leavis has made his 'essential discriminations' (p. 9) in the English
novel with such force and economy that he appears to have convinced almost everyone except himself[24] that there are no novelists worth reading apart from his great novelists. Yet closer in-
spection reveals that Leavis has identified at least two classes of
importance aside from the great: those under the general head
of permanent historical interest, and the anomalous geniuses,
Dickens and Emily Brontë. The first group, which includes the
chief novelists in the eighteenth-century tradition, are distinguished
by such epithets as, 'remarkable', 'distinguished', 'permanent',
'intelligent', 'impressive', 'important' and 'classic'. They are:
Bunyan, Defoe, Fielding, Richardson, Fanny Burney, Scott,
Peacock, Thackeray, Disraeli, Charlotte Brontë, Hardy, Joyce,[25]
T. F. Powys, L. H. Myers and Arthur Koestler. Significantly,
Leavis has another set of terms to describe the great: 'major',
'creative', 'unprecedented', 'significant' and 'pre-eminent'. It is
significant, too, that he does not use the terms 'create', 'creative',
'subtle', 'art' or 'artist' to describe the novel before 1800; but of
Jane Austen and her successors he uses them liberally. He implies
thereby that the novel did not become fully an art, a major literary
genre rivalling great poetry, until the nineteenth century. He was
soon to say so explicitly.[26]

In other words, Leavis does not aim to duplicate the literary
histories wherever these have been just. For instance, Fielding is
'important historically' because 'he leads to Jane Austen', and consequently he 'deserves the place of importance given him in the

literary histories' (p. 11). But 'standards are formed in comparison', he continues, and by the standards of technical subtlety and human complexity and depth visible in Jane Austen or George Eliot Fielding's art can hardly be called great: 'There can't be subtlety of organization without richer matter to organize, and subtler interests, than Fielding has to offer' (p. 12).

He implies that another test for saving the reader's time in this vast field, and so for deciding a novel's importance, might be whether or not a novel repays the labour spent in re-reading it. Accordingly *Clarissa* is a 'really impressive work', but, given the limitedness of its 'range and variety', Richardson makes 'prohibitive' demands on 'the reader's time' (p. 13). Likewise 'life isn't long enough to permit of one's giving much time to Fielding' (p. 11), and for the reader of Thackeray 'it is merely a matter of going on and on' (p. 31). Moreover, he questions his great novelists in the same way, wondering whether a large portion of *Adam Bede* (p. 49), all of *Romola* (p. 63), *The Ambassadors* (p. 178) and the early Conrad (p. 210) justify more than one reading. Not that Leavis expects his great novels to be easy reading: '*What Maisie Knew . . .* does certainly demand of the reader a close and unrelaxed attention . . . it never permits us to find it "easy to read as a novel" ' (p. 173).

Leavis, then, does not arbitrarily reject all save his great novelists. He makes his 'essential discriminations' and metes justice according to the highest standards, and with the strictest economy. He is invariably as forceful and incisive with a masterpiece of his great novelists, getting within a few pages to the heart of its significance without however simplifying its complex totality. A good example is his discussion of *The Portrait of a Lady*. Here, within six pages (pp. 163–9) and by means of a handful of key quotations and several carefully placed cross-references to other works of James's discussed in adjacent pages, he builds up a strong impression both of the total complexity of this long novel and of its place in James's *oeuvre*.

But very few readers have sympathised with Leavis's rigorous economy, or even understood the common-sense reasons behind it. Nor is it well understood that Leavis accords a special status to Emily Brontë and Dickens. Though they do not fit into his scheme, he calls them both 'genius' (pp. 29, 38), and does not lump them with the also-rans. For instance, it is all too tempting to take Leavis's description of *Wuthering Heights* as an 'astonishing work' and yet a 'kind of sport' for a convenient but mostly negative[27] equivocation that lets him out of coping with Emily Brontë. But Richard Chase has seen the justice of Leavis's judgement; that by it he does not mean to condemn Emily Brontë. Chase adds, though, that if Leavis were aware of the great American 'poetic' tradition he would have no difficulty in placing *Wuthering Heights* in it.[28] This is well said. Actually, Leavis is aware of the American tradition in so far as he relates James to it through Melville and Hawthorne (p. 145), but he would have done well to make Chase's point about *Wuthering Heights*.

Leavis is much more precise in his 'essential discriminations' with Dickens, as well as more favourable to Dickens than most readers have realised. He accepts *Hard Times* as a great novel and calls Dickens a 'great genius' for family entertainment—at, that is, his chosen level (p. 29). He was wrong in his overall judgement at this time, that 'the adult mind doesn't as a rule find in Dickens a challenge to an unusual and sustained seriousness' (p. 29), but there can be no reason for doubting the sincerity with which he made it, or for not perceiving that by it he distinguished Dickens above all those outside 'the great tradition'.

However, it is undeniable that, in excluding Emily Brontë and Dickens, Leavis narrowed and weakened his 'great tradition', for, apart from anything else, he left out the two most significant English precursors of Conrad. We can even see that Leavis seems half-aware that Conrad's affinities with Dickens have a greater importance than he allows. He writes in the opening chapter,

> As I point out in my discussion of him, Conrad is in certain respects so like Dickens that it is difficult to say for just how much influence Dickens counts. He is undoubtedly there in the London of *The Secret Agent*. . . . This co-presence of obvious influence with assimilation suggests that Dickens may have counted for more in Conrad's mature art than seems at first probable: it suggests that Dickens may have encouraged the development in Conrad's art of that energy of vision and registration in which they are akin.   (pp. 28–9)

He certainly goes on to demonstrate what he says here in the critique of Conrad, but without bringing himself to consolidate the link. He prefers on the grounds of Conrad's greater maturity to call his 'energy of vision and characterization' Shakespearean rather than Dickensian (p. 232). And yet the critique of *Hard Times* which follows is devoted to extolling Dickens's Shakespearean dramatic power, poetic energy and flexibility of mode!

All that we have been saying of Emily Brontë and Dickens points to the fact that, had Leavis at this time re-read Dickens and had greater confidence in his idea of 'the novel as dramatic poem',[29] he would have made *The Great Tradition* a different and very much more satisfying book. And this was to come: if we include Mrs Leavis's 'Fresh Approach to *Wuthering Heights*', the Leavises provided in *Dickens the Novelist* a revised version of *The Great Tradition*.

Meanwhile the exclusion of Dickens undoubtedly did much to encourage the notion that Leavis is unreceptive to delight and the comic spirit. But, even accepting the first part of this proposition as true, how true is the second part? A critic so perceptive, just, and persuasive as Lionel Trilling has argued that the whole proposition is true. Linking Leavis's treatment of Dickens with his treatment of Congreve, Sterne and Meredith, Trilling concludes that Leavis

> takes no proper account . . . of the art that delights—and enlightens—by the intentional relaxation of moral awareness, by its invitation to us to contemplate the mere excess of irrelevant life. Nor does he take any account of the impulse of sheer *performance*, even of virtuosity, which, whether we respond to it in acrobatics or in athletics or in prestidigitation or in the ballet or in music or in literature, is of enormous human significance.[30]

These enviably magisterial sentences contain issues that are debatable at much greater length than there is room for here. Suffice it to say, first, that there is no question in *The Great Tradition* of Leavis's lumping Dickens with Congreve, Sterne and Meredith. His point in endorsing Santayana's advice about Dickens[31] is that Dickens is a great genius for family entertainment, his chosen level of creation. For the rest, and with the exception of *Hard Times*, Dickens was 'innocent' of 'mature standards and interests' (p.147). By this description Leavis means that Dickens does not aspire to create art of mature subtlety, and 'innocent of', going with the endorsement of Santayana, constitutes a fondly 'placing' judgement, however wrong and limiting it proved to be. Leavis's attitude to the other three is very different. He implies that they do aspire to write with mature subtlety for a mature audience, but that in failing to do so they are immature in a pejorative sense. Secondly, literature being in question, it is scarcely credible that the *oeuvre* of Congreve, Sterne and Meredith can either individually or collectively be described as having 'enormous human significance'. Nor, thirdly, is it credible that Leavis takes only a solemn interest in, say, *Emma*, *The Europeans* and *Hard Times*. In fact he almost rhapsodises over Dicken's art in making Sleary's Horse-riding a central metaphor precisely of delight, wonder and creative performance in *Hard Times* (p. 254ff.).[32] From Leavis's affirmation of *Hard Times*, from his comparison of Congreve's Millamant with George Eliot's Gwendolen Harleth (p. 111), and from other places besides,[33] we may surely conclude that for Leavis the art that truly delights—and enlightens—is the art in which comedy and delight *intensify* moral awareness. And, if we think of Shakespeare, as Leavis invariably does in relation to his great novelists, this is an impregnable point of view.

In sum, I think that, when all the limitations of *The Great Tradition* have been weighed, Trilling makes the common mistake of putting a too narrow construction on Leavis's use of the word 'moral'. It is very true that Leavis writes with such urgency and intensity about the 'moral intensity' of his writers that the reader may easily feel he is the object of a 'Gospel Hall'[34] sermon. But it is uncritical to remain in such a posture. Leavis always means, and shows that he means, far more than a narrow puritanical outlook in his use of 'moral'. He invariably qualifies 'moral' with the terms 'life' and 'richness' and 'depth of interest' and 'human significance'. The 'marked moral intensity' of his great novelists has nothing to do with contracting or reducing life. On the contrary, it goes with a 'reverent openness before life': a capacity to look at and into life with imaginative sympathy rather than with prejudice, wonderingly rather than knowingly. At any rate, a closer look at Leavis's discussion of impersonality in his great novelists may help to show how little excuse there is for thinking his interest in literature narrow.

Leavis begins to identify the qualities of a great novelist in Jane Austen. Her interest in her art, he suggests, cannot be separated from her close interest in life. She works out her own technique (unlike Scott, whom Leavis has just been mentioning) to suit her subject-matter, and both the technique and the subject-matter derive from an 'intense moral interest of her own in life':

The principle of organization, and the principle of development, in her work is an intense moral interest of her own in life that is in the first place a preoccupation with certain problems that life compels on her as personal ones.   (p. 15).

But such an interest in her art and in life does not mean that her art is confessional, or a kind of personal therapy, for

> She is intelligent and serious enough to be able to impersonalize her moral tensions as she strives, in her art, to become more fully conscious of them, and to learn what, in the interests of life, she ought to do with them. Without her intense moral preoccupation she wouldn't have been a great novelist.   (p. 16)

Two major criteria emerge from these two quotations. The great novelist creates out of a deep, personal engagement with reality. The process is not one of self-indulgence, but rather of his striving toward a completer, more disinterested understanding of his relation to life. Consequently he achieves a vision of reality unvitiated by personality. This kind of impersonality, Leavis is to instance again and again, indicates the writer's maturity in his attitude to both literature and life. It is neither Eliot's 'escape from personality', nor Joyce's Stephen Dedalus's nail-paring indifference,[35] but rather the completion of personality described by I. A. Richards. The more, says Richards, 'our personality is engaged' in the objects of its interest 'the more we seem to see "all round" them', and 'the more *detached* our attitude becomes', so that 'to say we are *impersonal* is merely a curious way of saying that our personality is more *completely* involved'.[36]

Leavis went on to clarify what he himself meant in the first of the essays belonging to 'Notes in the Analysis of Poetry' called ' "Thought" and Emotional Quality'. There, by means of comparison and contrast of a large variety of poems by Wordsworth, Tennyson, Lawrence, Marvell, Lionel Johnson, Blake and Shelley, he aimed to demonstrate that, where the emotional life of a poem is seen to be controlled and objectified by the poet's thought, the result is a sincere, mature and impersonal evocation of reality; but that, where this has not happened, the result is personal indulgence and a falsification of reality. 'The "impersonal" poem', he says, 'unmistakably derives from a seismic personal experience'.[37] First-hand experience generates the emotional life in the poem and gives it vitality. But for the poem to become fully impersonalised and to be more, in other words, than a mere overflow of personal emotion, feeling must be controlled by the 'thought' or critical attitude which the poet takes towards it. The poet's thought, he says, varying his terms, is 'an element of disinterested valuation'; and he adds that in the completely impersonalised poem the poet's emotion is not seen as a thing apart from his thought: 'feeling is not divorced from thinking'.[38] As he remarks of Wordsworth's 'A slumber did my spirit seal', 'No one can doubt that Wordsworth wrote his poem because of something profoundly and involuntarily suffered—suffered as a personal calamity, but the experience has been so impersonalized that the effect . . . is one of bare and disinterested presentment.'[39] And what he goes on to say of the 'Metaphysical habit' applies directly to what he said of Jane Austen in the passage already quoted:

> The activity of the thinking mind, the energy of intelligence, in-
> volved in the Metaphysical habit means that, when the poet *has*
> urgent personal experience to deal with it is attended to and con-
> templated—which in turn means some kind of separation, or
> distinction, between experiencer and experience . . . to analyse
> your experience you must, while keeping it alive and immedi-
> ately present as experience, treat it in some sense as an object.
> That is, an essential part of the strength of good Metaphysical
> poetry turns out to be of the same order as the strength of all the
> most satisfying poetry.[40]

And, he might have added, of all the most satisfying novels. For, as he observes of their finest work, George Eliot, James and Conrad write out of 'urgent personal experience' but so as to maintain a 'distinction between experiencer and experience'. As he oftens puts it, it is a matter of the novelist's knowing the experience or situa-tion he portrays from 'inside' while he at the same time adopts a critical attitude to it from 'outside'. It amounts to a critical detach-ment which is sometimes ironic. Thus Leavis finds James's por-trayal of New England civilisation fine and effective 'because he is not merely an ironic critic . . . he both knows it from inside and sees it from outside with the eye of a professional student of civilisation who has had much experience of non-Puritan cultures' (p. 150). Similarly, Conrad's successes with *Typhoon* and *The Shadow-Line* result both from his knowing the Merchant Service 'from the in-side' and from 'the capacity for detachment that makes intimate knowledge uniquely conscious and articulate' (p. 208). The same is true of George Eliot in *Middlemarch*: so long as she controls from outside what she knows from inside—that is, from first-hand experience—she achieves 'the poised impersonal insight of a finely tempered wisdom' (p. 89). Hence her success with the portraits of her intellectuals, Casaubon and Lydgate. These are so successful because she herself knows very well the strain of intellectual life: 'Only a novelist who had known from the inside the exhaustions and discouragements of long-range intellectual enterprises could have conveyed the pathos of Dr Casaubon's predicament' (p. 75). She succeeds with Lydgate for similar reasons (p. 79). This knowing from the inside is what Leavis meant at the outset when he said that the great novelists have a 'vital capacity for experience': they explore reality at first hand. However, the novelist must control his explorations with critical detachment. Lydgate and Casaubon are strongly real because subjected to the 'irony that informs our vision of the other characters in these opening chapters' (p. 87).

In stressing irony as a means for distancing the novelist from his subject, the experiencer from the experience, Leavis anticipates much subsequent important theory on the novel, for he is talking essentially of the ironic distance which later theorists on the novel have written so extensively about, most notably Wayne Booth in *The Rhetoric of Fiction* (1961). Only, for Leavis, the great novelist combines irony with a rich sympathy and understanding of the reality he transmutes into art.

This process of working reality into art—the artist's technique, that is—Leavis characteristically calls 'realisation'; and it is a key element in his notion of impersonality. What Leavis means by 'realisation'[41] has been well understood by Vincent Buckley:

> Leavis is not a realist in any naive sense. The word 'realisation' is a very felicitous one; for it suggests the paradoxically dual nature of the quality he is talking about. It carries a suggestion not only of the creating, the bringing present, of some objective reality, but also of self-realisation, that kind of inner human activity which is perhaps better called, not self-expression, but self-recognition.[42]

This certainly ties in with what we have noted so far of Leavis's view of impersonality, and especially with his words on Jane Austen. It coincides with his remark that when George Eliot writes at her impersonal best it is with 'the genius that is self-knowledge and a rare order of maturity' (p. 90). And this happens when she draws on her self-knowledge in such a way as to 'realise' dramatically in her art realities she knows intimately from her own experience, as with Casaubon and Lydgate in *Middlemarch*:

> It is remarkable how George Eliot makes us feel his intellectual passion as something concrete. When novelists tell us that a character is a thinker (or an artist) we have usually only their word for it, but Lydgate's 'triumphant delight in his studies' is a concrete presence: it is plain that George Eliot knows intimately what it is like, and knows what his studies are. (p. 79)

Then, to make 'concrete' is to 'realise' as Leavis shows in a similar appreciation of Bulstrode, also from *Middlemarch*:

> The peculiar religious world to which Bulstrode belongs, its ethos and idiom, George Eliot knows from the inside—we remember the Evangelicalism of her youth. The analysis is a creative process; it is a penetrating imagination, masterly and vivid in understanding, bringing the concrete[43] before us in all its reality. (pp. 82–3)

We also note from this that 'realization' is a creative process, and that a failure to realise implies a failure to be truly creative.

Leavis can illustrate particularly well in George Eliot his key criteria for judging creativity—impersonality, realisation, concreteness, self-knowledge, maturity—because he finds her habitually failing to write impersonally. This happens when she fails to distance herself from a character in whom she has a special interest; with whom, rather, she identifies herself too emotionally, as Leavis finds she does again and again in her novels: with Maggie Tulliver, with Adam Bede, with Dorothea Brooke and with Daniel Deronda. In such cases she 'idealises' instead of 'realises'. For instance, he finds that Will Ladislaw in *Middlemarch* is not an independent dramatic reality, but, rather, a product of George Eliot's precreative 'idealising' imagination, and, furthermore, that the 'idealised' Will is merely a means for filtering to the reader George Eliot's self-idealisation in Dorothea Brooke:

> In fact, he has no independent status of his own—he can't be said to exist; he merely represents, not a dramatically real point

of view, but certain of George Eliot's intentions—intentions she has failed to realize creatively. The most important of these is to impose on the reader her own vision and valuation of Dorothea. (pp. 88–9)

And to 'idealise' is to indulge in sentimentality, as Leavis shows in bringing a similar criticism against James's portrayal of Milly Theale in *The Wings of the Dove*: 'she isn't there [i.e. real], and the fuss the other characters make about her as the "Dove" has the effect of an irritating sentimentality' (p. 175).

On the other hand, Axel Heyst in Conrad's *Victory* might well serve as a paradigm of the process of self-recognition that leads to a firm grasp on reality. Leavis certainly sees Heyst as an emblem of Conrad's creative sensibility. Heyst, he remarks, goes through a 'progressive self-discovery through relations with others', so that by the time of his death he has overcome his scepticism about life and gained a 'new sense of reality' which is a triumph of self-knowledge and a new maturity (pp. 223–30). His death gives the novel its title: it is a 'victory of life' and his career as a whole reflects Conrad's artistic achievement: 'The characteristic Conradian sensibility is that of the creator of Heyst' (p. 230). What Leavis means by this is that Heyst incarnates an answer to the questions that typically animate Conrad's art: namely, 'what do men live by? what *can* men live by?' (p. 42). And the answer is a 'victory of life', or, in other words, Conrad through Heyst affirms life. By extension he shows that life means more than mechanically existing or living in despair; that, rather, life has a meaning and a purpose in that it contains possibilities of hope for better things, of growth, and of spiritual renewal. He shows, in short, that life is both worth living and worth living for. *Victory* embodies very strikingly Leavis's conviction that great literature is an affirmation of life in that it articulates and celebrates man's finest spiritual potentialities.

Hard Times does so even more strikingly. The novel, which Leavis sees as a 'moral fable' depicting 'the confutation of Utilitarianism by life' (pp. 250, 260) and for which he inaugurated the analogy 'the novel as dramatic poem', plainly deserves a more central place in *The Great Tradition*. Quite simply, the evaluation and affirmation of Dickens's Shakespearean vitality, flexibility of mode, dramatic power, and poetry reads as the strongest passage in *The Great Tradition*:

There is no need to insist on the force—representation of Dickens's art in general in *Hard Times*—with which the moral and spiritual differences are rendered here [the description of Sissy Jupe and Bitzer in the schoolroom] in terms of sensation, so that the symbolic intention emerges out of metaphor and the vivid evocation of the concrete.   (p. 253)

... 'practical criticism' analysis ... would reveal an extraordinary flexibility in the art of *Hard Times*.   (p. 257)

To the question how the reconciling [of the various modes] is done—there is much more diversity in *Hard Times* than these references to dialogue suggest—the answer can be given by pointing to the astonishing richness of life that characterizes the book everywhere.   (Ibid.)

His flexibility is that of a richly poetic art of the word. He doesn't write 'poetic prose';[44] he writes with a poetic force of evocation, registering with the responsiveness of a genius of verbal expression what he so sharply sees and feels. In fact, by texture, imaginative mode, symbolic method, and the resulting concentration, *Hard Times* affects us as belonging with formally poetic works.   (p. 258)

Then comes this clinching judgement (on the passage dealing with the discovery of Tom Gradgrind disguised as a negro servant in the travelling circus) which justifies the original title for the critique:

The excerpt in itself suggests the justification for saying that *Hard Times* is a poetic work. It suggests that the genius of the writer may fairly be described as that of a poetic dramatist, and that, in our preconceptions about 'the novel', we may miss, within the field of fictional prose, possibilities of concentration and flexibility in the interpretation of life such as we associate with Shakespearean drama.   (p. 266)[45]

Yet Leavis himself was at the very moment of writing this labouring under preconceptions about the rest of Dickens's art. Nor had he yet fully grasped the significance of the critical breakthrough he had achieved with the analogy 'the novel as dramatic poem'. Otherwise, he would surely have kept it as his title for the critique instead of replacing it with the more neutral, more clinical-sounding 'Analytic Note'. By the same token he might well have printed here much more of his essay on *The Europeans*, which was his second in the series of 'The Novel as Dramatic Poem', instead of reprinting that essay much later in *'Anna Karenina'*.

But he was soon to realise what he had done. For with the analogy he found the way in to a new understanding of Lawrence's major novels and, ultimately, of Dickens's great full-length novels. Significantly it was with Lawrence, as well as with Shakespeare, that Leavis compared Dickens's art in *Hard Times*. Thus Dickens's protest against the utilitarian spirit in Victorian education matches Lawrence's similar protests; the symbolic contrast provided between Sissy Jupe and Bitzer is 'essentially Laurentian'; the way Sleary's horse-riding highlights the human degradation incurred by industrialism recalls a 'characteristic passage'[46] of Lawrence (pp. 251–6).

On the basis of these comparisons and the affirmation of Lawrence as the only modern successor to the great tradition, Martin Green claims, perhaps expressing the common view, that Leavis makes Lawrence the touchstone for *The Great Tradition*. But, as noted earlier, the invocations of Lawrence belong to the latest additions to the book. The central matter was written earlier, when we cannot be sure that Leavis had yet reached the conviction about Lawrence's stature *as a novelist* that he reports at the close of the opening chapter (pp. 34–7). The manifestly Laurentian criteria—'vital capacity for experience, a kind of reverent openness before life, and a marked moral intensity' (p. 17)—have been made to fit critiques of earlier conception. But they do not always fit, as has been pointed out of the sections on Conrad.[47] And the ambiguous and anomalous status of the analysis of *Hard Times* underlines the confusion of criteria: on the one hand, the novel is seen to accord completely with the Laurentian criteria, better perhaps than any other novel examined in his book; yet, on the other hand, it is Dickens's only adult masterpiece—the remainder of his work happily belongs to the genius of entertainment.

But undeniably the Laurentian criteria are there, pointing ahead to *D. H. Lawrence: Novelist*. And, meanwhile, it is, interestingly, a novel of Dickens's that provides Leavis with the key to discovering and articulating Lawrence's poetic significance; and the discovery will lead him back to a mature reappraisal of Dickens.

In sum, the critique of *Hard Times*, annexed half-apologetically in *The Great Tradition*, has become a landmark in Leavis's criticism. Looking back to it through the later criticism, we see that it provided a basis for a more stringent and up-to-date evaluation of two key conceptions: relevance and significance. For we watch Leavis come increasingly through the 1960s and 1970s to find that the truly relevant and really significant writers are those who defend human values and human life in the face of the dehumanising forces in, as he terms it, the 'technologico-Benthamite age', and do so not by overt propagandising but by creating insights into what human values are and by imagining and dramatising in a richly poetic art possibilities of living humanly. One such possibility is triumphantly figured for Leavis by Daniel Doyce, the inventive engineer in *Little Dorrit*, in his calm perseverance in the face of the dispiriting, faceless obstructiveness of the Circumlocution Office. So in the new phase Leavis's criticism becomes progressively sociological in direction, and more deeply rooted in the spiritual qualities of creative literature. He becomes more and more urgently interested in poetry and fiction that vindicate man's essential humanity and individuality. And in the process he proposes a new tradition of transcendently great writers coming after Shakespeare: Blake, Dickens and Lawrence.

As to the question why Leavis did not make Dickens a full member of 'the great tradition' at this earlier time, he has himself supplied the good, if astonishing, reason that he had not reread Dickens (*Dickens the Novelist*, pp. 1–2). And paradoxically it may after all have been fortunate that he had not done so. For we may believe that with Mrs Leavis's major contribution *Dickens the Novelist* gives a far more compelling and more rounded account of Dickens's genius than Leavis could have given on his own in *The Great Tradition*.

4 Q. D. Leavis and Major Women Novelists

The idea of 'the novel as dramatic poem' also revolutionised Mrs Leavis's approach, turning her from a theorist into a fully fledged critic of the novel. In the very next number of *Scrutiny* after that containing Leavis's critique of *Hard Times* we find her distinguishing two traditions of the novel in the following terms:

> While the novels of the eighteenth and nineteenth centuries, with few exceptions, were descended from Addison and Defoe, with some admixture of a debased stage comedy, there is quite another novel, created by Emily Brontë, Melville, Conrad, and Henry James, among others, which makes use of the technique of the dramatic poem.... To recognize in James's novels and *nouvelles* art of the same nature as *Measure for Measure*, to see that they are in a tradition of mediaeval and Elizabethan drama transmitted through Shakespeare, Ben Jonson and Bunyan (and so Hawthorne), is to make their meaning accessible, as it never can be if they are approached on the assumption that they are the same kind of thing as the writings of Trollope and Thackeray.[1]

These words look forward to Mrs Leavis's next considerable piece of writing and her first truly critical essay on the novel: her evaluation of Hawthorne as a dramatic poet.[2] I discuss this further in the appendix at the end of this study. Further, in almost every one 'of her critiques from here on she more or less directly applies the analogy 'the novel as dramatic poem': in her critical introductions to *Mansfield Park*, *Jane Eyre*, and *Silas Marner*, in her 'fresh approach' to *Wuthering Heights*, and in her chapters on *David Copperfield*, *Bleak House* and *Great Expectations* in *Dickens the Novelist*.

In so doing she had clearly profited directly from *The Great Tradition*. Before, she had written as a scholar and only incidentally as a critic of the novel. From the essay on Hawthorne onwards she writes as both critic and scholar, having assimilated her husband's critical methods into her own scholarly ones. Indeed, her development corresponds well with the description Leavis had used of the technical developments made by his great novelists: Mrs Leavis, as they, worked out her own 'appropriate methods and procedures' (*The Great Tradition*, p. 16). Consequently, she has remained a strongly individual critic of the novel, having essentially the same objectives as her husband, it is true, but reaching them in her own way. Also, this post-1948 Mrs Leavis is a much more effective writer on the novel, as we may see by comparing her writings on Jane Austen before and after that date.

Mrs Leavis's work in this latter period parallels and complements her husband's in other ways. Like Leavis, she engages in a revaluation of her earlier judgements of nineteenth-century novelists, and, like him, does so by reassessing the strongly positive contribution made by the Romantic movement. However, whereas her route is via Jane Austen, the Brontë sisters, and the Wordsworthian George Eliot in *Silas Marner*, his new understanding of the 'romantic' Lawrence takes him back to a further scrutiny of Blake. Their parallel investigations then most fittingly culminate in their joint book on Dickens.

In other words, there has all along been a close affinity between the Leavises in their work on the novel. They seem to have co-operated in a systematic revaluation of the English novel in two phases. The first phase covers roughly the existence of *Scrutiny*: from, that is, the early 1930s to the early 1950s. This might be called their 'classical period' in that their criteria seem decidedly weighted in favour of the eighteenth-century ideals of moral order and decorum, as *The Great Tradition* reflects in a spectacular way. Furthermore, it is more than probable that a major influence on Leavis in the writing of that book was, in addition to T. S. Eliot, his own wife. At least there is strong evidence for saying so: in general Mrs Leavis's advocacy of *The Great Tradition* and the way in which her early work led up to it; in particular, her excoriations of Dickens and Charlotte Brontë in *Fiction and the Reading Public*, her use of Jane Austen as an exemplar of self-disciplined writing in the same book, her *Scrutiny* essays on Jane Austen, to which Leavis refers the reader in lieu of providing his own chapter on this novelist who heads his 'great tradition', and Leavis's note of indebtedness to his wife in that book. The second and post-*Scrutiny* phase may be called their 'romantic period', except that this description seems too pat. It would be truer to say that in this later period the Leavises have sought to reconcile the chief virtues of classicism and romanticism—to see, for instance, how the predominantly 'classical' Jane Austen and the predominantly 'romantic' D. H. Lawrence[3] can both be called the successors of Shakespeare.

At all events, in the affinity of their work on the novel we see some of the reality behind the Leavises' dedication to each other of *Dickens the Novelist* on account of 'forty years and more of daily collaboration in . . . discussion of literature'.

It will have been noticed too that Mrs Leavis's writings complement her husband's in another way: namely, that, with exceptions, she has focused mainly on women novelists and he on men.

Mrs Leavis's essays on Jane Austen, the Brontë sisters, George Eliot, and Mrs Oliphant have then a central importance in her writings in that they show how she travelled from *Fiction and the Reading Public* to *Dickens the Novelist*—a large leap for readers who are only familiar with these two books. It would in fact be a boon if these scattered essays were collected into one volume as, perhaps, Mrs Leavis's idea of the great tradition of women novelists. Maybe she has such a volume in mind, for in the latest of these essays she sees *Miss Marjoribanks* as the missing link between *Emma* and *Middlemarch*. As usual she mounts a powerful argument. She notes that both Margaret Oliphant and George Eliot habitually wrote for *Blackwood's Magazine*, and that *Miss Marjoribanks* had come out early enough in the magazine—in 1866—to have made a large impact on George Eliot before she started work on *Middlemarch* two years later in 1868; and she adds that Blackwood had the 'highest opinion of *Miss Marjoribanks* and great hopes for it', and, moreover, that George Eliot's ironic attitude towards Dorothea in Book 1 of *Middlemarch* not only marks a new departure in her work but also strongly resembles Mrs Oliphant's attitude all through to her heroine, Lucilla.[4]

There can be little doubt that Mrs Leavis chose to focus on these women novelists because they were women examining the lot of woman in society in the age in which they lived and because they succeeded in transmuting this interest into art better than their sister novelists.[5] But, unlike numerous fashionable contemporaries, in so doing Mrs Leavis exhibits no precocious feminism. Rather, she studies them as in the first place major English novelists irrespective of sex, as these forthright words confirm:

I myself stipulate that any piece of female writing advocating equality of opportunity for the sexes should prove its author to have a highly developed character and a respectable intellect, to be free from mere sex-hostility, to have an at least masculine sense of responsibility and that capacity for self-criticism which impresses as a mark of the best kind of masculine mind, and over and above that to come from a woman capable of justifying her existence in any walk of life.[6]

Though Mrs Leavis addressed these words to her contemporaries in the late 1930s, and specifically to Virginia Woolf, there can hardly be any question that Jane Austen, Charlotte and Emily Brontë, George Eliot and Mrs Oliphant all passed her test.

Modern studies of Jane Austen date from the early 1930s, when R. W. Chapman published his first Oxford editions of the letters and the novels (in 1932 and 1933, respectively). But criticism of the novels unsweetened by Janeism begins with rare exceptions[7] a good deal later, most decisively perhaps with Marvin Mudrick's *Jane Austen* (1952). Mrs Leavis's 'A Critical Theory of Jane Austen's Writings',[8] comes out plumb in the middle of this twenty-year period and provides the watershed between the undiscriminating table-talk of earlier discussion of Jane Austen's art and the more rigorous criticism of Mudrick and his successors. As Edmund Wilson, so often the seer of striking literary developments, observed in 1944, the year the 'Theory' was concluded, Mrs Leavis illuminated Jane Austen's artistic development beyond all other critics.[9]

For almost another twenty years Mrs Leavis's 'Theory' went virtually unchallenged, which is surprising for a work so preponderantly speculative. That it did so testifies not only to the influence of *Scrutiny* but to the energy, detail, and essential justice of Mrs Leavis's argument that

Miss Austen was not an inspired amateur who had scribbled in childhood and then lightly tossed off masterpieces between callers; she was a steady professional writer who had to put in many years of thought and labour to achieve each novel and she took her novels very seriously.   (p. 4)[10]

'Labour' has an important value here. The 'Theory' attempts to reveal what lies behind the novelist's own comparison of her manner of composition to brushwork 'so fine . . . as produces little effect after much labour'.[11] By bringing out the truth of those last three words, Mrs Leavis wanted finally to rout those who flutter over or in various ways patronise Jane Austen's art. She had a number of targets: the Janeites, such as Mary Lascelles and Elizabeth Jenkins, who refused to accept the letters as 'representing the tone of the Austen household' (p. 66); those who thought with Caroline Spurgeon that the novels were miracles, or with Professors Elton and Garrod that the novelist did not develop, or with Bradley that the novels were 'exceptionally peaceful reading' (p. 1); or again those who believed with Lord David Cecil that Jane Austen could not appreciate 'pleasant worldlings like Mary Crawford' (p. 55), or with George Sampson (in *The Concise Cambridge History of English Literature*, 1941), that she was only a creator of comic characters (p. 62); and so on.

Yet for B. C. Southam Mrs Leavis had written a *tour de force*. He was the first to challenge the theory convincingly by challenging the scholarship on which it was based.[12] As R. W. Chapman's protégé in Jane Austen scholarship, he commands respect. With admirable reasonableness Southam objects both to the rationale for the theory and to its specific details. Thus, while agreeing that *Sense and Sensibility* is evidently the final version of an early prototype in letter-form (*Elinor and Marianne*), Southam cannot accept Mrs Leavis's assumption that all the novels are 'geological structures, the earliest layer going back to her earliest writings with subsequent accretions from her reading, her personal life and those lives most closely connected with hers, all recast'; or that they are 'palimpsests through whose surface portions of earlier versions, or of other and earlier compositions quite unrelated, constantly protrude' (pp. 4–5). Nor can he accept the specifics of Mrs Leavis's hypothesis that *Pride and Prejudice* has its epistolary prototype in *First Impressions*, that *Emma* was transformed from *The Watsons*, and that *Mansfield Park* derived chiefly from *Lady Susan* but with a letter-form draft intervening between the two. Southam objects that, since only sixteen pages of *Persuasion* survive in draft-form to show the exact nature of Jane Austen's working, Mrs Leavis's procedure must remain highly conjectural; that, since Cassandra Austen, a reliable guide with her memoranda, makes no record of draft-forms for any of *Northanger Abbey*, *Mansfield Park*, *Emma* and *Persuasion*, Mrs Leavis's assumption that the prototype to *Persuasion* was lost is pure assumption; and that, since the six novels give 'much the same events, and similar people . . . the art is in fine gradations', it is perfectly logical that there should be overlapping between them, giving the illusion of prototypes, but not necessarily according to Mrs Leavis's scheme.[13] Southam then focuses on the core of the theory, the transformation of *Lady Susan* into *Mansfield Park*, to which Mrs Leavis devoted half her space. She had proposed that the family drama between Henry Austen and Eliza de Feuillide was 'evidently the occasion of the draft of a novel'—*Lady Susan*—and then that this biographical fiction was the matrix for *Mansfield Park* (p. 29ff.). Southam denies this on the grounds of internal evidence in *Lady Susan* which shows that it was written before the family drama occurred. Secondly, he argues on the basis of Austen clannishness that Henry would not have allowed a biographical *Lady Susan* to remain in existence after Jane Austen's death.[14] Then, examining Mrs Leavis's genealogy of the characters in *Mansfield Park*, Southam pounces on the statement that Eliza de Feuillide 'had to be altered almost out of recognition' (p. 39) to become Mary Crawford, and comments that Mrs Leavis's method 'leaves us with the possibility of endless cross-relationships'.[15] He raises similar objections to *The Watsons—Emma* metamorphosis, conceding with Chapman that this, however, is more plausible.

In a later account Southam seems, however, to come closer to Mrs Leavis's position. He reveals that, 'had the *Austen Papers* been available to Mrs Leavis, her claim to identification' between Lady Susan and Eliza 'could have been stronger still'; yet, as if apprehensive of the implications of this, he insists again on 'the internal evidence that *Lady Susan* was already written by 1795, before these family events had taken place'; and he adds, 'Mrs Leavis takes it for granted that *Lady Susan* was composed later than 1797'.[16] Here Southam's accuracy and logic have deserted him. Mrs Leavis takes no such thing for granted, and in fact wrote of *Lady Susan*, 'I think we can decide on internal evidence that it was founded on events of the years 1795 to 1797, and was certainly written before the end of 1797' (p. 25). Whatever the precise date of *Lady Susan* vis-à-vis the affair between Henry and Eliza, how can Southam disprove Mrs Leavis's hypothesis that Mary Crawford in *Mansfield Park* seems to have been inspired by Lady Susan and Eliza? Again, Southam asks whether the ball scene in *The Watsons* does not more closely resemble the one in *Pride and Prejudice* than the one in *Emma*, as Mrs Leavis suggests—by which he implies that Mrs Leavis has overlooked this possibility. But Mrs Leavis had noted, 'The assembly ball in *The Watsons* is the first ball in *Pride and Prejudice*' (p. 16), reasoning, however, that it is closer to the one in *Emma* since 'Emma Watson's generosity to little Charles' is so suggestive of the 'much more subtle act of generosity' of Mr Knightley towards Harriet Smith (ibid.).

After all, then, Southam has not disproved the 'Theory' but only entered a necessary caveat as to Mrs Leavis's 'method of tracing':

> It is enough to illustrate that Mrs Leavis's method of tracing sources can be applied with equal effect to indicate the possibility of influence in a number of directions, some of them equally impressive but wholly inconsistent. It is, of course, possible that *Emma* may actually have been written out of *The Watsons*; but unless we discover stronger evidence of the change, this unlikely process of creation, as with the suggested transformation of *Lady Susan* into *Mansfield Park*, cannot be shown to have taken place.[17]

But Southam has made a much more telling criticism. He questions Mrs Leavis's reason for elaborating a theory of composition at all. She wrote, 'by examining how she worked we can determine what kind of novelist she was. By looking to see how she wrote a novel we can discover what her object was in writing it. Without such a preliminary no criticism of her novels can be just or even safe' (p. 23). To this Southam very reasonably rejoins that, since 'the six novels are complete and successful works of art', criticism has no need of such a preliminary; it can go to work on the texts:

> The major critical questions of interpretation and judgement are to be answered from the texts. There is no need for a theory of composition to tell us why they are so and not otherwise. There are no grounds for insisting that a theory of composition should be anterior to criticism.[18]

These words are irreproachable. They might, ironically, have been written by Leavis himself,[19] and would be approved by Mrs Leavis on most occasions. Why, then, did she go to such lengths to ensure that criticism should not be mistaken about the nature of Jane Austen's art? Quite simply she was determined to demolish the notion that the art was miraculous, limited and lightweight.[20] And she felt that this could best be done by *showing* what pains Jane

Austen took to perfect an art she was very serious about. Further-more, there lay Dr Chapman's Oxford editions freshly minted and scarcely appraised by criticism. If in her enthusiasm speculation exceeded probability, Mrs Leavis certainly gave a backbone to modern Jane Austen studies that was not there before she wrote the 'Theory'. As Arnold Kettle testifies, 'There is no longer, especially after Mrs Leavis's articles, any excuse for thinking of Jane Austen as an untutored genius or even as a kind of aunt with a flair for tell-ing stories that have somehow or other continued to charm.'[21] And in the same place Kettle gave credit to Mrs Leavis for showing

> how strong a part in Jane Austen's novels is played by her con-scious war on the romance. She did to the romance of her day (whether the domestic romance of Fanny Burney or the Gothic brand of Mrs Radcliffe) what Cervantes had done in his. *Pride and Prejudice* is as much an anti-*Cecilia* as *Northanger Abbey* is an anti-*Udolpho*.

Critics of even more recent date have found themselves able to neglect these things, and Mrs Leavis's theory in general, only by overlooking the fact that she substantially pioneered the tradi-tion of Jane Austen criticism to which they themselves belong.[22]

This is not true of Southam, who can mix rebuke with a gracious tribute to Mrs Leavis *as a critic*. 'Perhaps the strongest proof', he says of there being no need of a theory to validate criticism, 'is to be found, paradoxically, in the critical theory itself, where Mrs Leavis, if no "theorist," shows herself, in analysis and incidental remarks, to be the keenest modern critic of Jane Austen, someone to whom many more recent writers owe a considerable debt.'[23] If only—this intimates—Mrs Leavis had given more space to criti-cism and less to theory. What the 'Theory' most lacks is a com-panion group of essays giving critiques of the Austen novels. Fortunately the critical introductions to *Mansfield Park* and *Sense and Sensibility* go a good deal of the way towards filling this gap. In them is to be found the pick of the critical insights that were scattered through the 'Theory' but are now sharpened and amplified.

To examine the justice of Southam's tribute and assess Mrs Leavis's achievement as a critic of Jane Austen, we may compare these critical introductions with the pick of Jane Austen criticism in the years between the 'Theory' and their appearance: Marvin

Mudrick's *Jane Austen* (1952), Andrew Wright's *Jane Austen's Novels* (1953) and Lionel Trilling's essay on *Mansfield Park* (1954). My feeling is that Mrs Leavis takes the reader beyond Mudrick and Wright by virtue of three things: the depth of her analysis of the novels, the understanding she shows of Jane Austen's idiom, and the largeness of her perspective on Jane Austen as a novelist examining the society in which she lived. As for Mrs Leavis and Trilling, their accounts of *Mansfield Park* compare very favourably and agree in the important judgements. Because of this and because of the wide difference in method of dealing with the novel, both repay reading. Mrs Leavis's method might make hers the more stimulating of the two discussions for many readers, since, by means of quotation and analysis, she keeps the reader always close to what is happening in the novel, both technically and thematically; while Trilling is much more detached from the text.

To turn first to *Sense and Sensibility*, most readers would agree with Wright that this novel is 'a study of opposites' (Elinor's 'sense' opposing Marianne's 'sensibility') and that

> In a very superficial way the behaviour of the two sisters is strongly contrasted; but in a profounder sense both sisters are stirred by their respective suitors. Marianne has yet to learn sense, but already the sensibility of Elinor has been awakened. The elder sister may still be able to give counsels of sense; but she had already tasted the values of sensibility. . . .
>
> In the final—and most perfect—volume Elinor and Marianne become increasingly like each other, a process which makes both of them more rounded and complete people.[24]

But the demanding reader who expects to learn more about the 'process' by which the sisters become 'more rounded and complete',[25] and more therefore about 'sense' and 'sensibility', is left unsatisfied by Wright. More illuminating is Mudrick's observation that Jane Austen is in this book exorcising 'Mackenzian sensibility': 'the notion of sensibility as it appears in the Mackenzian novel, as a foolish, exaggerated, literary, indeed an emotionless emotionalism'.[26] Yet Mudrick too comes to odd conclusions. He claims that Jane Austen is telling the reader that 'not merely *false* feeling, but feeling itself, is bad', and that as a result she sees to it that 'Marianne must be humiliated and destroyed', and by the end

'Marianne, the life and center of the novel, has been betrayed; and
not by Willoughby'.[27] Indeed! Jane Austen wrote *Northanger Abbey*
to make fun of such uncritical readers. Wright's reading seems
in contrast positively sane.

Though giving only a page and a half to *Sense and Sensibility* in
the 'Theory', Mrs Leavis indicates a subtler novel than either of
these critics. She does so principally by what she says about Mrs
Jennings, whom Wright neglects entirely and whom Mudrick
dismisses as merely a 'vulgar gossip'.[28] Stressing with Wright that
the novel 'has a theme of deeper import' than 'sense versus sensibility', Mrs Leavis notes that 'Marianne has lacked "candour"',
that key word in Miss Austen's vocabulary, and her sin has consisted in an uncandid attitude to society and a refusal to take her
part as a member of society' (pp. 21–2). 'Mrs Jennings', she adds,
'stands for a sample of the social average', although at first this
lady is seen by the reader not through the novelist's eyes but with
Marianne's 'distorted vision' (p. 22). Marianne's view makes Mrs
Jennings a person 'indelicate in speech, and inelegant in manners,
and unrefined in spirit' (ibid.). However—and this is the crucial
point—from the time of Marianne's crisis with Willoughby

> Jane Austen contrives that the absence in Mrs Jennings of the
> qualities she [Jane Austen] valued most is seen to be offset by
> the presence of qualities that must, if only in theory, have been
> at least as much recommendation to her even when unsupported
> by elegances and distinctions—an unfailingly good heart, a
> well-judging mind, a shrewd grasp of the essentials of character.
> (Ibid.)

In other words, she shows Mrs Jennings to be a well-regulated
amalgam of sense and sensibility. For, as she further points out,
'It is from Mrs Jennings's mouth that the final verdicts on
Willoughby, Mrs Ferrars and her daughter, and other leading
characters proceed' (ibid.). Yet such critical insights as these crop
up only incidentally in the 'Theory', and too rarely.

But in her critical edition of this novel Mrs Leavis reverses her
procedure and subordinates theory to critical interpretation and
valuation. She shows how the novel investigates woman's place in
a society being rapidly changed by the impact of the Romantic
system of values on the pre-Romantic system. She suggests,
moreover, that all the Austen novels have this theme so much at

their centre that the last completed novel, *Persuasion*, marks almost a reversal of attitude in Jane Austen from that with which she started out in *Sense and Sensibility*; that, in other words, she had grown from an eighteenth-century writer, having the characteristic eighteenth-century values, into a nineteenth-century one.

Mrs Leavis makes these conclusions while analysing the plot of *Sense and Sensibility*:

> Besides dramatising an argument, the plot gives many opportunities for investigating the social attitudes of the new and old woman, and discovering how, when put into practice, the former compare with these latter. . . .
>
> Marianne is decidedly not silly, like the heroine of *Northanger Abbey*, she is merely misguided and inexperienced—'everything but prudent'. Prudence was the grand female virtue of the pre-Romantic system, so in flouting it (it is the old-fashioned moral) Marianne comes to grief. However, Jane Austen came to think less well of the prudential outlook as we can see in *Persuasion*. But Elinor is not 'prudent' from any meanness of nature—her brother is there to show the soul eaten away by prudence—she is on the contrary a fine, superior creature whose intelligent insight into the motives and ideas of her acquaintances has driven her to adopt something like the disillusioned attitude of a Chesterfield. [29]

Hence the book's title should be interpreted as follows:

> The 'sense' of the title is not opposed to 'sensibility' as has been generally assumed, for each sister has both—the contrast is in the way each directs these qualities. Marianne constantly exposes herself and her sister to vulgar comment by laying herself open to 'the ridicule so justly annexed to sensibility': the irony is directed against those who think sensibility a joke. 'Sensibility' is not meant to convey any suggestion of affectation or exaggeration, that is done by the word 'romantic'—'her opinions are all romantic' says Elinor. The Austen code respected sensibility, that is, profound feeling, but expected a stoic surface. (p. xv)

In these extracts Mrs Leavis exhibits the advantage of not confining one's attention to a particular element of Jane Austen's art. Wright and Mudrick specify a particular interest in structure and irony respectively, and, while they do not of course consider only these elements, yet they do seem at times to have blinkered themselves from other and wider considerations. Mrs Leavis, on the other hand, has a much more open-ended approach, her interest being ultimately in the meaning of the novels and in how Jane Austen has imaginatively dramatised her meaning in words. Consequently, she pays special attention to the novelist's use of language and her handling of idiom, as the above extracts show. And with this flexible approach Mrs Leavis can see Jane Austen through larger perspectives, as in the following:

> And all her novels are different because they are projections of different positions as Miss Austen matured and altered. The differences between the positions of Elizabeth and Jane Bennet in comparison with those of Marianne and Elinor Dashwood, and the relation of Marianne to Elinor compared with that of Elizabeth to Jane, and their creator's attitudes to them all, are revelatory of the general development in her inner life that led her from *Sense and Sensibility* to *Persuasion*—to a complete reversal of the inherited assumptions with which she began (those which had caused her to exaggerate playfully and pillory her own antisocial impulses in the person of Marianne) until she ends with a heroine, Anne Elliott, whose unhappiness and mistakes before the novel opens were entirely the result of following the prudential counsels of an older Elinor, Lady Russell. (pp. x–xi)

Then she finds that this novel has a place in the central tradition of English comedy: 'But the deeper comic level is that struck at the opening of the novel, by the masterpiece of meanness in the dialogue between John Dashwood and his wife: this is comedy in the line of Ben Jonson, and *Sense and Sensibility* links Jonson with Dickens' (p. xviii).

Mrs Leavis's critique of *Mansfield Park* surpasses Wright's and Mudrick's on similar grounds.[30] And comparison of her treatments of this novel in the 'Theory' and in her critical introduction reveals that Mrs Leavis has gained a much surer idea of the novel's stature as a work of art and of its place both in Jane Austen's *oeuvre* and in the tradition of the English novel.

In the 'Theory' she appears tentative and uncertain about this novel despite the usual buoyancy of her prose. She calls it 'that unsatisfactory, but instructive novel' (p. 23). It is unsatisfactory

because of its 'priggishness', because 'the morality is almost deliberately conventional and the moralising unbelievably trite',
because the author appears to contradict her own experience in
censuring the theatricals, and because of Fanny Price (p. 25).
However, she can account for, and so mitigate, these flaws with
data from her hypothesis about the genesis of the novel. Thus '*Lady
Susan* into *Mansfield Park*' means the expansion of 'a précis of a
melodrama' into an 'involved psychological study' (p. 40); the
pervasive moralising reflects a 'conscious change' in Jane Austen,
in whom a new 'deeply religious outlook . . . would acount for the
castigation of worldliness in the novel' (p. 51); and the 'unnatural
censure' of Mary Crawford can be explained since she is modelled
on the real-life Eliza de Feuillide, 'who was leading the favourite
brother [Henry Austen] into a wholly unsuitable marriage' (p. 55).

Much more interesting, however, is the more critical judgement
that the novel's faults and rough edges are symptoms of experimen-
tation by Jane Austen, and that *Mansfield Park* is transitional
between the early art and the late masterpieces. As a result the
Austen irony is becoming subtler, and technique and psychological interest more complex.

> There, as in *Emma* and *Persuasion*, we see her forgoing the im-
> mediate effect of witty rejoinder and humorous character to
> analyse motive and to build up total effects; in this new manner
> the human heart is investigated in a new way, every impulse
> noted and considered with respect, instead of inspiring the easy
> comments of the earlier automatic and rather unfeeling spright-
> liness. If the analysis in *Mansfield Park* annoys us by its ejacula-
> tory and panting manner, we must bear in mind that it was the
> forerunner of a new technique. . . . In the evolution of *Mansfield
> Park* we can see her discovering it.   (pp. 59, 61)

On this tantalising yet tentative note Mrs Leavis left discussion
of the novel in the 'Theory'. In the critical introduction she is much
more confident, confirming and consolidating such insights by
quotation and analysis—by, in other words, a critical appreciation
of the novel. Without jettisoning her theory of the novel's genesis
she now subordinates this to a critical reading of the text. The
results are striking. Though she still feels doubtful of Jane Austen's
attitude towards the theatricals, she can see that these play an

integral part in a novel in which Jane Austen is exploring the possibilities of a new, poetic art of fiction:

> But being a great artist she contrives a serious function for the play within the play: the prophetic irony of casting Maria for the tragic rôle of a seduced woman and Miss Crawford for the part of a woman lacking in feminine decorum, is a less obvious but more important contribution to the meaning of *Mansfield Park*, and a technique that Miss Austen could have found only in Shakespeare. We should indeed know, even without Edmund's and Mr Crawford's telling us, that our author was soaked in Shakespeare. Fanny's poets are Shakespeare, Cowper and Crabbe, her favourite prose-writers Johnson and Goldsmith, reflecting her creator's taste. While the mould and moral tone of the Johnsonian sentence can in *Mansfield Park* be found decisively influential, it is the frequentation of these poets which seems to me to have enabled Jane Austen to have risen, as an artist, out of the class of Fanny Burneys, Maria Edgeworths and Mrs Inchbalds of the age she grew up in. . . . *Mansfield Park*, in technique and subject and prose style and in its thoughtful inquiries into human relationships, looks forward to George Eliot and Henry James; so *Mansfield Park* is the first modern novel in England.[31]

'The first modern novel in England': in this judgement especially Mrs Leavis's essay intersects with Lionel Trilling's earlier and justly admired discussion of the novel. Trilling describes its modernity as follows:

> It was Jane Austen who first represented the specifically modern personality and the culture in which it had its being. Never before had the moral life been shown as she shows it to be, never before had it been conceived to be so complex and difficult and exhausting. Hegel speaks of the 'secularisation of spirituality' as a prime characteristic of the modern epoch, and Jane Austen is the first to tell us what this involves. She is the first novelist to represent society, the general culture, as playing a part in the moral life, generating the concepts of 'sincerity' and 'vulgarity' which no earlier time would have understood the meaning of, and which for us are so subtle that they defy definition, and so powerful that none can escape their sovereignty.[32]

Mrs Leavis offers no perspective so large as this—not because she cannot, but because she has apparently a closer interest than Trilling in the formal aspects of Jane Austen's art. Consequently she illuminates to advantage the 'how' of Trilling's sociological perspective. She shows how the new psychological depth of Jane Austen's examination of human nature compelled her to make technical innovations so that *Mansfield Park* is new and modern both in technique and subject-matter. In effect, the two essays complement one another. Again we need to quote generously from Mrs Leavis.

Of Edmund Bertram's and Fanny Price's relations Mrs Leavis says,

> What is really new is the attempt to work out a psychological analysis of feeling, which creates a new style; the very movement of thought and feeling is caught in the panting, ejaculatory sentences, often only disordered phrases, which register Fanny's emotions and Edmund's hesitations and doubts.
>
> (p. xv)

Fanny, Edmund, the Crawfords and the other young people in the novel belong to the new age, that of Byron and the Romantics, and Jane Austen has created her new psychological style to articulate and dramatise their 'romantic' questionings of the eighteenth-century world of decorum, epitomised in the novel by Sir Thomas Bertram and Mansfield Park:

> Jane Austen shared with Pope the Augustan vision of the place of the great country-house in the life of the nation, duly related, she shows, to the parsonage, farm and cottage. *Mansfield Park* seems to be an Adam-type mansion with grounds laid out by 'Capability' Brown, since Sir Thomas certainly belongs to that phase of our cultural history; his children, however, like the Crawfords, are of the new age, rebelling against the traditional proprieties and the restraints of country life and hankering after the dubious pleasures of the gay Regency world of Brighton and London. . . . Which is right? is not Miss Austen's subject, but: What is to be said for and against each? Our author holds no brief for the Past—Fanny is well laughed at for her Gothic yearnings at Sotherton Court, and that Elizabethan mansion is represented as a stifling museum where spontaneous life had died

and to which the Regency improver is rightly called, to mod-
ernise and open a prospect. (pp. xv–xvi)

Futhermore, Mrs Leavis observes in the new style a Shakespearean
dramatic-poetic energy, and appears therefore to imply that
Mansfield Park is the first notable instance in the English novel of
'the novel as dramatic poem'. If so, she adds force to Leavis's claim
that Jane Austen heads the great tradition. Also she intriguingly
anticipates her essay on *Jane Eyre*. There she calls the Brontë sisters
the pioneers of the English poetic novel. But Jane Austen, it would
seem, was already pointing the way, if less flamboyantly:

> The Sotherton episode is the finest and most original in the
> Austen novels, and I know nothing of the kind more remarkable
> in any English novel; if we met it in Kafka or Henry James we
> should at once recognise its wonderfully sustained but never
> obtrusive symbolism—perceive that its action is a pregnant
> microcosm. Yet there is not a phrase or image in it which is not
> meaningful, giving a forecast of the rest of the action (again a
> Shakespearian technique). All the action is symbolic—we have
> Maria contriving to slip round the locked gate with her lover, to
> Fanny's horror ('You will hurt yourself against those spikes',
> etc.), Julia scrambling after her, Edmund deserting Fanny for
> Miss Crawford, with whom he has a significant debate before he
> returns to his desolate cousin, and so on. At the time it reads like
> a bad dream, and we see its point when we find the pattern of
> events so exactly and awfully repeated, when Maria, imprisoned
> in matrimony, forces Mr Crawford to elope with her. The novel
> is as full of prophetic ironies as *Macbeth*: only on second reading
> do we note Henry Crawford's boast, 'I never do wrong without
> gaining by it'; and Tom's, that *he* can be trusted to 'take care
> that Sir Thomas's daughters do nothing to distress him'.
>
> (pp. xvi–xvii)

In this critique of *Mansfield Park* Mrs Leavis in effect reassesses Jane
Austen in the light of a new and more sympathetic understanding
of the Romantic movement, and her discovery that Jane Austen's
genius comprises 'romantic' as well as 'classical' virtues seems
clearly to have launched her into making the reassessment of the
Victorian novel which culminates in her essays in *Dickens the
Novelist*.

R. W. Chapman, the best-known of all Jane Austen scholars, remarked without elaboration, 'In *Mansfield Park* alone does Jane Austen tread the confines of tragedy.'[33] A final quotation shows how Mrs Leavis the critic gives meaning to the remark:

> With all his virtues Sir Thomas has been culpable towards his children; in forcing on them an appearance of conformity and leaving no outlet for their tastes, he has precipitated the tragedy—for *Mansfield Park*, alone of the Austen novels, is tragic (in spite of the appearance of a happy ending). The Mansfield stage is finally as strewn with corpses of ruined lives as the stage at the end of *Hamlet* with dead bodies. The tragedy of the Crawfords is of their own making, though involving Mansfield; they are the dangerous side of the new age (the age of Byron and Constant), and Crawford anticipates the latter's Adolphe in 'indulging in the freaks of a cold-blooded vanity too long'. His punishment, like Byron's, is to have outlawed himself from Mansfield Park. Maria seems to belong to the tragic world of Racine, a repressed but passionate woman tormented first by vanity and pride, and then by jealousy, into her own destruction. We are not spared the Dantean sequel, that they become each other's torment until they break apart and Maria is consigned to a yet lower circle in hell shared with Mrs Norris. The means Maria took to escape from the confinement of Mansfield has ironically produced a sentence of life imprisonment.
>
> (p. xvi)[34]

Confronting the Janeites at the outset of the 'Theory' Mrs Leavis wrote, '[Jane Austen's] inspiration then turns out to be, as Inspiration so often does, a matter of hard work—radical revision in the light of a maturer taste and a severe self-criticism, and under the pressure of a more and more clearly defined intention over a space of years' (p. 5). But in the light of her critiques of *Sense and Sensibility* and *Mansfield Park* one asks with B. C. Southam, Could not Mrs Leavis have enforced that thesis by means of a literary-critical examination of the achieved novels? And yet, on the other hand, did not the 'Theory', which seems to have been generally correct,[35] help Mrs Leavis to be a better critic of Jane Austen? No doubt. But the 'Theory' is at best a tantalising substitute for a full *critical* study of the Austen novels. There are no critiques of *Northanger Abbey*, *Pride and Prejudice*, *Emma* and

Persuasion to give a sense of completeness to Mrs Leavis's study of Jane Austen.

The key significance, then, of the 'Theory' is that with D. W. Harding's essay it challenged more cogently than any other document the prevailing 'sweet Jane' attitude to the novelist, and, in so doing, pioneered the revolution in modern Jane Austen criticism, a revolution which very soon extended to criticism of the novel in general, as has been noted of Leavis's revaluations of George Eliot and Conrad. Then, the chief value of the introductions to *Sense and Sensibility* and *Mansfield Park* is that they show Mrs Leavis's capability as a critic of Jane Austen—as, to repeat Southam, 'the keenest modern critic of Jane Austen'. As such Mrs Leavis is not concerned to emphasise any one feature as predominating in the novelist's art, as the handling of point of view or irony or style or characterisation. Her interest is more rounded. It consists in appraising Jane Austen as a novelist, who uses these and other elements and resources of fiction to give a sensitive record of the society of her age. This was an age of turbulent transition between the reasonable world of eighteenth-century decorum and the more passionate questionings of the Romantic period. It is in the way Jane Austen examines and registers the disturbances caused by the transition within the family community and within the individual in his relation to society that Mrs Leavis wants to have her achievement as a novelist appraised: as a novelist, in other words, in touch with the realities of powerful psychological and social change, and not just as 'the last exquisite blossom'[36] of eighteenth-century civilisation. Mrs Leavis's attitude to Jane Austen is neatly characterised by what she says of the unjust fate of 'the scrupulous couple, Edward and Elinor' in *Sense and Sensibility*: 'We must not expect comfort from Miss Austen. We go to her to be alerted and braced' (p. xviii). By the same token Mrs Leavis emphasises that Jane Austen's art is not static, but to a highly conscious degree experimental and continually developing.

The situations of Fanny Price and Jane Eyre are 'factually very similar',[37] as one critic reminds us. So, though on the basis of *Fiction and the Reading Public* one could hardly have foretold she would, it is scarcely surprising that Mrs Leavis proceeded next to revalue *Jane Eyre*. At first Mrs Leavis's judgements of Charlotte Brontë had been at best equivocal, and in general clearly disparaging of the novelist's emotional immaturity. In comparison with Jane Austen's predecessors, 'the novels of Charlotte Brontë . . . exhibit a

shameful self-abandonment to undisciplined emotion which makes
these latter seem the productions of a schoolgirl of genius', and,
again, whereas there is in Jane Austen a 'critical detachment that
stamps everything she wrote. . . . *Jane Eyre* is on the contrary a
fable of wish-fulfilment arising out of experience', and as such a
Victorian Romantic prototype of the modern bestseller.[38]

But in her introduction to *Jane Eyre* such sentiments become the
target of one of Mrs Leavis's characteristically scathing attacks:
'Yet though *Wuthering Heights* and *Jane Eyre* have always been accepted as powerful and impressive, it is not as works of art that they
are commonly thought of, rather as artless concoctions of uncon-
trolled daydreams'.[39] She directs this at Lord David Cecil, a
favourite target, and his 'standard work *Early Victorian Novelists*',
and she goes on to accuse him of showing 'an inability to read, to
see what is in fact staring one in the face' (p. 11). Yet the reader of
this does not have to be on his toes to see that Mrs Leavis's switch
from the past to the present tense is a shade too glib, that until now
her published opinion was what was 'commonly thought', that she
too apparently shared Lord David's inabilities, and that, in any
case, *Jane Eyre* has been revalued since his *Early Victorian Novelists*.[40]
By now, then, Mrs Leavis has undergone an almost total conversion in her attitude to this novel. Charlotte Brontë the 'schoolgirl
genius' has become, in virtue of envisaging and creating (with her
sister Emily) prose fiction as 'something as serious, vital, and
significant as the work of their favourite poets' (the Romantics and
Shakespearean tragedy), a 'great creative genius', 'curiously suggestive of D. H. Lawrence', and producing art that is 'more eman-
cipated than George Eliot's' (pp. 11–2).

What has happened to bring about this conversion? Was it
helped on by a surer appreciation of Jane Austen's 'romantic'
criticisms of the stifling tendencies of the Mansfield ethos, and of
the increasing psychological depth and poetic method of her art in
conveying these criticisms and these tendencies? Or was it that Mrs
Leavis rediscovered *Jane Eyre* much as Leavis testifies that he
rediscovered *Dombey and Son*—by rereading the novel in maturity?
Probably it was a combination of all these.

Where before so many readers, including herself, had seen *Jane
Eyre* largely as an artless, though powerful, melodrama, Mrs
Leavis now bases her claims for the novel as a mature and serious
work of art on a number of things. There is the theme, the 'urgently felt personal one . . . of how a woman comes to maturity in

the world of the writer's youth' (p. 11), and what this involves: 'examining the assumptions that the age made with regard to women, to the relations between the sexes and between the young and those in authority' (very topical, in the 1960s, one notes, though Mrs Leavis is not parading the novel as a *roman à thèse*); 'in addition, conventions of social life and accepted religious attitudes come in for radical scrutiny' (p. 13). Then, 'one of the interesting and original features of the novel is the use made of literature—books are referred to for their symbolic meaning' (ibid.). And in showing very convincingly in what ways the books that Jane Eyre either reads (Bewick's *British Birds*, *Gulliver's Travels* and *Arabian Nights*) or comes across (*Rasselas*) correspond either with her situation at the time or with the stage she has reached in her moral education, Mrs Leavis impressively anticipates her discussion of the Dickens illustrations in *Dickens the Novelist*. But in insisting that this novel is unquestionably a major work of art, Mrs Leavis's stress comes down on the poetic method of the parts, the poetic-dramatic unity of the whole, and the 'suggestive use of language and the magical quality of her writing, which distinguishes Charlotte Brontë equally from her predecessor Jane Austen and her successor George Eliot . . . and gave her the right to demand that "poetry" must be a part of all great art' (p. 26). And with her illustrations of Charlotte Brontë's poetic method Mrs Leavis not only gives a much more convincing account of the novel's total effect than Walter Allen, who talks vaguely of 'unity of tone';[41] she shows how well she has learned from her new insights into the processes of Jane Austen's art. In other words, her discussion of method in *Jane Eyre* should be compared with her discussion of method in *Mansfield Park*. Insisting that *Jane Eyre* is 'strikingly coherent, schematic (like *Wuthering Heights*) . . . the theme has, very properly, dictated the form', she continues,

> *Jane Eyre* moves from stage to stage of Jane's development, divided into four sharply distinct phases with their suggestive names: childhood at Gateshead; girlhood, which is schooling in both senses, at Lowood; adolescence at Thornfield; maturity at Marsh End, winding up with fulfilment in marriage at Ferndean. Each move leaves behind the phase and therefore the setting the characters which supplied that step in the demonstration—the novel is not an *éducation sentimentale* like *David Copperfield* but a moral–psychological investigation. A good deal

of the effect of the book depends on the reader's making out
associations, and the parts are not mechanically linked by a
plot as in most previous fictions but organically united (as in
Shakespeare) by imagery and symbolism which pervade the
novel and are as much part of the narrative as the action.

(p.13)[42]

Had Mrs Leavis contributed this essay to *Scrutiny* it would undoubtedly have appeared under the heading 'The Novel as
Dramatic Poem'. It is an impressive case for this novel as post-
adolescent reading—as even a work of art, in Leavis's phrase, 'addressed to the adult mind'.[43] And, no doubt, for many readers it
would be more impressive still for the insertion at some point of a
qualifying 'once I thought'.

Mrs Leavis was working on *Wuthering Heights* at the same time as
she was making up her edition of *Jane Eyre* for the Penguin English
Library series. The essay that appears in *Lectures in America* (1969) is
the final form of 'a mass of material on and about *Wuthering
Heights*'[44] which she took to lecture from at Harvard and Cornell
Universities in 1966. Her title 'A Fresh Approach' aptly conveys
the nature of her undertaking. Since she had always held this novel
in high esteem, from *Fiction and the Reading Public* onward, but
without more than incidentally touching on it, she is not revaluing
her own previous estimate. Nor is she concerned to establish the
greatness of a neglected novel. Her 'corrective' intention (p. 84)
even includes a protest that the novel is not flawless: 'Desperate attempts to report a flawless work of art lead to a dishonest ignoring
of recalcitrant elements or an interpretation of them which is
sophistical' (p. 86). She keeps personal correction to a minimum,
however. She does not, as often, parade Emily Brontë's critics for
some heavy artillery practice. As a result of the fresh assessment
Mrs Leavis concentrates upon providing, earlier valuations, interpretations and misconceptions of the novel are mostly corrected
implicitly.

She aims principally to give the novel in 'its relation to the social
and literary history of its own time', to learn its 'true nature' as a
novel—as, that is, a work of art dramatising individual lives in
their human relationships—and so discovering its 'human core'
and its 'truly human centrality' (pp. 137–8). The approach is exploratory, but implicitly revaluative. 'There is no agreed reading of
this novel at all', Mrs Leavis notes. And, like her husband, she

seeks not to impose a definitive reading but to invite recognition and perhaps agreement in respect of its central meaning, which she reasonably insists is its human meaning. This human meaning, she insists, is the sphere of a 'true novelist . . . whose material was real life and whose concern was to promote a fine awareness of the nature of human relations and the problem of maturity' (p. 135).

These are words Leavis might have written. Leavis has always, like Arnold before him, valued great works of art according to their human centrality, insisting on it more urgently in his later writings. But, again, what distinguishes Mrs Leavis's from her husband's criticism is a difference in method. It is not that she does not get to grips with the text, quoting, analysing and commenting in the method favoured by Leavis: she does all these with equal effectiveness. The difference lies in the apparatus of scholarship that she builds up as a support, or, rather, as a frame to her assessment of the novel. What she remarks in her Prefatory Note sums up the difference: she wants 'to put into circulation grounds for a responsible and sensitive approach to *Wuthering Heights* in its context (both literary and historical)' (p. 84). '. . . grounds for' and 'in its context (both literary and historical)'—those words indicate the scholarly material that will provide the background for the 'fresh assessment' she aims at. Leavis would make straight for the text for a fresh assessment.

To give this context Mrs Leavis brings together an impressive apparatus of notes, appendices and literary influences and parallels: ample scope for considerable theorising and guesswork. But, though she indulges in some of both, she makes all her data subsidiary to a single-minded progression through the various 'literary' layers of the novel to its human centre. Thus she takes stock of the 'literary' *Wuthering Heights* (itself multi-stranded) with the *Lear*-like violence and the Edmund-like cuckoo-in-the-nest quality of Heathcliff (p. 88ff.), the Hoffmannesque *Beauty and the Beast* opening to the story (p. 90ff.), and the 'Romantic image of Childhood' elements (p. 91ff.), and the strong savour of the Scott of the violent tales of Border-farmers in *The Black Dwarf* and *The Bride of Lammermoor* (pp. 100ff., 149ff.). Then she appraises the 'sociological' *Wuthering Heights* with respect to its related themes of social status in the Victorian world being dependent on money, and of the child's innocence being corrupted by a society so structured (p. 95ff.). As 'part of the explanation of Catherine's failure in life', Emily Brontë, Mrs Leavis notes, 'evidently had in mind the difficulties and dangers inevitable in civilizing children to enter the artificial world of class, organised religion, social intercourse and authoritarian family life' (p. 97). At this point the reader recalls Arnold Kettle's justly admired account of the sociological novel, grounded as he rightly insists on observed and concrete reality.[45] And, like Kettle, Mrs Leavis notes how the novel is 'very firmly rooted in time and place' (p. 98).

But for Mrs Leavis neither the literary nor the sociological *Wuthering Heights* is the 'real' novel:

> if we were to take the sociological novel as the real novel and relegate the Heathcliff–Catherine–Edgar relationship and the corresponding Cathy–Linton–Hareton one, as exciting but excentric dramatic episodes, we should be misconceiving the novel and slighting it, for it is surely these relationships and their working out that give all the meaning to the rest.   (p. 101)

At this point Mrs Leavis makes her approach truly fresh. She takes up Roché's novel *Jules et Jim*, which was published in 1953, a hundred years after *Wuthering Heights*, and argues on the basis of thematic and schematic correspondences between the two novels that 'the focus of the first half' of Emily Brontë's 'real' novel 'is most certainly Catherine and it is her case that is the real moral centre of the book' (p. 103).[46] She does not impose the theme of the French novel on Emily Brontë's. Rather, by means of a careful cross-examination of the two novels that is the substance of her essay (pp. 104–34), Mrs Leavis reveals how closely Catherine's 'case' in the nineteenth-century novel resembles Kate's in the twentieth-century one. Both novelists, she shows, are preoccupied with examining Woman in relation to the question 'What is it that people call Love?' (p. 114).

Mrs Leavis's comparison of the two novels, interesting as it is in itself, leads to even more interesting conclusions and insights with respect not only to *Wuthering Heights*, but also more generally to the art of the novel in the nineteenth and twentieth centuries. Thus she is able to remark of Catherine's 'case' that Emily Brontë developed 'out of a simple sociological conflict an original psychological exploration' (p. 105). Also, she can give a much more satisfying account than previous critics, than Kettle and Klingopulos, at any rate, of the second half of the book, as she shows how the relationship between Cathy and Hareton provides a centrally relevant criticism of Catherine's case and illuminates the central theme of maturity. And she is able to point up the significance of the other characters as well in this real human novel, even of the apparently insignificant Frances Earnshaw. In completely failing, as a 'foreigner', to understand 'the proper functioning of the small farm', and in inciting 'Catherine's vanity and egotism' towards 'the Lintons' idea of gentility' Frances 'belongs to the sociological meaning of the novel' (p. 136). But she also belongs integrally in the human novel: 'the novelist has something more profoundly human to convey through Frances. For one thing, before we are shown what Catherine makes of marriage we are given a norm to compare with' (p. 137). Then, in the use that Mrs Leavis makes of *Jules et Jim* she gives not only strong evidence that her reading is abreast with the modern novel but also some inkling as to why neither she nor her husband has found in the English novel, at least, any novelist of real importance after D. H. Lawrence. She plainly admires *Jules et Jim* and gives it distinction by including it with *Wuthering Heights* in a category of novels with *Women in Love*, *Anna Karenina* and *Great Expectations* (p. 138). In the same category, perhaps, but not in the same class: 'because with all its genuineness it gives so much more discomfort than satisfaction' (p. 115); 'because there is really no moral interest only a series of shocks and surprises' (p. 117); because Roché is indulgent with his Kate, unlike Emily Brontë with her Catherine, and because his novel is 'less instructive about the human problems both novels are concerned with', and this because Roché 'offers no more than a record of two men's experience of Woman' within 'a moral vacuum'—as against Emily Brontë's complex psychological and moral drama (p. 127). By criticising the twentieth-century French novel in these terms, Mrs Leavis in other words criticises the age which has produced it, an age in which to show a moral interest in human life invites ridicule and the label 'old-fashioned'. Instead the order of the day is to 'play it cool' and be clinically detached. This is Mrs Leavis's implication as she tries to pinpoint the essential difference between the two novels.

Why does one feel that in spite of its intensely painful scenes— painful in a great variety of ways—*Wuthering Heights* always repays rereading? It is easy to lay a finger on a passage that shows why what only disturbs in *Jules et Jim* moves us profoundly in the other novel, because instead of a clinical detachment we

get a delicate annotation of behaviour that convinces us that it is
not perverse but natural, human and inevitable.   (p. 115)

And she instances chapter 8 of *Wuthering Heights*, in which
Catherine at fifteen makes the transition from the Heights to the
Grange and goes through all the inner conflicts this entails. Here,
'moves' implies sympathy and what Leavis calls an affirmation of
life; but 'disturbs' implies destructiveness without ensuing recon-
struction. For both Leavises, great art must affirm life.

Last but not least, one notes from this essay how Mrs Leavis has
qualified her husband's judgement in *The Great Tradition* (p. 38)
that *Wuthering Heights* is 'a kind of sport' out of which 'a minor
tradition comes'. By the comparative references she makes not just
to *Jules et Jim* but also to *Great Expectations* and *Women in Love*, Mrs
Leavis has given the strongest possible grounds for considering
Emily Brontë's novel in the great tradition. And the inclusion of
this essay in the collaborative *Lectures in America* gives one excuse for
thinking that Leavis too would now concur.

Little need be added to what has already been noted of Mrs
Leavis's introductions to *Silas Marner* and to *Miss Marjoribanks*. She
deals with *Silas Marner* in much the same way[47] as with *Jane Eyre*
and with *Wuthering Heights*, and has a similar objective. That is, she
wants to invite readers of George Eliot's novel to see beneath the
'moral "faery-tale"', and in turn beneath the sociological novel
(village life *versus* urban life at the dawn of industrialisation)
beneath that, to the deeply human novel that dramatises with complexity in economy that there are mysterious 'laws of life'
motivating human behaviour.[48] So she comments on 'Cliff's story'
(Cliff who was like Marner after him an alien immigrant in the
district of Raveloe, and whose death in madness and childlessness
is 'an awful warning of what Silas's [fate] might be'),

So this parable within a parable is the clue to the whole, and Mr
Macey justly sums up in what might be an epigraph for the
novel: 'there's reasons in things as nobody knows on—that's
pretty much what I've made out.' There *are* laws of life, George
Eliot shows, and they were 'made out' in village life although
they can't be stated. In Mr Macey's narrative and its affiliations
with the rest of the book we have one example of the wonderfully
complex organisation and the unobtrusive structure of symbol

and theme which make the text of *Silas Marner* so dense and rich in meanings and yet so economical in words.[49]

Such economy, suggestiveness and complexity plainly put this novel, too, in the category of 'the novel as dramatic poem'.

> Though *Marner* prepares us for its successors *Middlemarch* and *Felix Holt* it is superior to these in an art of concentration that uses always the minimum—the loaded word and the uniquely representative act—an art which puts *Marner* with Shakespeare and Bunyan rather than with other Victorian novels.[50]

Finally there is the Introduction to Margaret Oliphant's *Miss Marjoribanks*, the major novel in her Chronicles of Carlingford and rated by Mrs Leavis above the comparable things in Mrs Gaskell's Cranford and Trollope's Barchester volumes. Of this I need only add to what has been said (p. 52 above) that, whether or not Mrs Leavis has succeeded in establishing the novel as the missing link between Jane Austen's *Emma* and George Eliot's *Middlemarch*, she has exhumed a novel of distinction which it is not ridiculous to compare with these masterpieces. Mrs Leavis does not exaggerate: the novel is witty, entertaining, and at the same time a serious criticism of, in her words, 'false Victorian values where women are concerned'.[51] Mrs Leavis's edition came out in 1969, published by Chatto and Windus in the Zodiac Press, the same publishers with the same press of another neglected classic (in 1955), this one edited and introduced by Leavis: Mark Twain's *Pudd'nhead Wilson*. Subsequently, in 1974, Mrs Leavis wrote an introduction for the *Autobiography and Letters of Mrs Margaret Oliphant*, published by Leicester University in their Victorian Library series. So a Margaret Oliphant revival seems already under way, started by Mrs Leavis.

5 F.R.Leavis and D.H.Lawrence

D. H. Lawrence: Novelist (1955) is aptly the central work in Leavis's criticism both of the novel and as a whole. It looks back to one of the earliest long essays Leavis wrote, on Lawrence, in 1930, which he then placed at the centre of *For Continuity* (1933); and it looks forward to his last book, *Thought, Words and Creativity: Art and Thought in Lawrence* (1976), in which he confirms his conviction of Lawrence's centrality as writer and thinker. The middle work strikingly shows, too, that all Leavis's interests and 'fields' as a critic—in literature, culture, society, education—have converged with the interests of the novelist who concerns himself most deeply with the modern world. 'The novel can help us to live, as nothing else can',[1] Lawrence had claimed, and Leavis in this book endorses Lawrence. He finds Lawrence's art overall an education in the broadest and deepest senses, both 'enlivening' and 'enlightening' (p. 9).

D. H. Lawrence: Novelist decisively revalues the early essay on Lawrence and becomes the sequel volume to *The Great Tradition*. Leavis links Lawrence with George Eliot and seems to complete his revaluations of the English novel. However, his new insights into Lawrence led him on to a further phase of revaluation. The key sentence in the book is, 'It is Lawrence's greatness that to appreciate him is to revise one's criteria of intelligence and one's notion of it' (p. 27). In perceiving Lawrence's affirmation of individual responsibility and creativity as a 'romantic' strength, Leavis revised his own criteria and notion of intelligence, and saw that he needed to re-examine the Romantic movement to distinguish Lawrence's true forerunners.

The later criticism—begun when Leavis was in his sixties—concentrates the inquiry into the nature of the highest form of creative impersonality. 'Disinterestedness' he sometimes calls it with Arnold, to emphasise that the quality he has in mind is not merely aesthetic, but applies to every sphere in life. It means an unselfish and imaginative devotion to making the conditions of life better, in the manner of Albert Schweitzer,[2] whatever one does. Leavis used the phrase 'the servant of life' in *The Great Tradition* (p. 23), and his later criticism intensifies his analysis of its meaning in the context of literature by a prolonged study of four poets and novelists: Lawrence, Eliot, Blake and Dickens.

The search to define creative impersonality in terms of human responsibility involved revising the 'great tradition', and crucially hung on deciding whether Lawrence or Eliot was the more creative and centrally human writer. This was a tough and deeply felt challenge, which Leavis tackled throughout a lifetime: Lawrence and Eliot were his contemporaries; he had ardently pioneered academic recognition for them, and they in turn had inspired him as a young thinker; yet they were deeply different, even opposed, in their beliefs. Making up his mind about them was thus for Leavis a quest for self-knowledge. In discriminating between Lawrence and Eliot, and discerning the defects as well as the virtues of each, Leavis sharpened his criteria, knew his own mind, spoke with a voice both distinctive and perhaps as influential as theirs, and in due time wrote of them with something like the impersonality he sought in them. And he helped himself to reach this point by means of his imaginative extension of the notion of 'the novel as dramatic poem'.

But Leavis's greater objectivity with Lawrence and Eliot came later and was fully achieved in the analysis of *Four Quartets* in *The Living Principle* (1975) and the exploration of Lawrence's thought and creativity in *Thoughts, Words and Creativity*—works which followed similar explorations of Blake and Dickens. In *D. H. Lawrence: Novelist* the search for objective criteria sometimes gets entangled in the thickets of personal loyalty; hence the passionate anger against Eliot and the passionate praise for Lawrence. Some readers have therefore reacted against the book, finding Leavis intolerably harsh with Eliot and not critical enough with Lawrence. Passages can be cited in their support, yet it is important to understand the issues that generated Leavis's heat. They are not trivial, and the book needs re-examination in light of them.

At first Leavis shared Eliot's reservations about Lawrence's romantic and mystical intensities (*For Continuity*, p. 117ff.), though even at the start he was weighing the poet and the novelist and preferring Lawrence's nonconforming courage to Eliot's

'Establishment' softness (pp. 155–7, 180). He also supposed, in
the Preface to this work, that he would 'never again' be able to give
Lawrence's works 'the prolonged and intensive frequentation' that
went into the long central essay on Lawrence (p. 2). But evidently
Eliot's publication of *After Strange Gods* in the next year, 1934,
jolted Leavis into changing his mind. Lawrence was being smeared
by the most influential living writer in English. Leavis rallied, reread Lawrence, and the result in due time was *D. H. Lawrence:*
Novelist, which emphatically revises the earlier judgement that 'the
man appears saner than the art' (*For Continuity*, p. 147).

Comparison of the two books shows how far Leavis had progressed in his criticism both of Lawrence and in general. Specifically as a critic of the novel he had developed a much clearer idea of
what he meant by impersonality, a key criterion. In 1933 he
thought most highly[3] of *Sons and Lovers* and *Lady Chatterley's Lover*,
strongly personal fictions, the one obviously a fictional autobiography and the other the fictional thesis of an intensely personal
philosophy of love. In 1955 he rates these much below *The Rainbow*
and *Women in Love*, now the supreme masterpieces by virtue of their
impersonalised complexity.

It should be added that already in 1933 Leavis felt sure that
Lawrence ranked above Virginia Woolf, Dos Passos and Joyce, his
most important contemporaries, though not above E. M. Forster.
He found that *A Passage to India* 'stands for qualities of intelligence
and civilisation that Lawrence has little concern for' (*For Continuity*,
p. 133), and that, in other words, Forster was reassuringly in the
'classical' tradition that descends from Jane Austen.

Leavis does not explicitly rank these novelists in *For Continuity*,
but his relative placing of them emerges by implicit contrast. Thus,
for instance, by placing the essay on Lawrence at the centre of the
volume he appears deliberately to signify Lawrence's superiority as
a novelist to all save Forster. Meanwhile, he does place Virginia
Woolf below Dos Passos, arguing that she does not achieve as
he does a broad human context for the action of her novels. The
author of *The Forty-Second Parallel* 'Unlike Mrs Woolf, his antith-
esis, . . . cannot be interested in individuals without consciously
relating them to the society and civilisation that make the individual life possible' (p. 102). A close interest in individual lives in
their social interrelations makes Dos Passos a serious artist, he
feels. And in *D. H. Lawrence: Novelist* he is to affirm such an interest

ıs a hallmark of Lawrence's genius as a novelist, making the point
ᵉpeatedly, as here of *The Rainbow*:

> No one could have been more profoundly possessed by the
> perception that life is a matter of individual lives and that except
> in individual lives there is no life to be interested in or reverent
> about, and no life to be served. . . .
>   The insistence on the individual, or 'fulfilment' in the in-
> dividual, as the essential manifestation of life carries with it a
> corollary; one that points to the specific vocation of novelist
> (rather than, what is so often proposed to us as Lawrence's, the
> lyric poet's) more unmistakably: it is only by way of the most
> delicate and complex responsive relations with others that the in-
> dividual can achieve fulfilment.   (pp. 105–6)

But Leavis cannot talk of Dos Passos's art in these terms, because
ıe finds it ultimately too contrived to be called great. He finds that
ıis technique, which he praises as brilliant, has not enough life in-
ᶠorming it, not enough of the artist's consciousness or human con-
ᵗern. It is too machine-like, and not human enough:

> It is more than a superficial analogy when the technique is lik-
> ened to that of the film. The author might be said to conceive
> his function as selective photography and 'montage'. That this
> method does not admit sufficiently of the presence of the artist's
> personal consciousness the device called 'The Camera Eye'
> seems to recognise—it any rate seems to do little else. What
> this judgement amounts to is that the work does not express an
> adequate realisation of the issues it offers to deal with. (*For
> Continuity*, p. 107)

The term 'realisation' is significant even this early in Leavis's
writings. Here he appears to mean two things: Dos Passos has not
ᶠully grasped or 'realised' the reality of the issues he engages to
depict, and consequently he has not created or 'realised' by artistic
means a total vision of reality. And for Leavis in 1933 a true
realisation, or true vision of reality, necessarily includes an
awareness of the human realities that the mechanised world stifles
and destroys. 'But Mr Dos Passos, though he exhibits so over-
whelmingly the results of disintegration and decay, shows nothing

like an adequate awareness of—or concern for—what has been lost' (ibid.). In other words, Dos Passos does not sufficiently affirm man's capacity to realise his human potential in and in spite of his mechanical environment. And consequently his subject-matter, the dehumanising oppressiveness of the machine world, appears finally to have made his art mechanical, Leavis feels.[4]

In contrast, Lawrence has an acute awareness of and concern for what has been lost. To show this Leavis quotes the passage from *Lady Chatterley* (ch. 11) beginning 'The car ploughed up the hill', which has become a *locus classicus* for his criticism. Also, Lawrence does write out of intense personal experience and his novels are intensely charged with life: *The Rainbow* and *Women in Love* too intensely so, Leavis felt at this time. It should be added that Leavis already linked Lawrence with Blake at this time on account of his Blakean 'vindication of impulse and spontaneity against "reason" and "convention" (*For Continuity*, p. 113).

Joyce, too, serves as an implied contrast with Lawrence at this time. Leavis can admire parts of *Ulysses* very highly: 'the description, for instance, of Stephen Dedalus walking over the beach, [has] a Shakespearian concreteness; the rich complexity it offers to analysis derives from the intensely imagined experience realised in the words' (*For Continuity*, pp. 208–9). But for the rest he finds that Joyce's effects are contrived and artificial as compared with Shakespeare's:

> Nothing could be 'righter' than Shakespeare's effects, but they are irreconcilable with this kind of deliberate, calculating contrivance and with this external approach. They register the compulsive intensity and completeness with which Shakespeare realises his imagined world, the swift immediacy that engages at a point an inexhaustibly subtle organisation.   (p. 210)

Shakespeare 'realises' while Joyce 'contrives'. And *Work in Progress/Finnegans Wake* only confirms for Leavis the tendency of Joyce's development: to pursue art as a substitute for a deeply felt vision of life.

> To justify a medium much less obtrusive in pretensions than that of the *Work in Progress* Joyce would have had to have a commanding theme, animated by some impulsion from the inner life

capable of maintaining a high pressure. Actually the development of the medium appears to be correlated with the absence of such a theme.   (p. 211)

Readers of *The Great Tradition* would do well to note this early essay: it shows that Leavis had tackled Joyce and not arbitrarily dismissed him. He had in fact examined him according to the highest standard, Shakespeare: a compliment to Joyce.

If by contrast Lawrence's novels do have a commanding theme and are animated by impulsion from the inner life, their very intensity disconcerted Leavis at this time. He found Lawrence's quest for essential reality making his art fanatical and inhuman, and not just in the obvious places in *Kangaroo* and *The Plumed Serpent*. Of *The Rainbow* Leavis exclaims: 'Lawrence's fanatical concern for the "essential" often results in a strange intensity, but how limited is the range!' (*For Continuity*, p. 117). And of a passage in *Women in Love* he remarks that 'Lawrence's preoccupation with the primitive fosters in him a certain inhumanity' (p. 114). This is where Leavis's early view of Lawrence most strikingly coincides with Eliot's. And this view leads him to wonder if E. M. Forster does not in his novels embody 'qualities of intelligence and civilisation' just as urgently needed in modern life as Lawrence's spontaneity:

It seems to me too easily assumed that *Lady Chatterley's Lover* represents greater health and vitality than *A Passage to India*. And if we accepted the first without reserves, how much of what is represented by the second should we have to abandon? It is plain that *A Passage to India* stands for qualities of intelligence and civilisation that Lawrence has little concern for.   (p. 133)[5]

The early account of Lawrence came to seem naïve, as Leavis had foreseen and now admitted (*D. H. Lawrence: Novelist*, pp. 1–2). And we may note that his early aversion to Lawrence's romantic intensities parallels Mrs Leavis's similar reactions to Charlotte Brontë and Dickens at this time. Then, just as Leavis saw beyond the conventional response to Lawrence and stigmatised it, so he and Mrs Leavis saw beyond the institutionalised Dickens—the entertainer and creator of Christmas fables—to discover the mature and subtle artist.

Between his appraisals of Lawrence, in 1938 Leavis wrote a

critique of Forster which he later reprinted in *The Common Pursuit*
A fine tribute, it also explains why Leavis has not numbered
Forster among the great novelists. Forster has a 'representative
significance' as a spokesman of 'the finer consciousness of our time
and the 'humane tradition', and *A Passage to India* is 'a classic' (*The
Common Pursuit*, p. 277). However, he misses greatness because
even in his best work he fails to achieve the impersonality of
dramatic realisation:

> Mr Forster's style is personal in the sense that it keeps us very
> much aware of the personality of the writer, so that even where
> actions, events and the experiences of characters are supposed
> to be speaking for themselves the turn of phrase and tone of voice
> bring the presenter and commentator into the foreground. . .
> His habit doesn't favour the impersonality, the presentment of
> themes and experiences as things standing there in themselves
> that would be necessary for convincing success at the level of his
> highest intention.   (p. 275)

This impersonality Leavis saw typically in fictions that can be
called dramatic poems—in *The Rainbow*, *Women in Love*, 'The Captain's Doll', *St Mawr*, as he discovered on reassessing these works.
And Eliot played a key part in the discovery. His criticisms led
Leavis to the centre of Lawrence's novels and to a new understanding of them. Eliot charged that Lawrence was a snob and
morbid about sex, lacked cultural roots, education, and sense of
humour, was incapable of ordinary thinking and a heretic, wrote
badly and could not make a work of art. Leavis replied that one
had to discard stale habits and educate oneself anew to appreciate
Lawrence's intelligence, and made *D. H. Lawrence: Novelist* largely
a systematic rebuttal of Eliot's charges. Thus he shows, for instance, that 'The Daughters of the Vicar' is a critique of snobbish-
ness, and in 'The Captain's Doll' 'humour and irony and all the
liveliness of a refined and highly civilized comedy' are essential to
its mode (p. 206). The analyses of *The Rainbow* and *Women in Love*
reveal richly complex and original works of art, such as make nonsense of Eliot's criticisms.

For many readers these analyses would have sufficed to promote
Lawrence and disprove Eliot. The attack on Eliot seemed personal,
gratuitous, and misplaced. Leavis was 'belligerently dogmatic', indulging a 'pet peeve',[6] and 'using the artist to 'air his own likes and

dislikes'.[7] One can see the point in such strictures, but the issues lie much deeper than their authors recognise.

Leavis rounded on Eliot for perpetrating a double betrayal, of both Lawrence and himself as creative thinkers of major importance. Eliot was denying Lawrence his birthright as a great artist and selling his own in the process. Moreover, there was a streak of humbug in Eliot's attitude to Lawrence: he praised Lawrence for speaking against 'the living death of material civilization', and denigrated his art in the same breath.[8] Furthermore, he did so from a safely distinguished Establishment[9] position. All this deeply hurt a man of Leavis's integrity. He was shocked to the core that Eliot, whom he had admired and looked up to as a major poet, critic, and spokesman for modern civilisation, could act so irresponsibly, and so badly demean his intelligence. At the same time he recognised the value of Eliot's misconceived criticisms:

> But it is, I think, worth inquiring at this point now, if I am right in sum about Lawrence's genius and achievement, a mind capable of Eliot's best criticism can have been so wrong in matters so important. It is worth inquiring because the challenge leads us to certain useful formulations regarding the nature of Lawrence's greatness and the significance of his work.   (p. 25)

A challenge, in other words, to clarify the nature of creative impersonality and to establish his independence as critic from Eliot. And had Leavis felt more independent—had he deferred less to Eliot, and to Lawrence, at this time, as he had good reason to do with a major critical achievement already behind him, he might have treated Eliot with more detachment and less heat—more in the spirit of the passage above. But he was still weighing these two geniuses, one of whom, Eliot, was meanwhile the mandarin of English letters.[10]

As for the affirmation of Lawrence, so fervent is this that many readers will feel with Roger Poole that

> Reading *D. H. Lawrence: Novelist* is rather like being submitted to prolonged indoctrination. It is not so much that life is shown to be present in Lawrence, as that it is insisted upon as being there, again and again. Ostensively, repeatedly Leavis points to this passage and that, indicating his conviction that this is virtually ineffable, that this is transcendent art.[11]

It is true that Leavis builds up an insistent recitative of praise, with phrases such as 'the peculiar Laurentian genius', 'the wonderfully originally artist', 'the superlative intelligence'. Conrad once called *Moby Dick* 'a rather strained rhapsody'.[12] Few would agree. But many readers will feel that the rhapsody in *D. H. Lawrence: Novelist* is sometimes strained. Yet that ought not to be the cue to pour cold water, as it is so easy to do now that Lawrence has been canonised a great novelist. For Leavis was pioneering for such recognition of Lawrence. The shock tactics he employed in *The Great Tradition* to promote awareness of the novel as great imaginative art are here redeployed in the attack on Eliot and the praise for Lawrence to promote awareness of Lawrence's greatness as a novelist. Mark Spilka seems exactly right in his summing-up of these matters of tone and recrimination in Leavis: 'We may quarrel with his exactions, we may question his inclusions and exclusions, we may deplore his ardours and recriminations: but Leavis remains, for all that, the ablest of Lawrence critics and the chief progenitor of his revival'.[13]

The engagement with Lawrence, and by implication Eliot, centres in the inquiry into the nature of creative impersonality; and the inquiry is made by extending the notion of 'the novel as dramatic poem'. Thus *D. H. Lawrence: Novelist* directly follows the 'Analytic Note' at the end of *The Great Tradition*, and Lawrence's art is implicitly linked with Dickens's.

But the link is only implicit. Dickens occupies a back seat, as in the earlier book, being cited with approval in the 'Note: Being an Artist' (pp. 310–11). Also, in the chapter on *Women in Love* Leavis mentions that Mrs Crick's 'disturbing queerness is evoked with that power of Lawrence's which sometimes reminds us of Dickens' (pp. 159–60). But what that power is and where it is to be found in Dickens, he does not say. Moreover, he says not a word about the creator of Dombey and Coketown where we might most expect him to: in the long perceptive analysis of Lawrence's critique of Thomas Crich, his family, and his workmen in the chapter 'The Industrial Magnate'.[14]

In other words, we deduce that Leavis has yet fully to gauge Dickens's significance as a novelist and as a precursor of Lawrence. Meanwhile he links Lawrence with George Eliot, yet not to his complete satisfaction. For instance, the general similarities between *The Rainbow* and *The Mill on the Floss* include the 'immense difference between the two authors', which Leavis pins down as the 'poetic intensity' of Lawrence's art as compared with George Eliot's. 'This intensity', he adds, 'is an extraordinary sensuous immediacy (it is no more merely sensuous than the charged intensity of Shakespearean poetry is)' (pp. 115–16). With hindsight we sense that Leavis appears to moot that there is more than George Eliot behind Lawrence. We recall that it was Dickens's 'poetic force of evocation' in *Hard Times* that made Leavis think of Dickens's art as Shakespearean, and Conrad's as Dickensian or Shakespearean. We remember, too, from that essay his declaration that readers could not hope to grasp Dickens's significances without revising their criteria and expectations of the English novel.[15] Lawrence's masterpieces demand such revision:

> They present a difficulty that is a measure of their profound originality. Lawrence's art in them is so original in its methods and procedures that at first we again and again fail to recognize what it is doing or what it is offering—we miss the point. And this technical originality was entailed by the originality of what Lawrence had to convey. The important truths about human experience are not necessarily at once obvious. . . . the worst difficulty we have in coming to terms with his art is that there is a resistance in us to what it has to communicate—if only the kind of resistance represented by habit; habit that will not let us see what is there for what it is, or believe that the door is open.
>
> (pp. 21–2)

In other words, Leavis opened the door to Lawrence by following the advice he had given to readers of *Hard Times*, and *D. H. Lawrence: Novelist* confirms that he made a breakthrough in his thinking about the novel via Dickens,[16] even though unwittingly at this time.

Mark Spilka has noted the aptness of Leavis's approach in this way:

> His guiding simile, the novel as dramatic poem, allowed him to examine fiction with the care and 'scrutiny' which he brought to poetry: to quote and analyze long passages to demonstrate the operative function of ideas, and to develop symbolic and experiential patterns. Then, too, by insisting on the dramatic nature of such fiction, he could keep fidelity with rendered life and temporal progression and avoid excessive symbol-hunting.

Later critics, notably William York Tindall, Eliseo Vivas and Angelo Bertocci, would treat Lawrence's symbols as implicative networks in the *Symboliste* tradition, and so freeze the novels into intellectual patterns or 'symbolic poems'. Although Lawrence clearly works through implication, his chief mode of progression is dramatic, and symbols merely integrate and focus that progression. Leavis's simile is more apt, and more likely to promote the kind of formal study Lawrence needs, given his fluid sense of relatedness and change.[17]

This is well put. And no doubt because Lawrence's chief mode of progression is dramatic, Leavis had insisted that his strength is a novelist's before all else, and hence the title he gives his book. But Leavis means much more by 'poem' than Spilka here conveys, though the remark that he scrutinises such novels as he would poems is very true. By 'poem' Leavis means far more, also, than isolable examples of poetic prose, imagery, symbolism, or other obviously poetical effects. He means the whole novel conceived as a poetic creation—as having the density and complexity of meaning and organisation usually associated with formally poetic works. He wants the reader to consider that every element in the novel—action, scene, episode, dialogue, character, irony, contrast, variety of mode and style, the very use of language, as well as symbolism, imagery and so on—has been so organised by the novelist as to result in a complex organism of meaning, and fertile with the richness of evocation he would expect in Shakespearean drama.[18] Such novels, then, are not novels of plot in the conventional sense. They do not yield their meaning only through what *happens* in the story as it unfolds, and through such traditional devices of plot as peripeteia and *dénouement*. Rather, plot, as the quotation in n. 18 suggests, means the total design, the whole imaginative vision. Nor are they novels of ideas as such, in which the novelist uses his story as a disguised essay about life. In the novel as dramatic poem, meaning is conveyed not only by the novelist's dramatic methods, but also by his sheer power of poetic evocation with words in the narrative parts which integrate the dramatic action. As Leavis remarks of the opening pages of *The Rainbow*,

It is not merely that George Eliot doesn't write this kind of prose. Lawrence is not indulging in descriptive 'lyricism', or writing poetically in order to generate atmosphere. Words here are used

in the way, not of eloquence but of creative poetry (a wholly different way, that is, from that of *O may I join the choir invisible*): they
establish an actual presence—create as part of the substance of
the book—something that is essential to Lawrence's theme.

(p. 102)

The distinction implied here in the phrase 'creative poetry' is interesting and important. By poem, poetry and poetic he means the
whole creative process entailed in his concept of impersonality
as it has been discussed in Chapter 3 above. 'Poetic' for him
is synonymous with, not 'poetical', but 'creative'.[19] Another
example from the critique of *The Rainbow* makes the identification
more explicit. He comments on Will's and Anna's visit to
Lincoln Cathedral:

> The sustained stretch of prose that renders Will's ecstacy [*sic*] is
> not 'poetic prose' in any ordinary suggestion of that phrase. It is
> a poem rising easily and naturally out of the almost in-
> credibly flexible[20] prose in which *The Rainbow* is written—
> prose characteristically Lawrence's, but different from that of
> any book of his before or after. It 'creates the concepts' with
> which it is concerned.   (p. 129)

In other words, Lawrence's kind of poetic prose creates substances,
meanings, concepts which are essential to his total vision. He does
not merely paint picturesque effects. And so it is not only by his insistence on the dramatic in Lawrence's art that Leavis avoids
'freezing' the novels, as Spilka suggests other critics do, but with
the idea of poem, too, figuring as the creative totality. To put it
another way, Leavis's approach is itself much more flexible and
open-ended because the process that he implies in the notions of
poem and poetic subsumes the effects which he can call symbolic.
Poem with poetic is an all-encompassing notion of which symbolism with symbolic may, it is true, be an important part, but only a
part. This, moreover, explains Leavis's shyness with the term
symbolism and its cognates. He finds it too restricting, conveying
to the reader too much a one-to-one, a this-stands-for-that, meaning. He wants the reader instead to see Lawrence's dramatic
poems as far more complex significances. For instance, he comments on the 'significance' of Gerald's and Gudrun's relationship
in the Highland cattle and rabbit episodes (chs 14 and 18) in
Women in Love:

To sum up the significance is another matter: the whole
remarkable chapter [14] is very complex, closely organized, and
highly charged. It will be noticed that I have avoided the terms
'symbol' and 'symbolism' in this discussion: to suggest the
rabbit and the cattle 'stand for' this and that would be to
suggest much simpler ways of constructing and conveying significance and much simpler significances than we actually have.
(p. 203)[21]

And of the incidents in chapter 4, 'Diver', from the same novel he
says, qualifying his own comment that the drowned pair have an
'anticipatory symbolism' (for Gerald and Gudrun later on):

But these effects work subtly in with the whole complex organization of poetic and dramatic means that forms this wonderful chapter, means that, in sum, are no more to be brought
helpfully under the limiting suggestion of 'symbolism' than the
Shakespearean means in an act of *Macbeth*.   (p. 205)

By seeing his two masterpieces as dramatic poems Leavis has
been able to exemplify strikingly the operation of impersonality in
Lawrence, and, more, he intimates that Lawrence's kind of impersonality in its self-transcending responsibility towards life has
religious and teleological significance. *The Rainbow* and *Women in
Love* are now seen as much greater works of art than *Sons and Lovers*
because Lawrence knows himself better and knows how to trans-
mute intensely personal experience into impersonal art. He can
do this, Leavis says, because he has put the 'catharsis' of *Sons
and Lovers* behind him, and in his new maturity he has a surer
grasp of realising by dramatic means, and so objectifying, the
issues of life that most concern him (p. 136). For instance, he notes
that the relation that Paul Morel has with his mother in *Sons and
Lovers* is still too transparently and poignantly autobiographical of
Lawrence's 'notorious relation' with his own mother. And, though
critics have called this Lawrence's 'misfortune', warping him for
life (ibid.), Leavis disagrees. He argues that in *The Rainbow*
Lawrence has fully understood his relation with his mother, and
distanced and impersonalised it in the relation between the child
Ursula and her father. Citing a passage from chapter 8, 'The
Child', which begins, 'Still she set towards him like a quivering
needle', Leavis comments,

Replace 'father' by 'mother', and 'he' by 'she' and this is Lawrence describing what happened to him in his childhood. I spoke above of his 'misfortune'; but the question forced upon us by the comparison between *Sons and Lovers* and *The Rainbow* is: What, for genius, is misfortune? The personal note of the earlier . . . book has vanished in *The Rainbow*; the catharsis was complete and final. . . . There is in fact no more impressive mark of his genius than what he did with his 'misfortune'; he turned it into insight. It was a triumph of supreme intelligence—the intelligence that is inseparable from imagination and self-knowledge.

In its use in *The Rainbow* the experience is wholly impersonalized. . . . it is experience that understands itself. (pp. 136–7)

Similarly, Leavis shows that Birkin in *Women in Love*, though clearly a self-portrait of Lawrence, is nevertheless so tested and criticised by Ursula and others that he is made at times to seem a parody of Lawrence. Consequently he has an independent dramatic status and provides 'one of the most striking proofs of creative power' in Lawrence (p. 183):

Self-dramatized in Birkin, the Lawrence who formulates conclusions ('doctrines') and ponders them suffers exposure to the searching tests and the impersonal criteria that the artist's creative genius, which represents an impersonal profundity and wholeness of being, implicitly and impartially applies to them.

(p. 184)

These extracts give the idea of impersonality as already seen in *The Great Tradition*: an objectifying, or 'realisation', of deeply-felt personal experience by critical and dramatic means. But, in his analysis of Tom Brangwen in *The Rainbow*, Leavis goes further, suggesting that impersonality in Lawrence has a deeply religious character. He does so by way of arguing that Lawrence is a greater novelist than George Eliot, because he shows a 'religious' sense of responsibility to life, she only an 'ethical' sense (p. 114). Leavis does not specify impersonality in connection with Brangwen. But he clearly links Lawrence with Brangwen, intimating that Brangwen's self-transcending discovery that the individual life he is is but a unity of the greater universe of life beyond and around him embodies Lawrence's religious and reverent attitude to life; and it

is this attitude translated into art which is the highest creative impersonality. Brangwen, in sum, is a paradigm of Lawrence's art.

> What, in fact, strikes us as religious is the intensity with which
> his men and women, hearkening to their deepest needs and
> promptings as they seek 'fulfilment' in marriage, know that they
> 'do not belong to themselves', but are responsible to something
> that, in transcending the individual, transcends love and sex too.
>   (p. 115)

This is clearly a definition of impersonality in a life situation, and
by extension, of the creative spirit in both life and art. Leavis's
terms are almost mystical, not because he is being purposely
portentous but because Lawrence's uncanny rendering of life
forces him to be allusive rather than explicit and definite. And this
is because 'life' itself, the 'something that . . . transcends love and
sex', is an undefinable mystery, and 'reverenced' as such by
Lawrence. As he has said just previously of 'The Daughters of
the Vicar', ' "reverence" and "life" . . . get their definition in the
course of the tale' (p. 78). That tale also contains a Lawrence-
reflector, Louisa Lindley, who in her staunch refusal either to give
up or be given up by her lover Alfred Durant, the collier and her
inferior in class, exhibits a class-transcending commitment to
essential human values that Leavis describes as 'a passionate sense
for what is real, and a firm allegiance to it' (p. 80). 'Her moral
judgements are unmistakably vital judgements' (p. 86). By 'what is
real' Leavis can only mean a grasp of what it means to be humanly
and spiritually alive, and the phrase 'firm allegiance' seems clearly
a different way of saying a religious attitude to life.

In *The Great Tradition* (p. 22) Leavis described Conrad as 'the servant of a profoundly serious interest in life'. Here, in the distinction he makes between Lawrence's 'religious' sense and Geroge
Eliot's 'ethical' sense, and in the marked increase in his commentary of the terms 'reverence', 'minister', and 'wonderful', Leavis
has advanced to a more assured recognition of the nature of the
highest kind of creativity in imaginative literature. The great
novelist or poet serves more than a serious interest in life: his art is
life-giving.

Creativity at this 'religious' depth is the rarest kind, Leavis will
continue to postulate in all his later books. And only a handful of
English writers have fully represented it in the past two centuries:

notably Lawrence, Blake and Dickens. Their work, he points out, is truly impersonal and religious, but Flaubert's, by contrast, in a counterfeit way; for in them art is made to serve mankind, while in Flaubert mankind is sacrificed on the altar of art.[22] The Flauberian impersonality proves to be, paradoxically, a fanatical self-consciousness.

T. S. Eliot presented a specially interesting challenge to define impersonality at the religious depth. He had long been for Leavis the major poet of the century, the exasperatingly equivocal critic of Lawrence, and also of course the author in 'Tradition and the Individual Talent' of the classical definition of impersonality. Yet Leavis had not by the time of *D. H. Lawrence: Novelist* engaged with *Four Quartets*. (Instead he had scored easy points against *The Cocktail Party*.) What, then, would Eliot's poetic achievement look like as a whole? After prolonged study[23] Leavis would conclude, in the long analysis of *Four Quartets* in *The Living Principle* (1975), that Eliot does not quite achieve Lawrence's or Blake's level of creativity. Yet neither is he another Flaubert.

For Leavis, Eliot fails to reach the highest creativity because he fails to recognise Blake's distinction between 'selfhood' and 'identity' and remains imprisoned in his 'selfhood' (*The Living Principle*, pp. 185–6). From his own prison he sees life for everyone as a prison—or, as the closing lines of 'Burnt Norton' tell, 'the waste sad time/Stretching before and after'. This for Leavis is to trivialise and negate life:

A poet who, offering to achieve and confirm his reassuring apprehension of a really and supremely real by creative means, dismisses all but the non-temporal 'now' as the 'waste sad time stretching before and after' stultifies himself. He is committed to discrediting the creative process he undertakes to demonstrate and vindicate. (p. 191)

Four Quartets, then, expresses a disturbing paradox:[24] the whole poem is implicitly anti-creative. Leavis multiplies the evidence. The line 'human kind / Cannot bear very much reality' (also from 'Burnt Norton', ll. 42–3) is propounded as universal truth. Leavis repudiates it (p. 177). Not that the modern world is not sick. Eliot (like Dos Passos) diagnoses its plight very well, but he goes wrong, for Leavis, in presuming that his own reaction to it is every man's. Eliot reveals an attitude of despair. He writes that all the world's discoveries have been already made 'by men whom one cannot hope / To emulate' and the modern poet has 'only learnt to get the better of words / For the thing one no longer has to say' ('East Coker', ll. 176–7, 184–5). For Leavis, this is to deny the truth in Blake's words 'Jesus was an artist', that every man is potentially creative; and Eliot slights language, which is not a thing to be got the better of, but the living medium of human creativity to be kept 'alive and continually renewed' (pp. 213 and 185). In sum, Eliot lacks the 'necessary impersonality' for truly constructive thought (p. 232).

By 'necessary impersonality' Leavis means the religious depth of a Blake or Lawrence. 'Religious' in these describes the individual's deepest convictions about life, sanctioned and tested by intense personal exploration of experience. But in Eliot 'religious' involves less personal responsibility: it describes the adoption by the individual of a tradition of faith outside himself, the adherence to a formal creed. Nor is Eliot's Christianity as given in the lines,

> The dripping blood our only drink
> The bloody flesh our only food:
> In spite of which we like to think
> That we are sound, substantial flesh and blood.

> ('East Coker', ll, 167–70)

inevitably the right kind: 'there is more than one Christianity', Leavis retorts (p. 207).

Leavis's 'no' to Eliot and his 'yes' to Blake amount to a rejection of Anglo-Catholicism and a vindication of Protestantism. For Eliot the solution to the world's ills is humble self-surrender to the God of a dogmatic creed. Any other course involves pride, and pride for Eliot, Leavis points out, can only be the Coriolanian hubris of the destructive 'selfhood'. Life is to be feared and endured till we reach the real reality which lies beyond the actual world. Leavis disagrees, invoking Blake. Reality is here and now, to be lived and enjoyed (in the fullest senses of those verbs), and creatively sustained by the Blakean pride of the creative 'identity'. This creative pride is part and parcel of the religious impersonality we perceive in Blake's remark of his paintings 'Tho' I call them Mine, I know they are not Mine—or in Lawrence, when he said, 'One writes out of one's moral sense—for the race, as it were' (pp. 45, 185ff., *et passim*).

None the less, Eliot's poetry has a very high formative value[25] for the critic in pursuit of true judgement: 'He compels one, as a genius can, to the kind of disagreement that, positively, is a sharpening of one's power to perceive and to realize, and a strengthening of one's thought, conviction and resolution', (p. 202). Words to set beside the admission of twenty-one years earlier that to understand Lawrence one needed to revise one's criteria and notion of intelligence.

Some critics have been troubled by Leavis's use of the term 'religious', arguing that it implies belief, yet in what, they ask, does Leavis's belief consist? For instance, Vincent Buckley comments on Leavis's analysis of *The Rainbow* that it 'leads naturally to the point at which he can associate artistic impersonality with religious belief'[26]—but belief in what? Buckley seeks an answer in Leavis's thoughts on what Lawrence does in *St Mawr*:

> What his art *does* is beyond argument or doubt. It is not a question of metaphysics or theology—though no doubt there are questions presented for the metaphysician and the theologian. Great art, something created and *there*, is what Lawrence gives us. And there we undeniably *have* a world of wonder and reverence, whose life wells up from mysterious springs. It is no merely imagined world; what the creative imagination of the artist makes us contemplate bears an unanswerable testimony.
> (*D. H. Lawrence: Novelist*, p. 246)

Buckley is bothered by 'bears an unanswerable testimony' and wonders whether Leavis wants readers to believe that Lawrence's art is its own sanction: an astonishing revelation, if true, for it would put Leavis straight into the Flaubert–Joyce school. But Buckley unfortunately illustrates the mischief of extracting a passage from Leavis (or any writer for that matter) while overlooking everything else he has written. And Leavis has repeatedly shown that Lawrence's great strength is his power of evoking the real world, of making the reader contemplate through the novel's verbal universe the real universe to which he belongs. '. . . no merely imagined world' then means a world neither fantastical nor idiosyncratic, but real and shared; and 'what the creative imagination of the artist makes us contemplate' is the reality or truth inhering in actual human experience.

Leavis would express his conviction of the religious quality of the greatest writers in similar terms in all his later books.[27] But the term 'religious' as he uses it never has a doctrinal colouring. It does not need one. The great poet, as n. 27 shows, needs no theological apology. It is enough for us to see that the terms we associate with the notion of religious—'reverence', 'wonder', 'mystery', 'life'— have meaning in actual experience *largely because of* the creative artist. The great poet quickens our sense of life as reverent, wonderful, mysterious—and so, whatever the odds, as full of possibility and hope.

This is a deeply romantic outlook and a far cry from the earlier Leavis of classical rigour. *D. H. Lawrence: Novelist* makes the transition, perhaps a little reluctantly. How are we to describe Lawrence's quality of knowing that there is something more to life than attitudes and ideas? Leavis asks,

> What else is there? Lawrence believes—knows—that there is, or should be, something else—he believes that 'sincerity' can have a meaning; and if this conviction, which carries with it a belief that irreverence and an incapacity for awed wonder in the face of life, are deathly, is 'romantic', then Lawrence deserves to be called that.   (p. 241)

And, if Lawrence is 'romantic', who are his most important forerunners?

In the next two decades—the post-*Scrutiny* years—Leavis found his answers. Lawrence had loosed him from classical bondage[28] to Eliot; and now led him back and on to a revaluation of the Romantic movement and the discovery of its spiritual strengths in Blake and Dickens. The result is a new transcendently great line in English literature composed of one poet and two novelists (or dramatic poets)—Blake, Dickens and Lawrence, with Shakespeare at the head. And, significantly, it is the adjective 'greatest' that Leavis repeatedly uses to describe them.

What this means is that Leavis has really travelled full circle to the beginnings of his interest in literature, but now knowing his mind. Dickens and Shakespeare, he writes at the outset of his critique of *Dombey and Son*, were the pre-eminent authors for his childhood. Then, later, in his 1930 assessment of Lawrence, it was with Blake that he particularly likened this puzzling contemporary genius (see *For Continuity*). Then, ironically enough when introducing a book named *The Image of Childhood*, he affirmed Blake and Dickens as the transmitters and champions of what was really and vitally human in the Romantic movement:

> The propriety of calling the ways in which Blake's genius, at its most impressive, expresses itself 'romantic' is fairly clear. The peculiar insistence on the individual spontaneous life, and on art as the typical manifestation of its creativeness—wonder being a characteristic expression, or sign, of fully human vitality—is the protest of genius against the world of Locke and Newton, Reason and reasonableness, 'weight and measure' and the Grand Style.[29]

The organic relation of this passage to the whole of *D. H. Lawrence: Novelist*, and back to the critique of *Hard Times*, is very plain. Leavis now realised that he had hitherto been too 'reasonable' and 'weighed and measured' too much in the classical—or, rather, in the neoclassical—spirit. For he now saw that the great Romantics had more than merely 'romantic' qualities in a narrow historical sense; they expressed truths of classical permanence: 'The vital truths that Blake vindicates, make him unmistakably a writer of the "Romantic movement"—of the Romantic climate and inspiration. But the truths are not the less vital for that, and the vindication added something to the human heritage'.[30]

Leavis's journey back to the Romantic period parallels Mrs Leavis's similar one;[31] so it was entirely fitting that the next major dealing of each with the English novel should be with Dickens, and jointly undertaken. Then followed Leavis's final judgements of first Eliot, then Lawrence, in light of the new perceptions of Dickens and Blake.

The last book, *Thought, Words and Creativity* completes the Leavis *oeuvre* most satisfyingly. Using Lawrence as the twentieth-century paradigm of the creative thinker in words, Leavis clinches his defence of literary studies as the basis of the humane education that man so much needs in the age of technology and statistics. Having developed his defence in public for half-a-century, he here unequivocally claims that only the great creative writer's thinking matters now; the alternative kind—mathematical-discursive thinking—has brought mankind to a dead end (though in a rare show of tabulation he wittily implies its subservient function):

Three propositions or constatations serve to convey what the theme is:

(1) There could be no developed thought of the most important kind without language;

(2) Our language is English, which has a great literature, so that one had better say: the completest use of English is to be found in major creative works;

(3) A major creative writer *knows* in composing and writing a major creative work his concern is to refine and develop his profounder thought about life (the concluding three-word phrase unambiguously eliminates mathematics).   (p. 20)

This book concludes Leavis's work with Aristotelian inevitability and propriety. Yet, after all, why Lawrence once more? The basic insistence on relevance, that the critic keep his thinking about literature relevant to life as it is lived now, commanded the return to Lawrence. It was twenty-one years, a whole generation, since *D. H. Lawrence: Novelist*. And that book had completed Leavis's thinking about literature and life in the context of the world of the 'thirties and 'fifties; it wound up the *Scrutiny* years. The rapidly changing world of the 'fifties and 'sixties—the 'technologico-Benthamite world' as Leavis devastatingly termed it—compelled Leavis to rethink the relevance of literature and to revalue the tradition in which he had placed Lawrence. He rethought and revalued by way of a sustained re-examination of his great writers as creative thinkers, advocating their thinking about life as the antidote to technologico-Benthamism. And *Thought, Words and Creativity* crowns this post-*Scrutiny* period of reassessment.

The key essay of the period[32] is the critique of *Little Dorrit* with its masterly analysis of Dickens's creativity as a 'potency of *thought*': the novel provides an 'inquest into contemporary civilization' which 'might equally be called a study of the criteria implicit in an evaluative study of life' (*Dickens the Novelist*, pp. 216, 219). And of life now, in our own day, Leavis plainly implies. Revealing the world of *Little Dorrit* as the Victorian embryo of our own, Leavis urgently appeals to us to consider which we need more today: the statistical thinking that spawns the Circumlocution Office and Merdle and Gowan, or the humane thinking that can conceive and create the novel which includes and indicts them.

In other words, the critique of *Little Dorrit* develops the theme of

Two Cultures?, but with much greater subtlety and cogency, for Leavis shows how a great novelist tackles the theme, thinking it through and embodying it in a complex poetic drama, instead of asserting it discursively as he himself had done. The analysis of relevance and creative thought here is also subtler and more cogent than any part of *D. H. Lawrence: Novelist*. Hence the necessity of analysing Lawrence afresh—after further examination of Blake, in *Nor Shall My Sword* (1972), and of Eliot in *The Living Principle* (1975) (which has for its sub-title *'English' as a Discipline of Thought*).

The wiser, more confident Leavis makes a better critic of Lawrence. He writes from a greater emotional distance from Lawrence, and so more self-collectedly, more as an equal. The rhetorical plangency of *D. H. Lawrence: Novelist* has gone for the most part. Also, Leavis can now find more significance in *The Plumed Serpent* as a transitional work, leading to the masterpiece *Women in Love*, than he had found before (pp. 34–61).

A good example of the subtler critic of Lawrence, and of creativity in the novel, occurs in the new reading of the Loerke–Gudrun–Ursula episodes in *Women in Love*. The analysis parallels that made in *D. H. Lawrence: Novelist* (pp. 176–9) and reaches the same conclusion: that these episodes crystallise for us the difference between real and pseudo-creativity. But, now providing fresh insight into the part Gudrun plays in the drama, Leavis makes much more explicit the dynamic relationship he sees between creativity and thought in Lawrence's art. Leavis now explains that Loerke's bogusness as an artist stems from a failure to think, unlike the novel that contains him, which is genuinely creative because deeply thoughtful about life. ' "Do you do nothing but architectural sculpture?" Gudrun asked him one evening. Perhaps the question betrayed a vague sense in Gudrun that Loerke's talk about architectural sculpture, and the relation of art to life, had hardly been thought' (*Thought, Words and Creativity*, p. 74). Ursula, by contrast, has more than a vague sense of the relation: she sees it clearly. 'I think', adds Leavis, 'we may fairly say that Lawrence intends us to identify with his own Ursula's attitude and her conclusion: "The world of art is only the truth about the real world, that's all . . ." ' (p. 77). For

Her phrase, 'the truth about the real world', obviously covers the intention of the Laurentian maxim: 'Nothing is important

but life.' Of course, Ursula is not a genius, and isn't capable of the context of penetrating and comprehensive thought that justifies Lawrence's: 'Art-speech is the only speech.' It is not enough, however to stop at saying this. One must go on to say that the full justifying meaning, the enforcement, of the maxim is to be found in the art-which-is-thought of the marvellously organic and comprehensive totality which is *Women in Love*.
(Ibid.)

This analysis closely parallels the analysis of Little Dorrit, Daniel Doyce, and Henry Gowan in *Dickens the Novelist* (p. 236ff.). Indeed, Leavis plainly sees *Women in Love* as Lawrence's *Little Dorrit*: 'It is significant that Lawrence's most complete and searching inquest into neo-Benthamite civilization should have for title *Women in Love*' (*Thought, Words and Creativity*, p. 82).

Lawrence's maxim 'Art-speech is the only speech' held a special interest for Leavis down the years. In *Thought, Words and Creativity* he explores its meaning most thoroughly, and thoroughly endorses it—as he does other favourite Laurentian maxims. He might well have sub-titled the book, adapting Lawrence, 'Art-thought is the only thought'.[33] This is another way of saying that in his last book Leavis re-examines Lawrence in light of those dicta of Lawrence's that came to have for him a proverbial force. That they did so, moreover, was not owing to an obsessive loyalty to Lawrence; Leavis tested Lawrence's dicta for their truth in the work also of Conrad, Eliot, Blake and Dickens.

It would moreover be wrong to think that Leavis sees no fault in Lawrence, either as novelist or as critic. A great virtue of his essay on *Anna Karenina* is the way he examines Lawrence's—and also Arnold's and James's—criticisms of Tolstoy. He does so with authority, enlarging his perspectives on them as writers in the process. James, for example, on account of an addiction to form and economy, is judged a lesser 'kind' of creative writer than Tolstoy.

6 The Leavises and Dickens

Dickens the Novelist (1970) has nearly 400 pages, of which Mrs Leavis has contributed over two-thirds. And even a glance at the detailed table of contents (Appendix B) makes the scope of her contribution strikingly clear. However, the jointly subscribed Preface reminds us that Leavis's three chapters were the foundation of the book—the critique of *Hard Times* having first appeared in 1947, that of *Dombey and Son* in 1962, and that of *Little Dorrit* being substantially lecture material Leavis had used while Chichele Lecturer at Oxford in 1964. Evidently Mrs Leavis later wrote her four chapters and six appendices around these on an *ad hoc* basis (pp. xi–xii).

But if Leavis's chapters were the bones of the book to which Mrs Leavis added the flesh, this is not made apparent as we read: the book is not disjointed. And, since Mrs Leavis did the adding, she must deserve the main credit for this; if the title of their book is definitive of its subject-matter that is chiefly owing to Mrs Leavis. For his part Leavis mainly focuses on Dickens's progressive maturity and subtlety as an artist and critic of Victorian civilisation. Mrs Leavis does this and more, also providing a detailed account both of Dickens's development as a craftsman of the novel and of his importance in the development of the novel as literary genre. In doing so she ensures that the transitions between his chapters and hers are smooth. Again, though the Leavises concentrate on Dickens's output between *Dombey* and *Great Expectations*, all the earlier and later novels are incidentally accounted for by Mrs Leavis. As Leavis puts it in the Preface, her final chapter on the Dickens illustrations 'adds to the direct discussion of the major work an appropriate recall of the earlier work out of which the great novelist emerged' (p. xii).

The jacket of the English edition of *Dickens the Novelist* features Phiz's vignette of Little Dorrit stepping out of the Marshalsea and

99

a man (the turnkey?) looking on from behind the half-open door. Did the Leavises or their publishers have this idea? And did they intend the vignette as an emblem of the book, with Little Dorrit's action signifying the Leavises' emancipation from their 'classical' rigour with Dickens? The whole tenor of this book, and of the Leavises' writing in general, makes such an idea too whimsically fanciful. Yet, consider Mrs Leavis's chapter on the illustrations and her opinion of Dickens's preface to *Bleak House*: 'instead of an irrelevant, and indeed misleading, preface . . . Dickens would have done better simply to have printed on the title-page: "These things are parables" ' (pp. 123–4). The Phiz vignette may be a kind of pictorial parable of *Dickens the Novelist*. However, what matters is the new light in which the Leavises see Dickens and the importance of their book.

Dickens the Novelist has a many-sided importance. It is the culmination of the Leavises' criticism of the novel. In judging Dickens to be 'the Shakespeare of the novel' (pp. xi, 355 *et passim*), they complete their map of significance in English fiction, and in English imaginative literature as a whole. Certainly no greater eminences remain uncharted by them. Nor do they call Dickens the Shakespeare of the novel idly or expediently. They enforce this judgement throughout by analysing each of six major novels as dramatic poems having the dramatic power with the complexity of meaning and richness of poetic organisation associated supremely with Shakespeare's plays. They demonstrate that the full-length Dickens novel provides, and passes, the ultimate test for the critical approach worked out by Leavis.

Also, the Leavises' first truly collaborative[1] book is their most satisfying and comprehensive study of a writer. And how fitting that the Shakespeare of the novel should be its subject. We may reflect, too, that its packed wealth derives in part from their childhood immersion in Dickens. Such immersion may well have led to their shelving the creator of Pickwick and Little Nell with other childish things as they reached for more obviously adult authors, as Leavis testifies of himself (p. 1). Yet the childhood memory of the Dickens 'magic', as Leavis calls it (ibid.), seems to come alive again in the sensitiveness and the passion with which the Leavises now relish the mature Dickens.[2] And for Leavis it was a childhood occurring little more than a generation after Dickens's death in an England that was still essentially the one Dickens knew.

The strength of the book then comes from the collaboration, which combines Mrs Leavis's scholarly-critical account of Dickens's evolution as a great artist of the novel with Leavis's forceful evaluation of Dickens's mature genius and its enormous relevance to England—and, more widely, Western civilisation—in 1970. The Leavises planned this book very shrewdly, selecting among Dickens's works so as to suit their particular strengths as readers and critics to bringing out Dickens's strengths. Their chapters overlap and harmonise to illuminate Dickens's significance and centrality both as novelist and as a creative genius, with Mrs Leavis, the stronger scholar of prose fiction, mainly focusing on Dickens in relation to the novel,[3] and Leavis, the more forceful critic and the educator with larger perspectives, ranging more widely so as to indicate Dickens's pre-eminence in literature as a whole.

Dickens, for Mrs Leavis, is at the very centre of creativity in the novel. And she has chosen well among the major novels to bring this out. Ostensibly, she focuses on only three, *David Copperfield*, *Bleak House* and *Great Expectations*. But she shows that these novels, which span Dickens's greatest years—years of enormous creativity in the novel as a whole—represent in sequence some of Dickens's boldest experiments with integrating plot, theme and narrative structure. Consequently they provide the best examples for a close scrutiny of Dickens's development from a popular bestseller to a mature and major artist of the novel. Then, in her chapter on the Dickens illustrations Mrs Leavis makes a further review of all the novels. As a result, her four packed chapters contain a balanced examination of the whole *oeuvre*. Abstract Leavis's pages and *Dickens the Novelist* remains a substantial and self-sufficient study; and one that includes more than Dickens. Mrs Leavis synthesises in a context of Dickens all the important insights she has made about novelists and the novel since *Fiction and the Reading Public*. She has finally found in Dickens a vantage-point for clarifying her perspectives on the field she has studied over a lifetime.

Moreover, she plainly sees Dickens as the centre of more than the English novel. The great assimilator and transformer of English geniuses as diverse as Bunyan, Smollett, Jane Austen and, of course, Shakespeare, and the great forerunner of Joyce and Lawrence,[4] Dickens is also 'Tolstoyan before Tolstoy' in *David*

Copperfield, and in *Bleak House* Dostoevskian before Dostoevsky
(p. 161). She also links *Great Expectations* with Hawthorne (p. 292),
and so with the American novel. With these and scores of like
comparisons and allusions Mrs Leavis makes one dazzling kalei-
doscope of all her insights into the novel, with Dickens always the
centre of each pattern. And consequently she gives the title of the
book an extra resonance. Reading Mrs Leavis we are made to feel
that the title of the book is definitive in more than one way: however much she traces Dickens's symbolic explorations of human
nature and the human psyche, Mrs Leavis never stops reminding
us that he is above all a *novelist* and as such 'the artist—the truth-
teller, the psychological realist' of the times in which he lived
(p. 79); at the same time we sense that he is *the* novelist.[5]

Leavis in his briefer contribution adds to the resonance by asking
us to see *the* novelist as one of the greatest because most percipiently
human thinkers of the past 300 years—since the world became
dominated by scientific thought. He does so especially in the critique of *Little Dorrit*, where he places Dickens with Blake and
Lawrence in the supremely creative and central human tradition
that Shakespeare heads. He justifies linking two novelists, a poet
and the dramatist in a common tradition on the grounds that they
are all as master creators in language great poets. For Leavis these
four constitute a central human tradition because of the way they
have kept alive in language what it really means to be human.
They attest in works, which are both created and creative, that it is
in man's nature to be individually and originally creative. But they
attest too that in being truly creative the individual displays a
more-than-selfish interest in what he does; he demonstrates human
responsibility, an interest in life and in the fate of man generally
that is disinterested. For Leavis, true creativity in literature is,
then, the labour, in itself creative, of keeping alive in language the
basic truth that to live humanly is to live creatively, which means
valuing life in human terms and showing a disinterested concern
for the lives of others. The really great writers accomplish by
poetic–creative means what Leavis describes in expository prose:

> To insist that the psyche, the individual life, is both of its nature
> creative and in its individuality inherently social is to insist that
> all human creativity is, in one way or another, collaborative, and
> that a cultural tradition is a collaboratively sustained reality in
> the way exemplified by a living language—by the language of

Shakespeare, of Blake and of Dickens (to adduce three highly individual and potently creative writers). (p. 273)

And 'with Blake and Dickens I associate Lawrence', Leavis adds,
'so that we have a line running into the twentieth century' (p. 275).

As Shakespeare's successors, Blake, Dickens and Lawrence
have kept alive for us today in their original poetic masterpieces—
supremely, for Leavis, in *Songs of Innocence and of Experience, Little
Dorrit* and *Women in Love*—what it really means to be human in a
world directed by science, the computer and statistical thinking.
Their importance, Leavis declares, is the importance they have for
us now, who so sorely need to be reminded of all that makes life
human. But, though they write of and for the world of system and
technology in which we now live, to grasp fully their human relevance requires an effort of intelligence and imagination—itself
creative, Leavis implies—to see into the language of poetry and
into the ways in which the great novel and the great poem can
dramatise a complex statement of basic human truths. Thus we
may see *Little Dorrit* as a rich and complex metaphor of life—of both
its death-dealing and its life-giving forces—that holds true not
only of Victorian civilisation but of our civilisation as well. We
should, for instance, note the chapter 'Fellow Travellers' (bk ii,
ch. 1), says Leavis:

> The effect is to bring out with poetic force the nothingness of the
> Dorrit–Gowan–Barnacle human world. But it is not merely that
> Society, as figured in its sheltered conceit by the party enjoying
> warmth, wine, food and the mutual assurance of its superiority,
> is, for us, exposed to the irony and the challenge it ignores. We
> who live in the technologico-Benthamite age can hardly miss a
> force the episode—that is, the chapter—has for our time; for the
> whole book forms an exquisitely nerved context, and Dickens's
> analysis is radical. . . . To those troubled by the vanishing
> of what humanity more and more desperately needs if it is not
> to be deprived of all that makes it human, the 'society' of or-
> ganisation, social science, 'welfare', equality and statistics is
> as empty a nothing as the 'Society' of manner and exclusiveness.
> (pp. 272–3)

But Dickens does not merely expose and criticise negatively in *Little
Dorrit*. The novel incarnates in Little Dorrit, Arthur Clennam,

Daniel Doyce, Cavaletto and others an affirmation of human life
and creativity. They enact and represent the life-giving qualities of
Dickens's creativity in the novel. The novel may be called 'a study
of the criteria implicit in an evaluative study of life' (p. 216), and
the heroine, Amy Dorrit, represents the human positives of 'reality, courage, disinterestedness, truth, spontaneity, creativeness—
life' (p. 237).

Much of the force of the critique of *Little Dorrit* derives from the
rich context which Mrs Leavis has chiefly provided of Dickens's
development as a novelist. On its own the essay would still be a
remarkably powerful assessment of the novel and of Dickens's
mature genius in it, and comparable to Lionel Trilling's essay on
the same novel, though in power of judgement surpassing even
Trilling's, I believe.[6]

On the other hand, Leavis has himself built up to these climactic
judgements through his critiques of *Dombey and Son* and *Hard Times*.
In the one he argues that Dickens made the transition from loose-
plotted popular melodrama to serious art. *Dombey and Son* is
Dickens's 'first essay in the elaborately plotted Victorian novel'
(p. 2), and a 'wholly serious "criticism of life" ' carried out by
'poetic means' (pp. 25–7). And he indicates how this novel anticipates *Hard Times*. Its 'criticism' is not directed at industrial
England, yet even so at an England 'whose prevailing
ethos'—'money-pride and money-faith, egotism, the closed heart,
class as "exclusion" '[7]—is 'that of *Hard Times*' (p. 7).

The critique of *Hard Times* now comes into its own in this new
context. Necessarily altered in minor ways, the most significant
change concerns the new title, '*Hard Times*: The World of Bentham', and its placing under this heading beside the chapter '*Little
Dorrit*: Dickens and Blake'. As Roger Poole has perceived,[8] the
new title and the new placing decisively alter the complexion of this
early critique which Leavis hesitantly appended to *The Great Tradition*. With these few changes he has brought it up to date with his
new thinking about creativity and relevance. Moreover, this essay
probably did as much to revolutionise criticism of Dickens and of
the novel as any single work.[9]

Leavis alludes to this new relevance of *Hard Times* in his opening
remarks on *Little Dorrit*: 'The significance focused with a sharp
economy in *Hard Times*—a significance the force and bearing of
which can't be too insistently impressed on an age of statistical
method, social studies and the computer—is at the deep centre of

Little Dorrit' (p. 213). In the previous chapter I indicated that the discovery of Dickens's importance to today's world had revitalised Leavis's criticism. With Dickens on his side he was able to make the case for literature as an education for life more powerfully than ever. And no wonder: he could not have enlisted a more impressive ally than perhaps the most widely known of all novelists.

Yet, in a rich play of inadvertent comedy, the Leavises wage a running battle with a reputation of Dickens and 'Dickensian' for which they, too, had been responsible. They contend against a generation or so of egregiously sophisticated Dickens criticism, and earlier generations of uncritical adulation of Dickens's obvious bestseller qualities, accusing them all of having spawned an endless variety of geniuses called Dickens, and above all the great entertainer, none of which, however, is the real master creator in the novel. But they too had contributed to this state of affairs.

Dickens the Novelist, then, masterfully corrects personal as well as traditional and widespread misapprehensions. It brings into sharpest possible focus Dickens's achievement as a wholly serious artist of the novel, rather than as merely a popular entertainer, or theatrical performer, or dreamer, pscyhological neurotic, social reformer, or whatever. The wealth of cross-reference to other *novelists* is an incidental yet constant reminder of the Leavises' aim.

After first publishing his critique of *Dombey and Son* in the *Sewanee Review* in 1962, Leavis wrote, 'For a number of years, one of my main preoccupations in writing and speech, has been the "challenge of Dickens"—the challenge he presents to criticism to define the ways in which he is one of the greatest of writers'.[10] This may seem rather pat, but it would be foolish to dismiss Leavis's claim out of hand or deny his sincerity. Ever since he inserted the essay on *Hard Times* in *The Great Tradition*, at, we now learn, Mrs Leavis's urging (*Dickens the Novelist*, p. xi), he must have had hard second thoughts about Dickens's overall achievement. As well he might: Dickens criticism began to burgeon around him soon after. Yet, even as late as 1963, Leavis was not alone in feeling that the time was long overdue for a forthright evaluation of Dickens's essential achievement. A year later, in 1964, Robert Garis, the American critic and scholar of Dickens, was to deplore the tendency of modern Dickens criticism, deriving from one of its champions, Edmund Wilson, to shy away from evaluation. Garis complains that critics derive from the terms of Dickens's art, from his images and symbols in particular, a certain meaning about human behavior and the human condition which has social and political implications. But these implications are seldom realized explicitly; no attempt is made to 'place' his meaning, much less to judge it.[11]

This state of affairs had resulted from a 'sophisticated scepticism about the relevance of art', Garis explains, adding, 'it is hard to find a critic who is interested in going beyond interpretation to judgement'.[12] He excepts Santayana and Orwell.

Garis's words sound like a prescription for *Dickens the Novelist*, which must have been well on in preparation at this date. The whole of the opening paragraph of the Leavises' preface reads like a response to Garis's summons, from the declaration, 'Our purpose is to enforce as unanswerably as possible the conviction that Dickens was one of the greatest of creative writers' down to the opening salvo on 'wrong-headed' American criticism of Dickens 'from Edmund Wilson onwards' (p. ix).

But the Leavises phrase their attacks much more strongly than Garis and, in fact, more strongly than the facts warranted. Worse, by their extreme candour about the errors of almost all Dickens critics and by their relative silence as to their own shortcomings the Leavises damaged their cause. They have encouraged readers to see *Dickens the Novelist* as a *volte-face*, and to plunder it and all their writings for contradictory statements about Dickens,[13] rather than to see it as an important, necessary, and long overdue revaluation of Dickens's central achievement in the novel and in literature as a whole. For that matter, we may well enquire whether *Dickens the Novelist* really is a sudden about-face, or not, rather, the climax of a long yet clearly discernible development in the Leavises' criticism of the novel.

It is true that Mrs Leavis wrote in *Fiction and the Reading Public* (pp. 156–7) that 'Dickens stands primarily for a set of crude emotional exercises', and Leavis in *The Great Tradition* that 'the adult mind doesn't as a rule find in Dickens a challenge to an unusual and sustained seriousness' (p. 29). And it is true that they have roundly denounced such notions in *Dickens the Novelist*. And many more and lengthier examples could be cited. But, however wrong and simplistic their earlier views of Dickens may have been, there is a danger of oversimplifying them. The Leavises' criticism of the novel, and of Dickens, is not a sequence of fixed, immovable

judgements, but a developing process of evaluation and revaluation, of which *Dickens the Novelist* is the late and triumphant flower-
ing. And we have seen that the crucial turning-point in this
development is Leavis's essay on *Hard Times*.

We have seen furthermore that this process began well before the
essay on *Hard Times*. In *Fiction and the Reading Public* (pp. 212–13)
Mrs Leavis felt, if somewhat tentatively, that 'great novels are
frequently doing something like good poetry', and suggested
that, since 'a novel, like a poem, is made of words', much of
I. A. Richards's technique in the analysis of poetry, in *Principles of
Literary Criticism*, could be applied to the novel. However, she was
not ready to equate great novels with great poetry, but only with
good poetry, and she added that Richards was not after all much
help, since 'a poem is so much more delicate and compact an
organisation than a novel'. In the next year, 1933, Leavis took this
matter a step further when he noted approvingly of a passage in
C. H. Rickword's 'A Note on Fiction' that

> This bringing together of fiction and poetry is the more richly
> suggestive because of the further assimilation it instigates. The
> differences between a lyric, a Shakespeare play, and a novel, for
> some purposes essential, are in no danger of being forgotten;
> what needs insisting on is the community.[14]

Leavis started to carry this out in *The Great Tradition* after he had
completed his major evaluations of English poetry. The 'major
novelists', he declared, 'count in the same way as the major poets'
(p. 10). And he proceeded there to discuss James's art as that
of a 'poet—novelist' (p. 143ff.), to draw attention to Conrad's
Shakespearean dramatic power (p. 216ff.), and finally, in his discussion of *Hard Times* as a dramatic poem, to include this key
observation:

> It suggests that the genius of the writer may fairly be described
> as that of a poetic dramatist, and that, in our preconceptions
> about 'the novel', we may miss, within the field of fictional
> prose, possibilities of concentration and flexibility in the inter-
> pretation of life such as we associate with Shakespearean drama.
> (p. 266)

A key observation in a key essay. Following it, Leavis broke

through his own preconceptions about Lawrence's difficult masterpieces and so progressed to *Dickens the Novelist*. In light of this it is
entirely natural that upon rereading Dickens he and Mrs Leavis
should arrive at the conclusion that Dickens is 'the Shakespeare of
the novel'.

We can also see that their attitude towards Dickens steadily
changes from 1932 onwards, so that *Dickens the Novelist* crowns a
progressive rediscovery of Dickens's Shakespearean art that is
more complex than a selection of contradictory statements makes it
look. True, progress was slow, but it was progress nonetheless. In
Fiction and the Reading Public Mrs Leavis certainly painted Dickens
as an arch-progenitor of the modern bestseller, but she also singled
out *David Copperfield* and *Great Expectations* as 'novels to be called
literature' (p. 158), meaning by literature serious works of art.
Six years later, she would liken Richard Jefferies to several 'peculiarly English geniuses',[15] also Dickens, and she would favourably compare a modern satire on the state-school system to
'Dickens's admirable satires on the old system in *Hard Times* and
Our Mutual Friend'.[16] And we saw that it was she who recommended
the inclusion of the essay on *Hard Times* in *The Great Tradition*.

For his part, Leavis made a much more positive overall judgement of Dickens in *The Great Tradition* than is generally recognised.
While excluding him from full membership, he nevertheless affirmed him as a great genius for family reading, implying that that
was his chosen level of creation. This is corroborated by another
and much earlier reference he made to Dickens, in 1933, in a review of Faulkner's *Light in August*:

> Dostoevsky was influenced by Dickens, but they are very dif-
> ferent. *Light in August*, which is more readable than William
> Faulkner's earlier books, should make it plain that he is much
> more like Dickens than like Dostoevsky. . . . Faulkner, in fact, in
> his vision of Good and Evil is like Dickens—at his best simple, at
> his worst sentimental and melodramatic. The brutal submorality
> of Christmas might have been significant in a Dostoevsky con-
> text and, so, interesting.[17]

As a judgement of Dickens this may not be very exciting, and
Leavis clearly preferred Dostoevsky as the mature artist. But in the
way he links Faulkner with Dickens Leavis pays Faulkner a compliment and implies one for Dickens. And the judgement that

Dickens is 'at his best simple' tallies with the later one in *The Great Tradition* that he is 'innocent' of mature standards.

Next comes the essay on *Hard Times* with its judgement which seems to extend to more of Dickens than only this novel: 'The final stress may fall on Dickens's command of word, phrase, rhythm, and image: in ease and range there is surely no greater master of English except Shakespeare' (*The Great Tradition*, p. 272). At any rate, from now on Dickens becomes firmly lodged in Leavis's mind as one of the 'successors of Shakespeare', with rereading and revaluation an increasingly strong probability. The following includes his first use of the phrase, the novelists he means, and his reasons:

> In the nineteenth century the strength—the poetic strength—of the English language went into prose fiction. . . . I will merely offer the proposition (sufficiently acceptable perhaps) that in Jane Austen, Dickens, Hawthorne, Melville, George Eliot, Henry James, Conrad, and D. H. Lawrence we have the successors of Shakespeare. I will add that I am not, in this proposition to be taken as saying, with extension to other writers, the kind of thing that is said about Jane Austen when she is compared to Shakespeare because of her power of creating characters. The same kind of thing is said about Scott—to note which is a way of intimating their nature. They point to novels that, because of their organization and their kind of significance, it is critically profitable to think of as 'dramatic poems': such novels are to be thought of, if organization and significance are to be understood, as grouping with Shakespeare's plays rather than with *Moll Flanders*, or *Tom Jones*, or *Tristram Shandy*, or the novel of manners. And in this line of fiction the actual influence of Shakespeare can, in different ways, be felt as a profound and decisive, if unmeasurable, presence.[18]

We have no means of telling whether he includes Dickens here on the strength of *Hard Times* alone or more. But sometime in the next ten years, 1952–62, the Leavises' rereading of Dickens began. Leavis's reference to *Little Dorrit* in *D. H. Lawrence: Novelist* (pp. 310–11) suggests that in 1955 it is already under way: 'Dickens's indignant sense that the Gowans of the literary world undermined his status and took the meaning out of his achievement produced this strikingly original addition to the panorama of social

falseness that is *Little Dorrit*.' And, as I have proposed in the
preceding chapter, Leavis returned to Dickens as a result of want-
ing to pin down more securely the sense in which Lawrence was a
'romantic' writer, and to see more clearly who were Lawrence's
true precursors in the Romantic contribution to nineteenth-century
literature.

Further speculation on the genesis of *Dickens the Novelist* seems
profitless. But it should be clear that the book did not suddenly
spring up in 1970.

Yet why was the revaluation so long in coming? Leavis gives his
own reason very frankly at the beginning of his critique of
Dombey. It was simply a case of not rereading Dickens as an adult,
he says, because

> With so much else before one that *had* to be read—so much that
> there was the need and the urgent impulsion to read, one
> remembered Dickens as the classic it was perhaps on the whole
> best to leave, piously and affectionately, to the memory and
> associations of the early acquaintance. (p. 21)

There is no reason for doubting the sincerity of this reminiscence,
which also confirms that the judgement of Dickens's 'innocence'
in *The Great Tradition* was a fondly, rather than a destructively
'placing' one. Up to *The Great Tradition* Leavis relied on a premature assessment of Dickens as a genius for premature reading.
Moreover, he amply vindicated his claim that there was 'so much
that there was the need and the urgent impulsion to read'. The
period 1930 to 1948 saw Leavis revaluing English poetry and the
English novel from Shakespeare to the present. But this task ought
to have included a rereading of Dickens. Instead he relied on early
impressions and judged Dickens to be a genius of a particular kind,
one for young readers and family consumption. And no doubt it
was a case of his having been saturated in the institutionalised—
the sentimentalist's—Dickens: Dickens the unrivalled portrayer of
Victorian childhood, of Christmas, of Sikesian melodrama, and of
Little Nell pathos.

Accordingly, it seems significant that both the Leavises admired
Santayana's essay on Dickens, and that Mrs Leavis wrote commendatory reviews of both Santayana and Orwell.[19] For though
these two treat Dickens more respectfully than Mrs Leavis does in
Fiction and the Reading Public, and read him more wisely and more

compassionately than she does, yet they too read him as the great entertainer overall, and some of their key judgements must have struck her as true. Indeed, her early attack on Dickensian vulgarity seems only a more devastating rephrasing of the following in Santayana: 'It is remarkable . . . how insensible Dickens was to the greater themes of the human imagination'; 'He was a waif himself, and utterly disinterested'; 'Nor had Dickens any lively sense for fine art, classical tradition, science, or even the manners and feelings of the upper classes in his own time and country'; 'But Dickens was no free artist; he had more genius than taste, a warm fancy not aided by a thorough understanding of complex characters.'[20] And she would have agreed entirely with Orwell that

> Except in a rather roundabout way, one cannot learn very much from Dickens. And to say this is to think almost immediately of the great Russian novelists of the nineteenth century. Why is it that Tolstoy's grasp seems to be so much larger than Dickens's—why is it that he seems able to tell you so much more *about* yourself? It is not that he is more gifted, or even, in the last analysis, more intelligent. It is because he is writing about people who are growing.[21]

That two writers so penetrating as Orwell and Santayana should judge Dickens so similarly almost twenty years apart (1921–1940), and so near in time to both *Fiction and the Reading Public* and *The Great Tradition*, suggests that the Leavises' earlier, yet varying, judgements of Dickens were not a freak but accorded with a view, widespread and of long standing among demanding English readers, that Dickens was naïve, primitive and clumsily sensational beside such sophisticated artists as Flaubert, James, Tolstoy and Dostoevsky. George H. Ford demonstrates that Dickens was so viewed by English readers in *Dickens and His Readers* (1955), a book that is indispensable reading alongside *Dickens the Novelist*, and any study of Dickens for that matter.

But why did Mrs Leavis at first attack so much more severely than either Santayana or Orwell? Was she, albeit subconsciously, purging the sentimentalist's Dickens *as a necessary preliminary* for a more detached and discriminating revaluation? Her advocacy of Leavis's critique of *Hard Times* makes this a possibility.

To return to *Dickens the Novelist*, at least two important questions remain. How, more precisely, do the Leavises justify calling

Dickens the Shakespeare of the novel? And what of importance in
Dickens have they neglected? A satisfying answer to the first question ought to make the second redundant. And such an answer
might well be sought by comparing *Dickens the Novelist* with Robert
Garis's *The Dickens Theatre* (1965).

Both the Leavises and Garis keep close to the truth as enunciated
by Leavis that 'the novelist's art is an art of using words',[22] but
with markedly different results. For Garis Dickens is a theatrical
genius, and the novels are stage performances in which Dickens is
the central performer. So he calls Dickens a verbal 'contriver', an
'artificer', 'a self-exhibiting master of language' who is 'always the
self-conscious virtuoso'.[23] There can be little doubt of Garis's
sincerity and seriousness, or of the relish he has for Dickens. But,
though he distinguishes very usefully between 'theatrical' and
'dramatic' art, his Dickens is no Shakespeare of the novel.

Speaking of the variety of possible interpretations of Iago, Garis
observes that in 'the Shakespearean theatre it is the audience's
responsibility to keep all these possibilities open and ready',[24] for
there is no author present to tell us how to respond. The art is
dramatic, speaks for itself, and furthermore, allows us to have
direct contact with the inner life of the *dramatis personae*. In short,
the Shakespearean impersonality of 'serious dramatic art' favours
'dealing with the inner life', for its elements are 'the self-
developing, continuous, and integrated illusion, the self-effacement
of the artist, the disinterested, morally intelligent search for the
centre of self of human beings'.[25]

The Leavises would entirely agree. But Garis argues that
Dickens's 'theatrical art' is not of this kind. It is 'not an appropriate mode for dealing with the inner life, nor is an artist who
works in this mode likely to be interested in the inner life'; the
elements of dramatic art are 'totally at variance with the procedures and attitudes of theatrical art'.[26] Rather, theatrical art is
robustly personal. Dickens is authorially and self-exhibitingly present in the theatre of his novels, and consequently we make little or
no contact with the inner life of his characters. Nor ought we to try,
for, if we do we respond improperly to Dickens's 'voice', we falsify
his art, we imagine a novel that is not Dickens's:

> If we are obedient to Dickens's voice, we simply have no time or
> energy to make contact with the inner life of Lady Dedlock as we
> do with Hamlet's; nor is there any occasion to, since we are

already making a satisfactory contact with Dickens. But if we are not obedient, and ponder privately on Lady Dedlock's inner life, we are simply making up our own novel, not attending to Dickens's performance in the Dickens theatre.[27]

For the Leavises this is to ignore that Dickens wrote at more than one level for more than one audience. 'It depends who "we" are!' Mrs Leavis caustically exclaims (p. 121). And Garis's theory 'virtually relegates Dickens's work as a whole' (p. 96).

The Leavises would agree with Garis's distinctions between 'theatrical' and 'dramatic' art, and they do agree that Dickens can be theatrical. But they contend that Dickens *developed* a wholly serious and subtly dramatic art, which, like Shakespeare's plays, has a multi-layered significance. They emphasise that at his best Dickens created dramatic poems in prose, which have all the qualities that Garis mentions of serious dramatic art, and which therefore we may understand fully only if we respond to them as to a play by Shakespeare. The challenge for criticism,[28] they assert, is to pinpoint this development, and to see by virtue of what qualities in which novels Dickens can be rightfully called the Shakespeare of the novel. For them Dickens begins to develop most strikingly in *Dombey and Son*, continues to experiment and progress triumphantly through *David Copperfield* and *Bleak House*, and reaches the summit of his art in *Hard Times*, *Little Dorrit* and *Great Expectations*. In the last novel he achieves 'the greatest mastery of his medium', says Mrs Leavis (p. 115).

This mastery, they say, is the reverse of theatrical. The great Dickens manifests, rather, the impersonality, flexibility and depth of Shakespeare's dramatic art. And they maintain that, if we listen for the authorial voice, as Garis advises, we risk doing precisely what Garis cautions us against doing: making up our own novel and not Dickens's.

To illustrate her point, Mrs Leavis tackles Garis's reading of Mr Meagles in *Little Dorrit*. Garis has claimed that we have to accept at face value Mr Meagles's sermon to Tattycoram, because it has Dickens's official backing. But we do so at risk of disastrously misreading Meagles, *Little Dorrit* and Dickens, Mrs Leavis rejoins, for we will have failed to appreciate Meagles in the context of the novel, how his speech and actions accumulate an ironic judgement against himself. Accordingly we miss the subtlety of Dickens's critical irony. In fact we misunderstand the nature of his art, which is dramatic and speaks for itself, and does so at one level for the conventional reader, and at another for the more observing:

> At one level . . . there is the desired sermon on duty and a heroine who seems to endorse it; on another, for Mr Garis, if he could see it, a less attractive, extremely complex case of the blindness and mistakes human beings are prone to when they are nice ordinary John Bulls, and a much more sensitive and difficult and character-demanding rôle for the heroine than following the strait path of Duty.   (p. 122)

And we may only appreciate the different levels of meaning if we see that the art which embodies them is dramatic, not theatrical. 'The scenes with Tattycoram and the scenes where the Gowans and Meagleses and Arthur or any of them, meet, are all splendidly realized dramatically and in no respect can they be dismissed as theatrical' (ibid.).

Leavis adds in his turn that in *Little Dorrit* Dickens was at the peak of his Shakespearean powers: 'That Dickens's finest work has the impersonality of great art . . . is at the centre of my theme' (p. 221). *Little Dorrit* 'enacts' a 'set inquest into Victorian civilisation', in which Dickens's 'essential social criticism doesn't affect us as urged personally by the writer':

> It has the disinterestedness of spontaneous life, undetermined and undirected and uncontrolled by idea, will, and self-insistent ego, the disinterestedness here being that which brings a perceived significance to full realization and completeness in art. The writer's labour has been to present something that speaks for itself.   (pp. 220–1)

And Leavis devotes his long essay to showing how the novel's moral valuations are revealed dramatically, through the drama of life enacted in it. So we come to recognise the life-affirming qualities of disinterestedness, courage, truth and human responsibility in Dickens's art not because Dickens instructs us to do so but by seeing these virtues enacted in the behaviour of such diverse characters in the novel as Little Dorrit, Clennam, Flora Finching, Pancks, Doyce and Cavaletto, and highlighted in the ways they contrast with the life-opposing qualities of selfishness, greed, snobbery, assertive will and system incarnated in Mrs Clennam,

Merdle, Henry Gowan, Casby, Rigaud-Blandois, the Barnacles, and others.

But the Leavises freely admit that Dickens could and did write theatrically, and so below his best. He had, too, a weakness for imitating Shakespeare. They emphasise that the challenge is however to pinpoint the evolution of the theatrical 'Boz' into the mature Shakespeare of the novel, and to recognise that, in so evolving, Dickens, like Shakespeare, brought his vast reading public along with him.

For the Leavises the dramatic poet begins to prevail over the theatrical melodramatist in *Dombey and Son*: '*Dombey and Son* marks a decisive moment in Dickens's career; he offered it as a providently conceived whole, presenting a major theme, and it was his first essay in the elaborately plotted Victorian novel' (p. 2). And, though the novel's unity is 'specious' (p. 27), in view of the melodramatic and sentimental indulgences of, for example, the Edith Dombey–Carker episodes, Leavis feels that Dickens's poetry holds it together. He has conceived a 'wholly serious "criticism of life" ' and carried it through by dramatic-poetic means (pp. 25–7):

The answer fairer to Dickens's genius would be to point to the poetic conception of his art that this first elaborate novel of his gives proof of, and to the inexhaustibly wonderful poetic life of his prose. One may not feel the faintest velleity of serious response to such effects as that in which the refrain 'Let him remember it in this room in years to come!' figures; yet they have their place in the wonderfully varied and flexible play of what, considering the use of language, and the use of imagery and symbolism and dramatic enactment, one has to call poetic means.   (p. 27)

Leavis himself has already pointed to, quoted, analysed, and commented on the opening two chapters, concerning Mrs Dombey's death and the hiring of Polly Toodles (pp. 2–7), Mr Dombey's exchanges with Mr Toodles at home and in the railway station (pp. 8–9), and Dombey's *tête-à-têtes* with Paul (pp. 14–19). He adds instances of Dickens's poetic-descriptive evocations of the Dombey house, and concludes,

Everywhere, in description and narrative and dramatic presentation and speech, we have exemplified that vitality of language

which invites us to enforce from Dickens the truth of the proposition that in the Victorian age the poetic strength of the English
language goes into the novel, and that the great novelists are the
successors of Shakespeare. In fact, it is hard not to see a
significance in the habitual way (the habit is very marked in
Dombey and Son) in which Dickens quotes from Shakespeare and
alludes to him—in the familiarity with Shakespeare he assumes
in the reader and in the evidence he gives of the active presence
of Shakespeare in his own creative mind. That he developed an
art so different from anything he could have learnt from Smollett
or Fielding—or Ben Jonson, in whom he was also interested, or
the theatre of his own time—was of course a manifestation of his
genius. . . . Looking at the characteristics of form and method of
the novel as Dickens was aspiring to create it in *Dombey and Son*,
we can see that the influence of the sentimental and melodramatic theatre was not the only dramatic influence that counted,
or the most profound.   (p. 29)

Mrs Leavis picks up the same thread in her critiques of the next
two novels, *David Copperfield* and *Bleak House*. True, in writing on
Copperfield she makes little direct reference to Shakespeare,
predicating rather Dickens's Tolstoyan art before Tolstoy. But, in
amplifying what she means by that, and in the context of Leavis's
account of *Dombey and Son*, she consistently implies comparison with
Shakespeare: as when apropos of the structure of *Copperfield* she
notes the parallel deaths of David's mother and of Dora as 'an excellent piece of symbolic thought' (p. 58); when she notes how
Dickens makes 'dreams and delirious states an important means of
exploring experience in his novels' (p. 64); and when she draws
such observations into the general one that *David Copperfield* can be
read at more than one level: 'a popular one (humorous, sentimental and moralistic) and that of art, complex, serious, poign-
ant, subtly suggestive, though devious in presentation and its
argument subterranean' (p. 67). These points belong to her central
argument, her 'serious view', that the whole novel is rich in symbolic action and meaning. She concludes,

But granted that *David Copperfield* doesn't offer us the richly impressive rewards of *Dombey*, there is, I claim, a verbal interest in
the later novel that shows Dickens's Shakespearean use of the
language. Dickens is a master of words because they are more

than mere words to him, they are feelings and associations and dark implications. (p. 101)

And she adds four pages of varied illustration from this and several other novels (pp. 101–4).

She next shows that *Bleak House* is even more Shakespearean in complexity and richness of symbolic meaning. In fact, Dickens can at times be too blatantly Shakespearean, she feels. Accordingly, she helpfully distinguishes between where Dickens merely imports or mimicks Shakespeare to thicken his 'poetical' evocations and where he creates real poetry in Shakespeare's way. For instance, she remarks of the obvious use of *Hamlet* in the scene in which Lady Dedlock awaits Mr Tulkinghorn, 'Perhaps the use of *Hamlet* and its dramatic irony is too blatant here, but it shows how Dickens's imagination was working' (p. 163, n. 1). Perhaps even a little theatrical, she means.[29] Then, more interestingly, she indicates how we may discern in *Bleak House* the 'progress towards a finer art . . . by juxtaposing the old and the new prose techniques which exist in it side by side' (p. 170). Quoting from the episode of Jo and Lady Dedlock at the public burial-ground, Mrs Leavis shows how in the passage of dialogue between these two Dickens has evoked dramatically, and with original poetic force, what he has merely hankered to convey by 'poetical' effects in the previous descriptive passage.

It will be seen at once that the dialogue between the disguised Lady Dedlock and Jo at the gate of the public burial-ground for paupers makes the laboured irony of the previous description of the funeral unnecessary, since the dialogue effects, by purely novelistic means without authorial comment, what the rhetorical passage tries to do, but does it much more effectively and economically. (p. 171)

She argues further that in the descriptive passage Dickens has merely assumed, with the 'Come night, come darkness' sequence, a Shakespearean blank-verse portentousness. But in the dialogue that follows Dickens has shed his borrowed robes and creates a real poetry of his own, which has a real Shakespearean compression. He has ceased to be literary and now writes out of his own experience. 'The interest of the first extract is the way it moves in and out of automatic writing, tending towards blank verse (Dickens's

greatest weakness and always associated with his vague reaching
for what Shakespeare would have done in his place)' (p. 172). But
in the second,

> Dickens ceases to write blank verse but instead becomes
> Shakespearean in a real sense because the gas-jet recalls him to
> an actual scene where he must have remembered it 'burning so
> sullenly' because of the 'poisoned air', and that the metal of the
> gate felt slimy from the horrible deposits—fumes from the decay-
> ing bodies and therefore 'witch-ointment' since it was with
> human grease and extracts from corpses that witches made their
> ointments. And he sees that the arresting light is a signal to every
> passer-by to stop and witness this outrage, thus *calling* 'Look
> here!'. The real poetry in Dickens's prose is always in some
> detail of a concrete experience which has lodged in and therefore
> touched off his imagination.   (pp. 172–3)

'And *Bleak House* is full of this poetry' (p. 173), says Mrs Leavis,
adding numerous examples concerning Krook, Skimpole, Boythorn, Miss Flite and others.

Leavis's critique of *Hard Times* comes next, now figuring as
the core text not only of Leavis's whole case for great literature as
the antidote for science and Benthamite philosophy, but also of the
Leavises' joint illustration of Dickens's Shakespearean genius.

It may at this point be objected that the Leavises' notes and implications about Dickens's Shakespearean genius are only notes
and implications and do not sufficiently support their claim that he
is the Shakespeare of the novel. In other words, some readers may
feel that they ought to have attempted a more detailed exposition.
But this would be to mistake the purpose of *Dickens the Novelist*,
which in common with the rest of the Leavises' writings is literary-
critical and not, primarily at any rate, scholarly. It would be to
confuse the functions of criticism and scholarship. The Leavises
aim to evaluate a writer's essential importance and for a more than
academic audience. If they provide a scholarly foundation for their
criticism, as I believe Mrs Leavis notably does in this book, that is
all to the good. But, in measuring Dickens's significance, they have
neither space nor occasion for a detailed textual comparison between Dickens and Shakespeare. Instead, they constantly refer us
to Dickens's Shakespearean resourcefulness with character and
plot, and reveal that his use of language in narrative and dia-

logue is dramatic and poetic like Shakespeare's. So alerted, the reader can then elaborate comparisons for himself and be himself a more discerning critic and scholar of both Dickens and Shakespeare. Thus Leavis remarks of *Little Dorrit,*

> I won't offer to elaborate the parallel between Shakespeare's development and achievement as the great popular playwright of our dramatic efflorescence and Dickens's as the marvellously fertile, supremely successful and profoundly creative exploiter of the Victorian market for fiction. There is clearly, however, a need to insist that Dickens no more than Shakespeare started from nothing and created out of a cultural void. . . . He read immensely, with the intelligence of genius, and his inwardness with Shakespeare, the subtlety of the influence manifest, and to be divined, in his own creative originality, can't be explained except by a reader's close and pondering acquaintance.
>
> (p. 214)

That last sentence does not mean an abrogation of critical responsibility, nor does Leavis take an easy way out. He and Mrs Leavis have repeatedly indicated the kinds of relationship they have in mind between the two writers. And Leavis indicates so again. He makes Dickens's impersonality 'the centre' of his evaluation of *Little Dorrit* (p. 221), and once more indicates the Shakespearean 'flexibility' of Dickens's art, pointing out that he wrote this novel in very diverse modes and yet integrated these to make a completely satisfying whole. Quoting a variety of passages including description (Clennam brooding on Blandois' disappearance), narrative (Merdle's death) and dialogue (Affery and Mrs Clennam, the Merdles, Physician and Chief Butler), Leavis encourages the reader to see how Dickens's prose is charged with 'the immediacy of actual sensations' and how his formal similes and symbolism work 'as immediately as metaphor' (pp. 263–9). He then concludes, 'There had been nothing like this poetic power of the great novelist's prose since Shakespeare's blank verse' (p. 265).

And the mere accumulation of examples cannot do Dickens justice, Leavis insists. We murder to dissect such a novel as *Little Dorrit*. Its richness needs to be savoured whole by 'close and pondering acquaintance' (p. 214). The critic cannot do it justice in expository prose, because its richness ultimately defies analysis, however exhaustive.

> A power that has of its nature such diverse manifestations forbids
> any offer to do it justice by assembling examples. It is a condi-
> tion—this is my point at the moment—of the flexibility of
> Dickens's art; of his ability to bring together in the service
> of one complex communication such a diversity of tones and
> modes. (p. 265)

Here Leavis makes a key point about Dickens and the nature of the
greatest creative literature. By its poetic force and complexity such
literature resists all attempts to reduce its meaning to neat defini-
tions. No philosophical system or aesthetic theory can pin down a
work of art: that is the force of Leavis's observation, which of
course explains his own aversion to philosophy and theory. Instead
he suggests that the best that the reader can do is intelligently to
ponder his own experience of living and reading, and keep open the
door to surprise, change and further maturing. Great literature,
being an intelligent re-creation of life, can no more be reduced to a
formula or analysed with mathematical precision than life itself, he
insists. It is a controversial position, but one of basic common
sense and completely human.

In the light of the earlier critiques we may feel that Mrs Leavis's
single reference to Shakespeare in the essay on *Great Expectations* is
reminder enough of the genius at work in that novel, of which she
has already commented that Dickens achieved in it 'the greatest
mastery of his medium' (p. 115).

> Of course it is in the working out and presentation of these in-
> quiries [into 'guilt and shame' and 'what is "real"'] that the
> value of the novel lies, in the minute particularities of the indivi-
> dual life which are yet so skilfully invented as to carry overtones
> of allegory and to be exemplary. The pertinacity and concen-
> tration of Dickens's mind on his theme has made the two ques-
> tions, in which the third is implied, so interwoven as to be
> inseparable eventually, and his Shakespearean genius as a
> creator has produced the wonderful plot which is not only ex-
> citing to read and faultless in execution but strikingly classical in
> its peripeteia. (p. 288)

What of importance have the Leavises left out? The question
ought to be absurd, if they have been successful in their account
of Dickens as the Shakespeare of the novel. But it has been force-

fully asked by a Briton acting on the highly laudable motive of apologising for the bad manners of his compatriots, the Leavises, in so rudely chastising American criticism of Dickens. (How Dickens would have relished all this!)

In his résumé of the British and American approaches to Dickens over the past forty years, Robert Giddings[30] also distinguishes very usefully between the two literary traditions to which these approaches belong.

He justly lauds American criticism for opening readers' eyes to Dickens's poetic imagination. The Americans, he says, and they mainly, have immensely enriched our understanding of Dickens by unlocking the treasures of symbol, myth, fairy-tale and psychological magic to be found in the novels. This they have been enabled to do by the long 'transcendental/symbolic' tradition behind them, a tradition which has its roots in 'the old English way of looking at things . . . from Shakespeare's England', and which, miraculously surviving the blights of Augustanism, was most recently stimulated by the New Critical belief that literature is a 'pattern of *language at work*' (pp. 48–9). This is very true and well said.

On the other hand, British criticism characteristically denies and distrusts the imaginative, poetic Dickens, Giddings says. Belonging, rather, to a tradition, the 'logical/classical' one of Augustan rationality, that 'places great emphasis on tradition', it believes that 'creative literature, far from being the spontaneous imagining of the artist, comes somehow from other literature' (p. 48). Consequently, modern British critics have too readily adopted T. S. Eliot with his ' "tradition" complex', and have indeed become so 'hidebound with "tradition" ' that their Dickens has 'little of the comedy, none of the psychological magic, little of the poetry, originality, fable, fairy-tale, myth, or hidden power' (pp. 48–9). But he concedes that British criticism is strong historically (p. 51).

While this is also true and helpful in its general drift, Giddings's laudable diplomacy becomes badly inaccurate when he blames Leavis for being the arch-propagator of English insensitivity to Dickens the poet. He calls 'moral awareness' the 'keynote' of English criticism, and adds,

> If you expect literature to give you moral awareness, the next question will be *what sort of morals* are we to be made aware of? And this is what happens: lit. crit. becomes obsessed with what

literature teaches you, namely, the mainstream of bourgeois morality. It makes itself as essential a part of the superstructure as religion, education, entertainment, sport. It teaches that sex is naughty, money is wicked, science reduces life to mechanisms, and all the rest of it: right then, we look for literature which teaches us *that*, and then seek academically or critically to justify the merit and respectability of that literature. In other words, we become obsessed with the *what* of literature, and lose interest in the *how*. We can actually see that is what happened in the establishment of 'The Great Tradition', which had no place for Dickens.   (pp. 50–1)

This, to put it politely, is the routine misconception of Leavis. Leavis never simplifies great literature, or its value. His homage to Eliot and to Augustan Classicism has been more than compensated for by his deep sympathy with the romantic imagination in Lawrence, in Blake, in Keats, in Wordsworth and in Dickens. He has always posited Shakespeare as the touchstone of all his critical judgements of both poetry and the novel. He has always insisted on the inseparability of form and content, of the *what* and the *how* of literature. *The Great Tradition* contained in the critique of *Hard Times* the first essay in criticism explicitly to treat a novel in terms of a play by Shakespeare. And, though he excluded Dickens generally, it was not for the reasons Giddings implies, but because he had not begun to reread Dickens. Furthermore, Giddings has failed to see the central contradiction in his argument: namely, that it is supremely the poetic imagination that reveals how 'science reduces life to mechanisms'—as Leavis has for so long contended, and as Giddings himself contends in lauding the American tradition.

Significantly, Giddings also neglects to mention the work of Robert Garis, the one notable American who has reacted against the symbol-hunters in Dickens criticism who descend from Edmund Wilson. For he thereby neatly and ironically dispatches into the wings *the* two studies, the Leavises' and Garis's, which have sought most conscientiously to do what his article pleads for in Dickens criticism: to find the centre of Dickens's achievement by readings that are neither too symbolic nor too logical, that in other words avoid the extremes of the American and British approaches and achieve instead a happy balance of the two.

Giddings's criticisms have even less warrant with respect to

Mrs Leavis, who goes much beyond her husband in elucidating the 'how' of Dickens's art as well as in identifying and explaining the more-than-rational elements of fantasy, dream, folk-tale, myth and psychological eccentricity. Both the Leavises undertake the central thesis of pinpointing Dickens's development from a writer of popular fiction to a serious novelist, and of showing that in the major novels he combined the roles of entertainer and subtle artist. However, the accounts of the technical side of this development, the evolution of Dickens's thought from novel to novel, his contribution to the novel as literary genre, and hence his relation to contemporary Victorian novelists as well as to those preceding and coming after him—all these matters are substantially and impressively dealt with by Mrs Leavis.

A cardinal point in the thesis is that Dickens could not be the great writer that he is without having been a deep thinker, who dramatised in his fictions a profound insight into human nature and human need in the civilisation in which he lived; and that as such he is a psychological realist, a novelist; and not some other species of writer. We saw that Leavis devoted his critique of *Little Dorrit* to showing that novel as an 'enterprise of thought' *Dickens the Novelist*, p. 216). Mrs Leavis begins her critique of *Bleak House* with a rebuttal of the notion that Dickens was incapable of thought (p. 118ff.)—an interesting parallel to Leavis's opening to *D. H. Lawrence: Novelist*. She illustrates the development of Dickens as serious thinker and novelist in a multitude of ways. For instance, in her first appendix, 'Dickens and Smollett', she shows in a note on Captain Cuttle from *Dombey and Son* that Dickens's Smollett-like characters have, after *Pickwick Papers*, an essential thematic function in the novels to which they belong and are no longer the figures of fun and whimsy they would have been in Fielding and Smollett. Cuttle, she explains, is a 'necessary element' in Dickens's critique of 'that Victorian idea of Property as a value and its acquisition an end in itself' (pp. 30–3).[31] Secondly, she notes that *David Copperfield* includes a reworking of the orphan story that is much more 'realistic' and less obtrusively symbolic and melodramatic than in *Oliver Twist* (p. 93ff.). In the same passage she distinguishes usefully between fairy-tale and folk-tale, arguing that what we may be tempted to see as fairy-tale in the magical aspects of David's history is more properly to be seen in terms of folk-tale or myth. For the 'miracle' that is David's 'self-made' life embodies more 'the folk's experience of the truths of existence in allegoric forms' than the elements of 'escapism' characteristic of the fairy-tale (p. 92). 'There is nothing of the fairy-tale in *Oliver Twist*', Mrs Leavis says, implying the same of *Copperfield*. She adds moreover, that the qualities in Dickens that we tend to see as belonging to the fairy-tale and akin to Hans Andersen's tales are likely to be something of deeper psychological importance, because 'Andersen's Tales cover a very wide range of forms, in which the fairy-tale counts for less than the satire, the fable, the folk-tale, and the record of childhood experience through a child's consciousness' (p. 91).

Mrs Leavis illustrates the growth of the serious novelist and thinker in other ways. She notes that Dickens's prose style changes with the growing intensity and complexity of his mature critiques of Victorian civilisation: by *Bleak House* 'the rhetoric of indignation and satire' of the earlier novels has been discarded in favour of a more subtly evocative dramatic-poetic mode; Swift and Carlyle have been exchanged for Shakespeare as his model (p. 125ff.). Similarly, she shows in the appendix on Dickens's exposure scenes (appendix C to ch. 2) that the serious artist makes a much more economical and subtle use of these than previously. The earlier novels abound with such scenes and they are mostly stagy and melodramatic, purely for entertainment purposes. But they become in the major novels more and more inherently dramatic, and so more truly surprising. In *Bleak House*, 'The true surprise in the novel is a wholly novelistic one (not in the least theatrical or stagey but psychological and truly human), . . . Sir Leicester's unpredictable reaction to what affects his honour and his family's standing' (p. 114). In *Little Dorrit*, 'Miss Wade's case is . . . avoided as a theatrical occasion . . . being delivered in manuscript to Arthur Clennam to read' (p. 115); and in *Great Expectations* the exposure scenes between Pip and Magwitch and Pip and Orlick are 'much more interesting than in any other of his novels' (p. 115). Meanwhile, in tracing this aspect of Dickens's art, Mrs Leavis provides a useful résumé of the whole *oeuvre*, which she does again through the pages of her three critiques, and finally, once more, in the chapter on the illustrations of the novels. Again, in the account of *Bleak House* Mrs Leavis notes that Dickens as mature novelist has in the delineation of psychological abnormality forsaken caricature for sociological realism: 'Mr. Tulkinghorn is another masterly study in abnormality, though completely a human being—Dickens has

outgrown the stage of throwing up inexplicable monsters like
Fagin, Quilp, Squeers and Pecksniff' (p. 160).[32] She goes on to say
that Tulkinghorn is more rather than less terrifying for being
human.

Most impressive of all, perhaps, is the way Mrs Leavis illuminates Dickens's explorations of theme through characterisation, for she shows as she does so how each of the novels, though
unique, evolves out of its predecessor(s). Here again her account of
Bleak House is exemplary: the novel she finds 'the most impressive
and rewarding of all Dickens's novels' she shows to be particularly
rich in the evolution of theme through character (which is perhaps
not surprising since it is the chronological centre of Dickens's
oeuvre). Thus, for instance, she sees Esther Summerson as an
unsentimentalised variant of the 'good angel' Agnes Wickfield
(p. 159), a prototype of Amy Dorrit, and an alternative to Miss
Wade in *Little Dorrit*, Esther accepting her illegitimate status with
patient good nature and Miss Wade reacting to her stigma with ag-
gression and resentment (p. 280). Then, in this novel in which
theme is more important than plot (p. 125) Skimpole, 'unnecessary
to the plot but essential to the theme' (p. 148), is in one sense
Micawber reconsidered in a 'context of social responsibility' and in
another Dickens's demonstration that the writer as artist is 'not less
concerned' for others in society 'but more': Skimpole is thus the
prototype of Henry Gowan (pp. 153–4). Meanwhile, the fact that
Skimpole is also a failed doctor fits with Mrs Leavis's analysis that
the doctors Allan Woodcourt and Bayham Badger are the symbolic
saviours of a society diseased by litigation in the cause of self-
interest; and this in turn leads to her appendix on the symbolic
function of the doctor in other Victorian fictions. Other transmog-
rifications are noticed by Mrs Leavis: Betsey Trotwood's 'amus-
ing eccentricity' towards trespassers has become in Mr Boythorn's
manic aggressiveness 'part of a serious and central argument'
(p. 134); Mr Bucket is 'the precursor of the concept of the Split
Man' that Dickens launches with Pancks in *Little Dorrit* and
elaborates as Wemmick in *Great Expectations* (p. 139); and the
Smallweed children are the utilitarian prototypes of Bitzer in *Hard
Times* (p. 155). And so on: Mrs Leavis is constantly tracing such
relationships and evolutions to show the development of Dickens's
thought from novel to novel, like Shakespeare.

And always she returns to her insistence that Dickens's interest

in human behaviour is neither that of the theatrical manager no
that of the amateur psychologist, but that of the great novelist wh
thinks about 'the *why* of human conduct':

> Dickens sees people as at once the products and symptoms o
> their society and the producers of it. Similarly he shows his in
> terest in ethical matters by exploring the behaviour of characters
> chosen for the purpose, in such a way as to undercut theory anc
> extend our views by presenting situations in a new light, disturb-
> ing our preconceptions and prejudices. (pp. 279–81)

Hence Boythorn is less a stage part or a psychological grotesque
than a reflector of an actual Victorian mania for litigation; anc
Wemmick as split man represents a fractured attitude toward
work and home life actually held in Victorian times, and only
then.

It seems thus entirely in keeping that Mrs Leavis should be so
economical in her valuable comparison of *Great Expectations* with
The Pilgrim's Progress and *The Scarlet Letter* (p. 320ff.). As with her
examination throughout of Dickens's symbolic powers, she apparently feels it is enough to suggest the essential affinities between
these masterpieces—to say of Pip's meeting with Orlick that 'the
ordeal that culminates in the admission of guilt, and in repentance,
suffering, humiliation and a fight for life was in a popular English
literary tradition treating spiritual experience' (p. 321); or
Magwitch's trial 'that we must identify Pip's society with Bunyan's Vanity Fair' (p. 323); and, of the whole novel, that like
Hawthorne's it describes 'the human condition: we cannot escape
the necessity for prison and the graveyard' (p. 331)—and to leave
the reader to work out for himself the correspondences and the differences in greater detail. And we may suppose that this is just:
itemising and stone-turning can quickly degenerate into pedantry,
and, though Mrs Leavis proves herself a busier and abler il-
luminator of Dickens than her husband, she shares his aversion to
pedantry. Meanwhile, in likening this novel to the supreme
allegorical masterpieces in the English language, she has most effectively indicated the depths of Dickens's intuitions and insights
into human nature. And, in showing that Dickens combines
allegory with 'a novel overtly realistic in parts' (p. 321) she has
distinguished his originality from Bunyan's and Hawthorne's. Incidentally, Pip's self-confrontation in his ordeal with Orlick, which

is emblematic of the whole novel, dramatises in mythic form the process of impersonality as the Leavises see it in great writers.

At least two important conclusions can be drawn from Mrs Leavis's pages on Dickens: that 'the other of the collaborating pair' (p. xi) has come fully and impressively into her own as a critic of fiction, and that Dickens's creative energy and variety is matched only by Shakespeare's in the English language—hence once more the aptness of the Leavises' description of him as 'the Shakespeare of the novel'.

Dickens the Novelist affirms a whole critical approach and a whole critical belief. With Dickens the Leavises have by now more than adequately tested and attested the truth in Lawrence's claims that the novel is 'the book of life' and 'the highest example of subtle inter-relatedness that man has discovered', and that 'the Bible . . . and Homer, and Shakespeare . . . are the supreme old novels'.[33] They have vindicated their belief that literature matters in so far as it communicates a deep interest in life, and that therefore literature cannot adequately be discussed or judged according to uniquely aesthetic values any more than life can. In so doing they have convincingly shown that aesthetic considerations necessarily entail moral or human ones, and that art and criticism which deny them become impoverished. For they have demonstrated that Dickens's art is great *because of* the perceptions of human reality it embodies, and that, conversely, these perceptions have significance because of the poetic art that embodies them.

In linking Dickens with Shakespeare they have reconfirmed in the strongest possible way that the greatest writer 'realises' in a unity of form and content not a private art-world but a vision of human[34] reality.

Georg Lukács reaffirms the Leavises in the matter of 'realisation', and incidentally exposes the flippancy of the usual anti-Leavis dialectic:

Every true work of art arises out of the particular and real alternatives of its time. The means for the dynamic rendering of these alternatives is what we are accustomed to call style, which requires a two-fold investigation. One must consider first the *what* of the human content in the alternatives and in the meaningful responses to these alternatives; and second, the *how* in artistic expression, the way in which the human reactions to the world are articulated and fixed aesthetically. By 'realization' Cézanne meant the indissolubility of the *what* and the *how* in works of art.

Today people repeatedly condemn any serious emphasis on the *what* as inartistic. The approach is justified only where the *what* is divorced from the artistic *how* and rendered autonomous. It can never be autonomous, however, except when life itself compels the articulation. . . . But that is an expression of life and at best the raw material or impulse for art, not art itself. . . .

It would be still more incorrect to make the artistic *how* formally and semantically autonomous. What exalts Shakespeare above his contemporaries is his indissoluble unity of the *what* and *how*; any separation of the two is unimaginable in his art.[35]

So have the Leavises claimed of Dickens at his best, and of every poem or novel they have judged to be great.

Roger Poole feels that Leavis is unique among English and American critics but very like Lukács in upholding 'Realistic criticism'.[36] He may be entirely correct, and certainly the affinities between Leavis and Lukács can be very quickly substantiated from the Preface to *Writer and Critic*. But, in addition to ideological considerations, there is an important difference of method between the Leavises and Lukács. The Leavises demonstrate criticism in action. Habitually, they confront a literary work, quoting from it, analysing it, and commenting on it in a way that reveals the process of their criticism, shows the reader how he may practise criticism for himself, and encourages him to reread the work in question. Such criticism speaks well of the attitude of its practitioner. On the one hand, it promotes the belief that criticism is not a mystical process in the keeping of a hierophantic few, but rather a pursuit for anyone with intelligence and awareness, or even with the desire to become more intelligent and aware. And, on the other hand, such criticism betokens an innate modesty in the critic who, as we have seen of Leavis with *Little Dorrit* and *Women in Love*, says that the masterpiece he points to is far more important than anything he can say about it, since it conveys by poetic means and as a poetic whole what the critic can only allude and point to in discursive prose. In contrast, Lukács mostly reveals not the process but the conclusions of his criticism. And, illuminating though these are, I wonder whether his method can be as stimulating as the Leavises', and even whether he can stimulate as many readers.

The Leavises have consistently identified the masterpieces of

English literature by reasoning that they are masterpieces not merely because of their aesthetic intricacy but because they illuminate and enrich the experience of living. So in the end they have given the most telling answer one can give to the most basic question of all in regard to literature: why read?

Where, in conclusion, are we to place Leavis as a critic of the novel and as a critic in general? Such a question could only be asked in an age of science and specialisms. In earlier ages it would have been enough to call Leavis a critic and everyone would have known what he was: one endowed with common sense and moral tact and skilled in logic who, while making his criteria clear and clearly based on an ethical view of reality, undertook to advise readers what was worth reading and what was not. It would then have been for his readers to interrogate their own common sense and moral tact to decide whether he gave good advice or bad, whether he was a good or bad critic. The habit of previous ages made it possible for Eliot to define criticism as 'the common pursuit of true judgement'.[37]

But in the present atomised age of science and specialisms, literary criticism has itself become atomised into numerous camps of specialists speaking in divers tongues to initiates.[38] Consequently, the critic of common sense and moral values has also been made to seem a special case. Tolerated often as an anachronism who quaintly appeals to irrelevant moral standards, if, like Leavis, he speaks with force he can be treated as an obnoxious wasp in a garden of aesthetic and academic delights. Yet Leavis has done more than anyone else in the present age to give meaning to Eliot's phrase. His writings as a whole have been a painstaking effort to re-establish true judgement as the central concern of both the specialists and the intelligent general reader. He has sought to redefine evaluative criticism and to preserve its centrality in the twentieth century. And his values are permanent values.

It is necessary to recite these truisms because any assessment of Leavis must stress that he is a critic of common sense, who appeals to basic human values common to all readers and in a language easily accessible to all.[39] He does not pursue novel theories for arriving at literary truth any more than did Johnson or Arnold before him. He seeks, as they did, to remind readers of common-sense truths and values; and an important truth for Leavis, living in an age of specialisation, is that great literature is no more the preserve of initiates in or outside the university than life itself is. The early books, *For Continuity*, *Culture and Environment* and *Education and the University*, make this point repeatedly and urgently. Accordingly he has made it the object of his specifically literary criticism to distinguish the most valuable literature of the past because he believes that it can educate in man, who has increasingly dehumanised himself by science, a fresh awareness of all those human qualities that make life creative in moral and spiritual terms and give it a meaning that defies scientific analysis. So, if we call Leavis a critic of common sense, we do so realising that the term has both the usual and a special significance. Not only does his criticism exhibit an utterly common-sense attitude to literature and to life, it voices a constant plea for a return to common sense: for a recovery of those humane qualities that bring people together as a community of human beings rather than as merely economic interdependents.

Yet even such reasoning scarcely saves Leavis from looking like the Victorian anachronism he has been painted to be.[40] We need to see on methodological grounds that Leavis is no mere echo of Arnold or Coleridge or Johnson. We need to see that, if he has kept alive the great tradition of evaluative criticism and kept it in the centre of the modern critical map, he has done so by giving it a twentieth-century precision and idiom and by bringing to it a sociological interest entirely of his time. He is in fact keener in literary analysis than his precursors both because he is forced to be, in order to command an audience, and by choice, because he believes in literary criticism as a pedagogic discipline of the humane intelligence. He has also a keener historical insight than his predecessors for the good reason that he lives after them and so commands a greater historical perspective than they. Consequently, he has made evaluative criticism a more scientific procedure than hitherto without, however, making it into a science. He has far too much respect for the uncategorisable nature of imaginative genius to do that.

Of all the schools of criticism in the twentieth century, Leavis has the strongest links with the formalists and the sociological critics. He has almost no connection or sympathy with either biographical or psychoanalytic criticism. Believing implicitly in Lawrence's dictum 'Never trust the artist; trust the tale', he considers it an impertinence to see great art as thinly concealed autobiography or simply as the projection of the artist's neuroses. Accordingly he rejects Middleton Murry's biographical readings of Lawrence and Edmund Wilson's Freudian readings of Dickens. In fact, his concept of artistic impersonality makes it impossible for him to have links with either of these schools; and it is hard to believe that his criticism suffers as a result. Our appreciation of Shakespeare's art would scarcely be enhanced through biographical or psychoanalytic exegesis, even were enough of his life known to open the possibility. And for Leavis Shakespeare is the exemplar of impersonality and the touchstone for all literary judgements. Nor does he show an appreciable interest in the mythological approach to literature; Mrs Leavis shows more in her readings of *Jane Eyre*, *Wuthering Heights* and *Great Expectations*. This would be a weakness in his criticism only if he claimed to give definitive readings of poems and novels, or if he failed to point the reader to the greater depths of a work of genius than those levels he specifically deals with. But he makes no such claim, and a chief article of his creed is precisely that a masterwork by Dickens or Lawrence has levels of meaning that resist exact analysis.[41] And meanwhile he has made it his chief concern to distinguish such literature from shallower kinds.

Remaining, then, are the formalist school, which includes the various New Critical groups and the neo-Aristotelians at Chicago; the sociological school, which includes the Marxists; and the traditionalists associated with T. S. Eliot. Leavis's links with the last are self-evident. *Revaluation, The Great Tradition, D. H. Lawrence: Novelist* and *Dickens the Novelist* all exemplify Eliot's belief that only by establishing a tradition can we connect the literature of the present with the literature of the past and so better understand both the present and the past. However, Leavis has interpreted tradition more flexibly than Eliot, finding places for 'romantic' and 'classical' writers in his tradition, whereas Eliot's tradition is rigorously classical. Leavis may even thereby have enlarged readers' notions of the term 'classical'.

But the key to Leavis's imposing centrality in twentieth-century criticism lies in the way he manages to combine the formalist and the historical–sociological approaches. His criticism assimilates their strengths but avoids their weaknesses. He combines the close analysis of language and structure of the one with the keen sociological interest of the other, without falling into the formalist trap of stressing form at the expense of content or into the sociological trap of stressing content at the expense of form. His insistence that a work of art 'should contain within itself the reason why it is so and not otherwise' (*The Common Pursuit*, p. 224) would make Leavis a formalist were it not that he sees with the historical critic that 'the reason why it is so' has an inescapable historical significance. 'Creative geniuses' are 'peculiarly alive in their time—peculiarly alive *to* it', he says of Conrad (*The Great Tradition*, p. 32) but implying the same of all great writers. Hence he deplores the formalist's tendency to explore verbal analysis for its own sake and his inability or unwillingness to complete the work of criticism by directing analysis towards a value-judgement of the total work of art, of both its form and its content.[42] Leavis would join with the most devout Marxist in attacking the formalist's 'inbred attention to sheerly technical properties which robs literature of historical significance and reduces it to an aesthetic game'.[43] But Leavis is no Marxist: his interest in literature avoids ideological, political, and socio-economic considerations and reaches for its moral and spiritual value. By the same token, 'significance' for Leavis cannot be circumscribed by the term 'historical'—at any rate, as associated with the historical critic. And, since he insists in a quasi-formalist spirit that works of art enact their moral valuations, he cannot see the need for the literary critic to evaluate a work of art in terms of its socio-historical origins. He does not, then, see the historical critic's 'genetic' researches as a *sine qua non* for evaluation.

Leavis combines the formalist and historical approaches to greatest effect in his work on the novel and particularly when using the approach understood by the phrase 'the novel as dramatic poem'. In fact, one may see at once how well this phrase unifies the two ways of seeing a novel favoured by the formalist and by the historical critic: that is, the novel as poetic structure but also as dramatic rendering of man's social interrelations. But in practice Leavis directs his analysis of both formal aspects and social drama—of the novel as poem and as social criticism—to a total value-judgement that lies beyond the scope of the purist of either of these schools. For instance, the critique of *Little Dorrit* could not have been written by either the formalist or the historical critic, although parts of it reflect the interests of each. For neither one would evaluate the moral dimension of this novel as Leavis does. In other words, only a non-specialist who, like Leavis, fully acknowledges the moral value of literature and has affinities with several schools of criticism could have written the critique of *Little Dorrit*, or any of his criticism for that matter.

Mrs Leavis, on the other hand, and to her great credit, has stronger affiliations than her husband with the formalists and the sociological critics, pursuing the 'genetic' interests of the latter in all her work, and in *Dickens the Novelist* examining Dickens's craft in greater detail than does Leavis. All in all, she does much more than Leavis to inform the reader about the novel in all its variety as a literary genre, as we can see again in her essays on Dickens and in her account of *Wuthering Heights*. Wherefore I would call Mrs Leavis much more than Leavis a specialist or expert in criticism of the novel, and indeed, endorse Leavis's tribute to her, 'It's my wife (who's very different from me—hence our lifelong collaboration is historic) who's the authority on prose fiction. She's both critic and scholar. I think that, on the novel, she has no rival in the world.'[44]

What finally distinguishes Leavis from all other critics, including Mrs Leavis, is the passion with which he believes in the spiritual qualities in great imaginative literature. The Schweitzerian[45] note in his exaltation of novels and poems that 'affirm life' and writers who show 'reverence before life' makes his criticism distinctive and compellingly central. What makes *Dickens the Novelist* the Leavises' best book on the novel is that they have harmonised their strengths to affirm Dickens as the supreme English novelist.

Appendix A
The Leavises and Other Literatures

Those who delight in discrediting or diminishing Leavis's achievement commonly cite his provinciality and bad manners for the *coup de grâce*. But they usually give themselves away instead. To call Leavis provincial is patently absurd; and the charge of bad manners is nine times out of ten highly debatable.

René Wellek, a doughty combatant, calls Leavis 'provincial and insular' on account of three things: his 'concern with the English provincial moral tradition which he apparently finds in Shakespeare, in Bunyan, in Jane Austen, in George Eliot, and D. H. Lawrence, all countryfolk'; his 'concern for his students, for the controversies of his university'; the fact that 'besides English and American, he seems to have no interest whatever in another literature'.[1]

This is a caricature of Leavis, not the truth. The first proposition neatly omits James and Conrad, to go no further; and as if Leavis's interest in Shakespeare, and in promoting the great novelists, both American and English, as Shakespeare's successors, could be called provincial or insular! The second proposition trivialises the author of *Education and the University*. (Ironically, there is an essay printed along with Wellek's in which Northrop Frye, with all the appearance of making new insights, discusses the university as a centre of spiritual authority in the modern world—Leavis's theme for more than twenty years before.) The third proposition, even if true, ignores a key premise with Leavis, that to say anything of weight the student of literature must become thoroughly at home in his own literature *first*, before he branches out into other literatures. He made this point at the outset of his career in *How to Teach Reading: A Primer for Ezra Pound* (1932) as part of a general caveat against

Pound's cosmopolitan dilettantism. He then reprinted the *Primer* in
Education and the University.

It would be truer to say that Leavis's interest in literature and in
the university is broad, the reverse of provincial. But breadth of interest with Leavis is not a matter of accumulating authors like
luggage-stickers, but of bringing out the human significance of the
few writers in the English language who manifest such significance:
Shakespeare, the major poets, and Shakespeare's successors in the
novel: Jane Austen, Dickens, Hawthorne, Melville, George Eliot,
Twain, Henry James, Conrad and D. H. Lawrence.

To see more precisely how unprovincial this interest is we
need only glance at Leavis's principal objectives in writing on
James, Conrad and Mark Twain; at Mrs Leavis's in writing on
Hawthorne; and at both the Leavises on Tolstoy. In doing which,
we may see once again how useful it is to examine Mrs Leavis's
work alongside her husband's.

In *The Great Tradition* Leavis wanted to emphasise that the great
James owed more to the American and English traditions of the
novel than to the continental tradition—more to Hawthorne and
Jane Austen than to Flaubert and Turgenev (see esp. pp. 144–5).
He then reinforced this point by discussing *The Europeans* as a dra-
matic poem, showing that James at his best was more than a
Flaubertian stylist and had a Shakespearean power. He similarly
contrasted the Shakespearean Conrad with the Flaubertian one
(*The Great Tradition*, pp. 210–6).

Next Mrs Leavis clarified how James can be linked with
Shakespeare through both Jane Austen and Hawthorne. In her
critical introduction to *Mansfield Park* she showed how Jane Austen
was reaching for and achieving a dramatic-poetic power that re-
sembled Shakespeare and strikingly anticipated James. Then she
said that 'the essential Hawthorne' is a poet who created the 'literary tradition from which sprang Henry James on the one hand
and Melville on the other', and who can have 'gone to school with
no one but Shakespeare for his inspiration and model', for, rereading his best work,

One is certainly not conscious of a limited and devitalised talent
employing a simple-minded pedestrian technique; one is constantly struck by fresh subtleties of organisation, intention, expression and feeling, of original psychological insight and a new

minting of terms to convey it, as well as of a predominantly dramatic construction.[2]

And she backed this claim with searching analysis of Hawthorne's key works. The essay is a key one in Mrs Leavis's criticism, being her first essay using (implicitly) the analogy 'the novel as dramatic poem'.

Meanwhile, it is unwise to scoff at Leavis's use of Flaubert. One might as well scoff at James's opinion of Flaubert, which critics never seem to do. Leavis constantly invokes Flaubert in full recognition that he is *the* master of 'style' and 'form' in the novel judged purely according to aesthetic standards, but in full recognition too that the Flaubertian novel lacks the Shakespearean depth of subject-matter, unlike the great novel by Dickens or Conrad or James. And surely he could not better show the Shakespearean genius translated into the novel than by contrast with a master of the novel in another language. Without his citations of Flaubert, and without his essay on Tolstoy, certainly Leavis's criticism of the novel would have looked narrower.

Mrs Leavis's aim with Hawthorne is paralleled by Leavis's aim with Mark Twain generally, and in particular with Twain's *Pudd'nhead Wilson*: aims that reveal an attitude the reverse of provincial or insular. Primarily Mrs Leavis wanted the English academic world to open its eyes to the fact that Hawthorne was a great writer. Likewise Leavis wanted English readers to see that *Pudd'nhead Wilson*[3] has the same pedigree as *Huckleberry Finn*. But in the process the Leavises found themselves having to chide and correct American criticism for not having given these great writers their due. Mrs Leavis found Hawthorne restricted semi-apologetically to the inferior genre of 'allegory' by even the best American critics, F. O. Matthiessen and Yvor Winters, and Leavis found that the conventional account of Twain made him only a great novelist of the American frontier. On the contrary, say the Leavises, these are writers who transcend frontiers amd genres, who though deeply American belong to the world,[4] and who in developing American idioms do so out of Shakespeare's language. 'The language of Hawthorne and Lincoln and Mark Twain is the language of Shakespeare', Leavis insists, and 'Shakespeare belongs no less to America than to England'.[5] What attitude could be less provincial?

The Leavises have written sporadically on American fiction since only in response to real and specific need: where they have seen a Shakespearean achievement undervalued or misread. They have otherwise a high regard for American criticism of its native fiction.[6] Confirmation of this is provided in Mrs Leavis's recently published 'new perspective'[7] on the later Melville—the first and only account of Melville by either of our critics. Acknowledging American critics in general and Richard Chase in particular, she finds even so that the later Melville has suffered from two classes of reader: the Hawthornes (father and son), who labelled the post-*Moby Dick* output as 'incomprehensible' and 'morbid' (pp. 197 and 209), and modern readers who abuse their superior training in criticism by playing over-ingenious games with Melville's symbols and meanings at the expense of attending to his truth-telling about American life in the 1850s. Thus, though 'a consensus of at any rate American literary criticism' finds that *The Confidence-Man* 'contains Melville's most mature prose writing and some of his most interesting thinking', interpretations are often 'ill-judged' and, for instance, 'an inordinate amount of misplaced ingenuity has been devoted to discussion of exactly who the "avatars" of the Confidence Man are' (pp. 211–2). This is to slight Melville's art, Mrs Leavis insists. His technique is not a device to fool the reader: it serves the ends of a 'serious and responsible creative mind'—a diagnosis of American society and values (p. 206). Here we see the familiar Leavisian concern with ends as well as with means, and with what ends the means are intended to serve: the truly creative writer invents and fashions his techniques, even ironic and comic ones, for deeply serious purposes—as does Melville. And, when it comes to unravelling Melvillean subtlety, Mrs Leavis reads as acutely as any. Her 'new perspective', then, enables readers (who need) to correct their overall view of Melville. The years 1853–6 are 'fertile years' (p. 198) in which, though land- and family-bound and disheartened by the reception given to *Moby Dick* and *Pierre*, Melville commits himself with unquenched creativity to fresh concerns. Thus in *The Piazza Tales* he works out new techniques for exploring social themes and examining the place of art in American life, as Hawthorne before him and James after. These tales are in many cases 'try-outs' for the 'ironic masterpiece', *The Confidence-Man* (pp. 197–9). The habit of posing alternative answers to particular problems (such as Bartleby's 'No' to a life of drudgery as against Helmstone's 'Yes' in *The Fiddler*, and the opposite outcomes of confidence in *Benito Cereno*), are seen to have become the 'all-embracing technique' of ambiguity in *The Confidence-Man* (pp. 199–207).

In the masterly tracing of this development, the scholar co-operates with the critic and *vice versa*. In a resourceful reading of *Cock-a-Doodle-Do!* Mrs Leavis reveals how Melville drew upon Wordsworth (primarily 'Resolution and Independence', but two sonnets as well) so as to fashion a tale which both parodies Wordsworthian trust and yet at the same time affirms the consolatory powers of art. And she provides new insight into what Melville was about in *The Confidence-Man*, not only through the analysis of technique in the tales but also by her skilled reference to a wide variety of fictions that we can for different reasons see as this novel's analogues. The result is a perspective which places the 'Masquerade' among classics of satire and of the novel of philosophical speculation, and even distinguishes it apart and above these, it would seem. This is because Melville does not spare himself in his comprehensive criticism of society: the portraits of the woodenlegged man and the bachelor woodsman show 'humour directed against himself and self-awareness', qualities which are 'unusual in satirical writers' (p. 222). The novel may be bitterly ironic, but it is the work of a courageous and creative spirit, Mrs Leavis argues. Melville shows that he 'thirsts for honesty, courage, honourable conduct, love, integrity, true friendship, true charity, social justice, and that he is agonised because these necessities of life seemed to be victims of the spirit of his age, or even of social life in any age' (p. 223). In light of Melville's discouragement to find a responsive reading public after so much creative effort, we should not be surprised, Mrs Leavis concludes, at the 'predominantly ironic and painful' cast of the 1853–6 phase, but rather that 'these works display so much humour, humility, sensitiveness'; and it is 'natural' that Melville should 'direct his talents in *The Confidence-Man* to isolating the sources of blight and corruption in his age' (pp. 227–8). So understood, Melville emerges very favourably indeed: 'closer to Conrad than to Swift or Samuel Butler' and 'not imprisoned in a moral void like the author of *L'Étranger*, or in contempt and disgust like Swift, or in a neurosis like Kafka, or even in the joylessness of *Rasselas*' (p. 223).

Negative art, affirmative artist—or, negative art can be great when affirmative in spirit: that is what Mrs Leavis appears to be saying. This is a very interesting judgement. It decisively qualifies her own dismissal of *The Confidence-Man* as 'pessimistic or nihilistic' in her discussion of *Great Expectations* (*Dickens the Novelist*, p. 289). And, though it parallels somewhat Leavis's equivocal judgement of Swift as a great, though destructive, writer, we detect a more flexible attitude in Mrs Leavis or at any rate we get confirmation of her authoritative influence upon her husband's reading of fiction. For with this essay Mrs Leavis has filled a gap in our reading of their criticism: she had in 1947 remarked Melville's place in a tradition of the poetic novel (see above, p. 25) and he in turn referred to Melville (*The Great Tradition*, p. 145) as linking Hawthorne and James in the American tradition and also named him among Shakespeare's successors; but these claims were merely stated, presumably in deference to the critical justice accorded Melville by his modern compatriots. We see, moreover, how far Mrs Leavis has travelled since *Fiction and the Reading Public* and *The Great Tradition*.

It is worth recording Mrs Leavis's sense of decorum when she tackles an American author:

> For an English person to offer an opinion on Hawthorne, much more an evaluation of his *oeuvre*, must be felt in America to be an impertinence. But the excuse that would justify writing on Hawthorne, in an English context—that he is, except as author of one 'Puritanical' novel, unread and unrecognized, will, it seems to me, serve here too if somewhat modified. To me, a tremendous admirer of long standing of much of Hawthorne's work, it appears that the essential nature of his achievement has not been isolated and established critically. . . . I should like to present my own reading of his work, if only to get endorsement from others.[8]

What happened to turn this gracious Mrs Leavis into the ungracious Mrs Leavis of *Dickens the Novelist*? The chief reason according to Leavis[9] seems to be that American critics have not shown a reciprocal tact in writing on British authors. And no doubt he could substantiate this many times over, beginning with Harry T. Moore on Lawrence. Yet, when all is said, neither American critics in particular, nor Dickens critics in general, can be made the scapegoat for the Leavises' vexation at the critical slowness to recognise Dickens's greatness. They too were responsible, as they must have felt. Accordingly, in *Dickens the Novelist*, which contains side by side the best of their criticism and the worst of their temper as critics,[10] the Leavises are as much vexed with themselves as with those they attack. Hence the intensity of their polemics, but not the justification for them.

Tolstoy, like Flaubert, has a crucial importance in the Leavises' criticism of the novel. Like Flaubert, and like the American novelists, Tolstoy has helped to broaden their perspectives on the English novel, to see it through foreign as well as English eyes. Only, Tolstoy helped immeasurably more than Flaubert in the achievement of this larger perspective. For many years—from at least the time of *The Great Tradition* (see p. 140) till *Dickens the Novelist*—*Anna Karenina* seems to have been for the Leavises *the* touchstone, *qua* the novel, for judging all other novels, European and American. But it was so, Leavis explains, in virtue of Tolstoy's Shakespearean creativity: because of his 'great creative power in the tradition of the novel that owes so much to Shakespeare' (*'Anna Karenina'*, p. 15). Then later the Leavises discovered in Dickens the Shakespeare of the novel, a great European novelist,[11] and a master of the Tolstoyan novel before Tolstoy.

In sum, the Leavises have examined and judged the English and American successors to Shakespeare by the broadest and most exacting standards: by comparing them with each other, with Flaubert, with Tolstoy, and with Shakespeare. What could be less insular and less provincial?

But perhaps in accusing Leavis of provincialism and narrowness critics mean as well that Leavis's criteria permit him to value only writers who affirm life. Lionel Trilling evidently held this view, and Kingsley Widmer, for whom 'morality . . . does not provide an adequate perspective on art'.[12] R. P. Bilan represents this criticism against Leavis when he says, 'Leavis can praise only those writers whose response to life is unquestionably positive and who affirm—even if in an exploratory manner—positive values.' This makes Leavis unlike Lawrence, who could admire art having destructive force, and unsympathetic to writers such as Beckett, Hardy and perhaps Melville.[13] But 'only' is Bilan's word: he merely reissues a Leavis-myth. It is simply not true to say that Leavis can 'only praise those writers whose response to life is unquestionably positive'. The critiques of Swift, Dos Passos and above all T. S. Eliot make that very plain. Nor is Leavis unlike Lawrence: both know and demonstrate the value of demolition, but Lawrence's art (like Leavis's criticism) is devoted in

the last analysis to regeneration—as Kingsley Widmer himself
has shown.[14] Also, while we do not know what Leavis may have
thought about Beckett, we do know that he valued Hardy's poetry
very highly but his novels below the great—much as Hardy himself
did. We know, too, that Leavis included Melville among 'the
successors of Shakespeare'.

It would, then, be much truer to the facts of Leavis's criticism to
recall that it was devoted to distinguishing the highest creativity in
literature. And this, for Leavis, is in art that transcends modern de-
creation and nihilism.[15] Leavis reminds us that in Shakespeare and
his greatest successors creativity is not just de-creative but life-
affirming as well. The greatest writers give meaning to the term
'creative'.

Appendix B
Dickens the Novelist:
Contents

Notes

Chapter 1: Introduction

1. Notable exceptions are Vincent Buckley in *Poetry and Morality: Studies on the Criticism of Matthew Arnold, T. S. Eliot and F. R. Leavis* (1959); Fr Martin Jarrett-Kerr in 'The Literary Criticism of F. R. Leavis', *Essays in Criticism*, II (1952) 351–68; and George Steiner in *Language and Silence* (1967).
2. Bertrand H. Bronson, Introduction to Samuel Johnson, *'Rasselas', Poems, and Selected Prose* (New York, 1958) pp. ix and xi.
3. See Leavis's essay 'Johnson as Critic' in *Scrutiny*, XII (1944) 187–204; repr. in *'Anna Karenina' and Other Essays* (1967).
4. *The Common Pursuit* (Harmondsworth, 1962) p. 200.
5. I. A. Richards, *Principles of Literary Criticism* (1960) pp. 60 and 36–7.
6. 'There is an irony for me in recalling that in the 1930's the case for the steady academic disfavour I enjoyed was "We don't like the books he lends undergraduates" '—*Nor Shall My Sword: Discourses on Pluralism, Compassion and Social Hope* (1972) pp. 30–1. One of these was apparently *Ulysses*; see *Letters in Criticism*, ed. John Tasker (1974) pp. 97–9.
7. See *For Continuity* (1933) p. 52.
8. '*Scrutiny*: A Retrospect', *Scrutiny*, xx (1963) p. 1. It is interesting to consider Leavis's social criticism, which cannot in the end be severed from his literary criticism, in the tradition of public protest of Zola's 'J'accuse' (in *L'Aurore*, 13 Jan 1898), of Sartre, and of, now, Solzhenitsyn and Sakharov.
9. *Dickens the Novelist* (1970) p. 273.
10. Ibid., p. 274.
11. *D. H. Lawrence: Novelist* (Harmondsworth, 1964) p. 19.
12. Ibid.
13. As C. H. Rickword testifies, 'Modern opinion, commonly assuming that the novelist expresses himself primarily through character, tends to regard story as more or less incidental'—'A Note on Fiction', *Calendar for Modern Letters*, Oct 1926; repr. in F. R. Leavis (ed.), *Towards Standards of Criticism* (1933) p. 34.
14. As Mrs Leavis says, 'The technical perfection of the novels of Mr George Moore does not prevent them from being faultlessly dead'—*Fiction and the Reading Public* (1932) p. 233.
15. Leavis may be anti-theory for himself, but he does not deny a place for theory. Only he believes very strongly that evaluative criticism precedes theoretical criticism. As he says to René Wellek in defence of his procedure in *Revaluation*, 'But I am sure that the kind of work that I have attempted comes first, and would, for such a theoretical statement to be worth anything, have to be done first'—*The Common Pursuit*, p. 214.

16. *Fiction and the Reading Public*, p. 233.
17. Introduction to *Towards Standards of Criticism*, pp. 15–16.
18. Henry James, *Selected Literary Criticism*, ed. Morris Shapira (Harmondsworth, 1968) pp. 83–88.
19. He wrote this as an introduction to Morris Shapira's edition of James's criticism referred to in note 18. Book and introduction were first published by Heinemann in 1963.
20. *Fiction and the Reading Public*, p. 233.
21. See ibid., pp. 212ff., and in the next chapter.
22. *Towards Standards of Criticism*, p. 21.
23. Ibid., pp. 19–20.
24. For instance: 'The technique of the novel is just as symphonic as the technique of the drama and as dependent, up to a point, on the dynamic devices of articulation and control of narrative tempo. . . . More important, then, than what may be called the tricks of narrative is the status of plot and its relation to the other elements of a novel, particularly its relation to character, in solution'—'A Note on Fiction', ibid., p. 34.
25. See Leavis's approving references to *The Wheel of Fire* (which came out in 1933) in *The Common Pursuit*, pp. 142 and 166.
26. See *English Literature in Our Time and the University* (1969) pp. 4–5 and 29–30.
27. *Education and the University* (1948) p. 110.
28. Cf. 'As the inner sense of stress, tension and human need changes, English Literature changes—not merely (I mean) by accretion; the contour map, the chart of organic structure, changes'—*English Literature in Our Time*, p. 7. This comment helps explain his late return to Dickens and his reluctance to commit himself to a philosophical system to sanction his judgements. He preferred to remain flexible and open to the possibility of new growth inside himself.
29. T. S. Eliot, *The Use of Poetry and the Use of Criticism* (1933), repr. in *T. S. Eliot: Selected Prose*, ed. John Hayward (Harmondsworth, 1953) p. 51.

Chapter 2: Q. D. Leavis: *Fiction and the Reading Public* and *Scrutiny*

1. *The Great Tradition* (Harmondsworth, 1962) p. 9.
2. *Sewanee Review*, LIX (1951) 179–205 and 426–58.
3. 'Scrutiny: A Retrospect', *Scrutiny*, XX, p. 13.
4. For example, by comparison with Jane Austen Virginia Woolf is 'less spiritually fastidious' (*Fiction and the Reading Public*, p. 233), but her irony is 'far more subtle' (ibid., p. 325).
5. Cited in her bibliography, but otherwise unmentioned, is a book by W. C. Phillips, *Dickens, Reade, and Collins: Sensation Novelists* (New York, 1919). Phillips's subject is 'A Study in the Conditions and Theories of Novel Writing in Victorian England', and there are many resemblances between what he and Mrs Leavis write of this period. However, while Phillips is careful to pursue an impartial inquiry, and also to distinguish Dickens from his lesser imitators, Mrs Leavis seeks to reveal the originators of cheapness in fiction and does not refrain from acid value judgements: 'The critical reader is never in any novel before 1820 made uncomfortable by crudities of feeling as he is in reading Dickens, Charlotte Brontë, Kingsley, or by the vulgarity and puerility that he

winces at in Dickens' (*Fiction and the Reading Public*, p. 130).

6. As she seems at one point to imply of Dickens: 'Even Dickens, to take a leap to the beginning of another phase of popular fiction, was a great deal more than a member of his own public' (ibid., p. 246).

7. Ch. 4 of Leavis's 1924 thesis is 'Growth of a Reading Public'.

8. She is to qualify this in implicitly approving Leslie Stephen's judgement that 'Sterne represents a comparatively shallow vein of thought. . . . He is too systematic a trifler'—'Leslie Stephen: Cambridge Critic', *Scrutiny*, vii (1939); repr. in *A Selection from 'Scrutiny'* (Cambridge, 1968) vol. i, p. 23. And Stephen's judgement lies behind Leavis's footnote in *The Great Tradition* (p. 11) about Sterne's 'irresponsible (and nasty) trifling'. In 'nasty' Leavis also condenses Stephen: 'Sterne's sudden excursions into the nauseous are like the brutal practical jokes of a dirty boy who should put filth into a scent bottle'—*Hours in a Library* (1894) vol. iii, p. 152.

9. 'Poise' is another favourite word of both Leavises and appears to have been a legacy from Richards: 'Impulses which commonly interfere with one another and are conflicting, independent, and mutually destructive, in [Coleridge] combine into a stable poise'—*Principles of Literary Criticism*, p. 243.

10. 'The conscious cultivation of the novel as an art meant an initiated audience' (*Fiction and the Reading Public*, p. 169).

11. 'Though Defoe is by no means prelapsarian, his lack of sophistication in those quarters where our literary experience leads us to anticipate it is equally engaging, so that contemporary critics are inclined to credit him with an artistry which he never possessed' (ibid., p. 105).

12. 'The Relationship of Journalism to Literature: Studied in the Rise and Earlier Development of the Press in England' (Cambridge, 1924) pp. 282 and 290. This discrimination and this tribute lie behind Leavis's footnote on Defoe in *The Great Tradition* (p. 10), in which he says, 'Defoe was a remarkable writer'. Later critics fasten on this as evidence of Leavis's narrowness, and of his unconcern for eighteenth-century fiction. Arnold Kettle calls it 'Dr Leavis's "brush-off" footnote', and contends that it 'along with a couple of others in the same work, has had more influence in keeping students of English literature away from the eighteenth-century novel than any other pronouncement'—'In Defence of *Moll Flanders*', *Of Books and Humankind* (1964) p. 56. Clearly Kettle has neither read Leavis's doctoral dissertation nor scrutinised the footnote and must have very acquiescent students.

13. For example: 'One of the first difficulties the twentieth-century novelist encounters is the language-problem. . . . The idiom that the general public of the twentieth-century possesses is not merely crude and puerile; it is made up of phrases and clichés that imply fixed, or rather stereotyped, habits of thinking and feeling at second-hand taken over from the journalist' (*Fiction and the Reading Public*, p. 255). Sterne and Richardson, on the other hand, profited from an elastic idiom (ibid., p. 141).

14. Richards, *Principles of Literary Criticism*, p. 138. The definition is, 'This texture of expectations, satisfactions, disappointments, surprisals, which the sequence of syllables brings about, is rhythm' (p. 137).

15. Curiously, Mrs Leavis makes no reference, other than in her bibliography, to C. H. Rickword's 'A Note on Fiction' (1926), though it made suggestive links between the novel and poetry.

16. According at least to Stanley Edgar Hyman in *The Armed Vision* (New York, 1955) p. 305.

17. *Scrutiny*, v (1936) 181.

18. Ibid., xi (1942) iii.

19. 'Henry James's Heiress: The Importance of Edith Wharton', ibid., vii (1938) 261–76; repr. in *A Selection from 'Scrutiny'*, vol. ii, p. 134. Further page references will be to the latter source and appear parenthetically after the relevant quotations.

20. 'Hardy and Criticism', *Scrutiny*, xi (1943) 230–7; repr. in *A Selection from 'Scrutiny'*, vol. i, p. 296. This review provides insight into Leavis's reasons for excluding Hardy from *The Great Tradition*. Both Leavises in effect pay tribute to American criticism of Hardy, in particular to Arthur Mizener's critique of *Jude the Obscure* (*Southern Review*, Summer 1940), and agree with Herbert J. Muller's overall judgement, in the same number of this review, that Hardy is good reading for the pre-adult reader.

21. ' "Femina Vie Heureuse" Please Note', (a review of Ruth Adam, *I'm Not Complaining*), *Scrutiny*, vii (1938) 81. Mrs Leavis rates Ruth Adam's account of the modern state school very highly, comparing it with 'Dickens's admirable satires on the old system in *Hard Times* and *Our Mutual Friend*' and with the chapter 'The Man's World' in Lawrence's *The Rainbow* (p. 85).

22. 'Lives and Works of Richard Jefferies', *Scrutiny*, vi (1938) 435–46; repr. in *A Selection from 'Scrutiny'*, vol. ii, pp. 204 and 210.

23. W. J. Keith, *Richard Jefferies: A Critical Study* (Toronto, 1965) p. 129.

24. 'Henry James: The Stories', *Scrutiny*, xiv (1947) 223–9; 'Note on *The Great Short Novels of Henry James* [by Philip Rahv]', ibid., pp. 305–6; 'The Institution of Henry James', ibid., xv (1947) 68–74.

25. Thus she too opposes the fashionable exaltation of *The Ambassadors* and *The Turn of the Screw*, and favours the work of the middle period: *The Portrait of a Lady*, *The Europeans* and *Washington Square*. Compare *The Great Tradition*, p. 154.

26. 'The Institution of Henry James', repr. in *A Selection from 'Scrutiny'*, vol. ii, pp. 212–13.

27. 'When he took as the subject of a novel his most vital interest—the problem of how to live as a man of letters, the literary world being what it is, without sacrificing your integrity of purpose—he produced his one permanent contribution to the English novel'—*Scrutiny*, vii (1938) 73–81; repr. in *A Selection from 'Scrutiny'*, vol. ii, pp. 84–5. Mrs Leavis admires Somerset Maugham's *Cakes and Ale* for similar reasons in this review. And Leavis mentions Gissing in almost identical terms in *The Great Tradition*, p. 170.

28. *A Selection from 'Scrutiny'*, vol. ii, p. 88.

29. Ibid., pp. 88–9. '. . . all the other kinds' includes novels for the sociologist, such as Trollope's and Wells's; 'bogus traditions', as in Scott, Stevenson and George Moore; and propagandist novels, such as Charlotte Brontë's and Aldous Huxley's.

   Interestingly, Leavis too praised *The Egoist* in his essay on E. M. Forster in the same number of *Scrutiny*; and, strangely, did not edit the essay for reprinting in *The Common Pursuit* (see pp. 263–4) though he had gone on to demolish Meredith in *The Great Tradition*.

Chapter 3: F. R. Leavis and *The Great Tradition*

1. D. H. Lawrence, 'Morality and the Novel', in *D. H. Lawrence: Selected Literary Criticism*, ed. Anthony Beal (1961) p. 110.
2. Samuel Johnson, *'Rasselas', Poems, and Selected Prose*, p. 258.
3. Actually there is no serious problem of tone. With the exception of his strictures on Lord David Cecil in the first chapter, Leavis concentrates on the texts of his writers, and treats critics respectfully.
4. These are the years of the Second World War and its dismal aftermath. Leavis had gone to the First War, and had been profoundly disturbed, as Ronald Hayman records in 'Leavis at 80', *New Review*, II (Oct 1975). How the Second World War may have affected his attitude when he was drafting *The Great Tradition*, it is hard to say. But certainly he would not have found conditions favouring a study of novels in which the author trifles with life, however wittily or elegantly. Rather, it was a time for the chief virtues of George Eliot as Leavis records them: 'nobility' and 'compassion' (*The Great Tradition*, pp. 88, 92); and for pondering the questions that Conrad continually asks and seeks to answer: 'what do men live by? what *can* men live by?' (ibid., p. 42). Not that Leavis would in peaceful times exchange George Eliot for, say, Meredith, and Conrad for Sterne. But the war years did compel everyone to concentrate on essentials with unusual urgency, as Leavis does in this book on the novel.
5. 'The Appreciation of Henry James' (review of F. O. Matthiessen, *Henry James: The Major Phase*), *Scrutiny*, XIV (1947), repr. in *A Selection from 'Scrutiny'*, vol. II ; and 'Henry James's First Novel' (review of *Roderick Hudson*), *Scrutiny*, XIV (1947).
6. Leavis has recorded his own sense of their importance, by having them reprinted twice, in *A Selection from 'Scrutiny'*, vol. I , and in *The Living Principle: 'English' as a Discipline of Thought* (1975) where he added a brief section on prose.
7. See his Introduction to *Daniel Deronda* (New York, 1961).
8. *For Continuity* includes material on Wells, Dreiser, Bennett, Dos Passos, Lawrence and Joyce. He wrote a review of Faulkner's *Light in August* in *Scrutiny*, II (1933) 91–3, and a full-length critique of E. M. Forster in *Scrutiny*, VII (1938) 185–202. The latter he reprinted in *The Common Pursuit*.
9. Whether Leavis used Lawrence the novelist as the touchstone for *The Great Tradition*, as Martin Green avers in *The von Richthofen Sisters: The Triumphant and the Tragic Modes of Loves* (1974) pp. 205 and 310, is more debatable given the chronology of its composition (see pp. 48–9).
10. See the essay 'Sociology and Literature' in *The Common Pursuit*, pp. 195–203.
11. I discuss Leavis's relative 'placing' of these two in the course of a longer examination of *For Continuity* in Chapter 5.
12. Granville Hicks, *The Great Tradition: An Interpretation of American Literature since the Civil War* (New York, 1935).
13. Or, as Vincent Buckley interprets Leavis, 'Dos Passos' view fails at the point of spiritual crisis, and never becomes vision'—*Poetry and Morality*, p. 186.
14. René Wellek, 'The Literary Criticism of Frank Raymond Leavis', in Carroll Camden (ed.), *Literary Views: Critical and Historical Essays* (Chicago, 1964) p. 189.
15. When he began to revalue Dickens, Leavis observed, 'I would without

hesitation surrender the whole *oeuvre* of Flaubert for *Dombey and Son* or *Little Dorrit'*—*Letters in Criticism*, p. 96. This, too, implies a high valuation as well as criticism of the French novelist.

16. See also Leavis's Foreword to *Nostromo* in the Signet Classic edition (New York, 1960), where he expands the comparison to good effect.

17. See the important essay 'Johnson and Augustanism' in *The Common Pursuit*, and particularly the judgement that Johnson 'cannot appreciate the life-principle of drama as we have it in the poetic—creative use of language—the use by which the stuff of experience is presented to speak and act for itself' (p. 110). The subject is Johnson's deficiency as a critic of Shakespeare.

18. Ibid., p. 110.

19. See most recently John Gross in *The Rise and Fall of the Man of Letters* (1969) pp. 275ff.

20. According to Richard Stang in *Discussions of George Eliot* (Boston, Mass., 1960) pp. vii–viii; and R. W. Stallman in *The Art of Joseph Conrad* (East Lansing, Mich., 1960), p. xviii. Leo Gurko in *Joseph Conrad* (New York, 1962) p. 167, credits Leavis with having first discovered the importance of *The Secret Agent*. Leavis's achievement with James must largely be his demonstration that James belongs as indisputably to the great English as to the great American tradition of the novel.

21. Matthew Arnold, 'On Translating Homer', *Essays Literary and Critical* (1928) p. 249.

22. 'How to Teach Reading' (1932), *Education and the University*, p. 110.

23. 'My aim does not comprise exhaustiveness; on the contrary it involves a strict economy. It is . . . to give, as it were, the essential structure'—*Revaluation* (Harmondsworth, 1964) p. 10.

24. Among the commentaries I have read, only George Orwell in the *Observer* (6 Feb 1949) seems to have noticed that Leavis approves of more than the select few.

25. He wrote a brief critique of Joyce in *For Continuity*, which I discuss in Chapter 5. More surprisingly, he does not mention Forster, whom he had distinguished in a long critique in *Scrutiny*, VII (1938) 185–202. But he was to reprint this in *The Common Pursuit*.

26. 'In the nineteenth century the strength—the poetic strength—of the English language went into prose fiction'—'The Americanness of American Literature' (1952), *'Anna Karenina'*, p. 145.

27. Even George Orwell (*Observer*, 6 Feb 1949) understood Leavis to be damning Emily Brontë's 'talent' as of a 'bad kind'.

28. Richard Chase, *The American Novel and Its Tradition* (New York, 1957), pp. 3–4.

29. Significantly he did not reprint the critique of *Hard Times* under this head, nor did he refer to G. D. Klingopulos's essay on *Wuthering Heights* as a dramatic poem, though it too had already appeared, in *Scrutiny*, XIV (1947) 269–86.

30. Lionel Trilling, 'Dr Leavis and the Moral Tradition', *A Gathering of Fugitives* (Boston, Mass., 1956) p. 104.

31. 'In every English-speaking home, in the four quarters of the globe, parents and children would do well to read Dickens aloud of a winter's evening!' (*The Great Tradition*, p. 29). According to *Dickens the Novelist* (p. 10) this was Leavis's own childhood experience.

32. The following might be compared with Trilling's sentence: 'Representing human spontaneity, the circus-athletes represent at the same time highly-developed skill and deftness of kinds that bring poise, pride, and confident ease—they are always buoyant, and ballet-dancer-like, in training' (*The Great Tradition*, p. 254).

33. For instance, in what he says of George Eliot's art with Klesmer in *Daniel Deronda* (ibid., p. 133ff.), of James's comedy in *The Bostonians* (p. 151ff.) and of the ironic comedy in *The Secret Agent* (p. 236ff.).

34. V. S. Pritchett in a review of *The Great Tradition* for the *New Statesman* (15 Jan 1949).

35. See T. S. Eliot, 'Tradition and the Individual Talent'; and Joyce, *A Portrait of the Artist as a Young Man*, ch. 5.

36. Richards, *Principles of Literary Criticism*, pp. 251–2.

37. *A Selection from 'Scrutiny'*, vol. I, p. 211.

38. Ibid., pp. 215–16.

39. Ibid., p. 212. We may see that Wordsworth's famous description of poetry as 'emotion recollected in tranquillity' has a close bearing on Leavis's concept of the process of impersonality.

40. Ibid., p. 220.

41. What Georg Lukács says of Cézanne seems to me to apply equally to Leavis: 'The rendering of the many-sidedness and many levels of visible reality as well as of what is not directly visual but is transmitted through various mediations is what Cézanne was accustomed to call "realization" '—*Writer and Critic* (New York, 1970) p. 10.

42. Buckley, *Poetry and Morality*, pp. 163–4. The whole chapter 'F. R. Leavis: Reality and Sincerity' is pertinent and illuminating.

43. John Kilham is dissatisfied with Leavis's use of 'concreteness' as an evaluative term, complaining that he uses it indiscriminately for the psychological novel of George Eliot and for the novel of pattern of Conrad—*British Journal of Aesthetics*, V (1965) 14–24. But I think that Kilham wants too much to have the term applied with a scientific precision, and does not allow that just as reality has many sides and levels so it can be realised in art in many different ways. And see Leavis's discussion of 'realization' in *Education and the University*, p. 76ff., where he shows with Shakespeare that the term cannot be used with technical precision.

44. Leavis has already given examples of what he means by this, referring to *The Waves* and *The Years* as 'works that offer something like the equivalent of Georgian poetizing'. 'Even *To the Lighthouse*', he went on, 'which may be distinguished among her books as substantially justifying her so obviously "poetic" method is a decidedly minor affair—it is *minor* art' (*The Great Tradition*, p. 144).

45. Again notice how Leavis invokes the master of style in the novel: 'Dickens, we know, was a popular entertainer, but Flaubert never wrote anything approaching this in subtlety of achieved art. Dickens, of course, has a vitality that we don't look for in Flaubert' (ibid., p. 270).

46. This is the description in *Lady Chatterley's Lover* (ch. 11) of the drive through Tevershall, beginning, 'The car ploughed uphill through the long squalid straggle of Fevershall, the blackened brick buildings, the black slate roofs, glistening their sharp edges, the mud black with coaldust, the pavements wet

and black.' Except for the car it might be Coketown. Leavis quoted the passage repeatedly in his writings, almost talismanically.
47. See p. 34 above. R. P. Bilan has noted Leavis's hesitation about Conrad in *Nostromo*—'what are his positives? It is easier to say what he rejects or criticizes'—and comments, 'Leavis makes Conrad appear to be more of an affirmative writer than he actually is only by leaving his questions about *Nostromo* unanswered and shifting his discussion to *Victory*—*Novel*, a (Spring 1976) 208–9.

Chapter 4: Q. D. Leavis and Major Women Novelists

1. 'The Institution of Henry James', *Scrutiny*, xv (1947) 68–74; repr. in *A Selection from 'Scrutiny'*, vol. ii, pp. 212–13.
2. 'Hawthorne as Poet', *Sewanee Review*, 5a (Spring and Summer 1951) 179–205 and 426–58.
3. Leavis's early misgivings about Lawrence included disagreement with him over Jane Austen (see *For Continuity*, p. 133).
4. Introduction to *Miss Marjoribanks* (1969) pp. 11–2.
5. Like her husband, Mrs Leavis posits that the great writer has a vital capacity for experience. Consequently she cannot take Charlotte Yonge (for instance) seriously, but calls her 'a day-dreamer with a writing itch that compensated her for a peculiarly starved life'—*Scrutiny*, xii (1944) 152–60; repr. in *A Selection from 'Scrutiny'*, vol. i, p. 147.
6. From a review of *Three Guineas* by Virginia Woolf, *Scrutiny*, vii (1938) 203–14; repr. in Eric Bentley (ed.), *The Importance of 'Scrutiny'* (1964) p. 387.
7. Particularly D. W. Harding, *Scrutiny*, viii (1940) 346–62.
8. Parts I and II in *Scrutiny*, x (1941–2) 61–87, 114–42, and 272–94; Part III in *Scrutiny*, xii (1944) 104–19. All parts are reprinted in *A Selection from 'Scrutiny'*, vol. ii, which is my source for quotation.
9. Edmund Wilson, *A Literary Chronicle: 1920–1950* (New York, 1950) p. 304.
10. Cf. the observation of R. W. Chapman's successor: 'We see that the six novels stand at the end of a long apprenticeship. . . . They were the rewards of laborious composition, of trial and error, the art of the novelist won through many years of highly conscious experiment'—B. C. Southam, *Jane Austen's Literary MSS* (Oxford, 1964) p. vi.
11. Letter 134 to J. Edward Austen (16 Dec 1816), reprinted in *Jane Austen: Selected Letters*, ed. R. W. Chapman (1955) p. 189.
12. Marvin Mudrick had entered a caveat about 'many of her aesthetic deductions' and certain 'dubious biographical particulars', but without controverting the theory itself—*Jane Austen: Irony as Defense and Discovery* (Princeton, NJ, 1952) pp. 260 and 263.
13. B. C. Southam 'Mrs Leavis and Miss Austen', *Nineteenth Century Fiction*, xvii (1962) 21–3.
14. Ibid., pp. 27–8. He also adds in his later book that Cassandra's sense of decorum could not have permitted her to do so—*Jane Austen's Literary MSS*, p. 143.
15. Southam, in *Nineteenth Century Fiction*, xvii, 30.
16. Southam, *Jane Austen's Literary MSS*, p. 142.
17. Ibid., p. 148.

18. Southam, in *Nineteenth Century Fiction*, xvii, 32.
19. Compare Leavis's very similar objections to Quentin Anderson's biographical explanations for parts of James's late novels: '[The critic] is concerned with the work in front of him as something that should contain within itself the reason why it is so and not otherwise'—'Henry James and the Function of Criticism', *Scrutiny*, xv (1948); *The Common Pursuit*, p. 204.
20. Compare D. W. Harding's testimony: 'Chiefly, so I gathered, she was a delicate artist, revealing with inimitable lightness of touch the comic foibles and amiable weaknesses of the people whom she lived amongst and liked. All this was enough to make me quite certain I didn't want to read her'—'Regulated Hatred: An Aspect of the Work of Jane Austen', *Scrutiny*, viii (1940) 347.
21. Arnold Kettle, 'Jane Austen: *Emma*', *An Introduction to the English Novel* (New York, 1968) p. 86.
22. Notably A. W. Litz, *Jane Austen: A Study of Her Artistic Development* (New York, 1965); Howard Babb, *Jane Austen's Novels* (New York, 1967); and Douglas Bush, *Jane Austen* (New York, 1975).

   Moreover, as Robert Liddell rightly deplores, 'serious criticism of Jane Austen has lately suffered from separatism'—*The Novels of Jane Austen* (1965) p. xi. Mrs Leavis has not been guiltless in this. Liddell specifies that she ignored Mary Lascelles's work and that R. W. Chapman ignored Mrs Leavis's. He could have included other instances, such as Andrew Wright, who, in his *Jane Austen's Novels: A Study in Structure* purports to give a comprehensive annotated bibliography but omits all mention of Mrs Leavis.
23. Southam, *Nineteenth Century Fiction*, xvii, 32. Gallant words and timely in view of note 22, and showing that caveats can be courteous.
24. Wright, *Jane Austen's Novels* (Harmondsworth, 1962) pp. 42 and 96–7.
25. Concluding with the Leavis-like question, 'Does sense solve every problem, does sense deal adequately with life?', Wright answers, 'the "lesson" of the book is that neither mode is adequate, each contradicts the other—and there is no happy medium' (ibid., p. 99).

   Not only does this contradict his notion that the sisters are by the end 'more rounded and complete', but Wright seems finally to waive all understanding of the finer distinctions between sense and sensibility.
26. Mudrick, *Jane Austen*, p. 90.
27. Ibid., pp. 91–3.
28. Ibid., p. 78.
29. Introduction to *Sense and Sensibility* (1958) pp. xiv–xv. All further references will appear parenthetically after the relevant quotations.
30. See below, note 34.
31. Introduction to *Mansfield Park* (1957) pp. xiii–xiv. All further references will appear parenthetically after the relevant quotations.
32. I quote from the reprint of Trilling's essay in the *Pelican Guide to English Literature* (Harmondsworth, 1957) vol. v, p. 128.
33. R. W. Chapman, *Jane Austen: Facts and Problems* (1948) p. 200.
34. Mudrick's analogies seem thin in comparison: 'Poverty is the passive enemy that destroys the will and makes choice impossible', he remarks of Fanny in her parents' home in Portsmouth (vulgarity is Mrs Leavis's and Trilling's diagnosis, which is much closer to the mark), adding, 'This is the final lesson,

the confirmation of Fanny's faith. If in Jane Austen's parable, Mansfield Park is Heaven and the Crawfords' London Hell, Portsmouth is the Limbo of the morally unborn'—*Jane Austen*, p. 174.

35. Compare Southam again: 'We see that the six novels stand at the end of a long apprenticeship. . . . They were the rewards of laborious composition, of trial and error, the art of the novelist won through many years of highly conscious experiment'—*Jane Austen's Literary MSS*, p. vi.

36. Lord David Cecil, *Jane Austen* (Cambridge, 1935) p. 21.

37. Peter Coveney, *The Image of Childhood* (1967) p. 106. This book was originally published under the title *Poor Monkey* in 1957, the year in which Mrs Leavis published her edition of *Mansfield Park*. It is a book much admired by both Leavises: Leavis wrote the Introduction for the revised version, and she mentions it as 'the invaluable book . . . by P. Coveney' in her essay on *Wuthering Heights*—F. R. and Q. D. Leavis, *Lectures in America* (1969) p. 91, n. 2—which she gave in lecture-form in 1966, the year of her edition of *Jane Eyre*. But how far Mrs Leavis was affected by Coveney's book in her mature conversion to Charlotte Brontë is best left as a question.

38. *Fiction and the Reading Public*, pp. 130 and 237.

39. Introduction to *Jane Eyre* (Harmondsworth, 1966) p. 11. All further references will appear parenthetically after the relevant quotations.

40. Though not, it must be admitted, as completely or as convincingly as by Mrs Leavis in this introduction. However, compare from a more recent standard work: 'No one should be led by their obvious imperfections to underestimate these novels [of Charlotte Brontë], which reflect—in their best passages—the workings of an acute and intensely individual mind'—D. A. Traversi, 'The Brontë Sisters and *Wuthering Heights*', *Pelican Guide to English Literature* (Harmondsworth, 1958) vol. vi, p. 256.

41. Walter Allen, *The English Novel* (Harmondsworth, 1958) p. 190.

42. Cf. also: 'The scene of the meeting [between Jane and Rochester for the first time] (as strangers ignorant of each other's identity) is symbolic as well as dramatic; he cannot get home without leaning on her shoulder and it is through her that he has hurt himself slipping on the ice (in due course he is to try to persuade her into a bigamous marriage with disastrous results)' (Introduction to *Jane Eyre*, pp. 16–17).

43. A favourite phrase which he uses at the end of his critiques of both James and Conrad in *The Great Tradition*, pp. 191 and 248.

44. *Lectures in America*, p. 84. Further references will appear parenthetically after the relevant quotations.

45. 'There is nothing vague about this novel. . . . The realisation is intensely concrete'—Kettle, *An Introduction to the English Novel*, p. 130. Note the Leavis-like phrasing.

46. Two corrections of former readings are implied in this. First, it is not Heathcliff who is the real centre: he belongs too much to the literary novel, 'being made up of so many inconsistent parts that the novelist evidently was in some perplexity to make him cohere enough' (*Lectures in America*, p. 107). Secondly, and contrary to Klingopulos, whose essay in *Scrutiny* (1947) Mrs Leavis admires, *Wuthering Heights is* a moral tale, Mrs Leavis insists: 'Catherine is judged by the author in the parallel but notably different history of the daughter who, inheriting her mother's name, and likenesses both

physical and psychological, is shown by deliberate choice, and trial and error, developing the maturity and therefore achieving the happiness, that the mother failed in' (p. 88).

47. As with *Wuthering Heights*, she gives the literary and historical context of *Marner* with a plenitude of notes that includes illuminating comparisons with Shakespeare, Bunyan, Wordsworth, Dickens, Richard Jefferies and Turgenev.

48. She also implicitly corrects her earlier valuation of the novel when she compared it with Edith Wharton's *Summer* (in 'Henry James's Heiress', *Scrutiny*, VII), and Leavis's valuation in *The Great Tradition*: '*Silas Marner* has in it, in its solid way, something of the fairy-tale' and it is a 'charming minor masterpiece' (p. 58). He was, however, in a footnote added in 1959, to revise his 'stresses on "minor" and "fairy-tales" ', calling these 'infelicitous' (p. 60).

49. Introduction to *Silas Marner* (Harmondsworth, 1967) p. 23.

50. Ibid., p. 14. Mrs Leavis adds, 'It is very evidently the source of Hardy's novel-writing, but he never any where equalled the characterisation of Raveloe and the talk in the Rainbow.' The reason for quoting this has to do with the next chapter. It must be a surprise to many readers that Leavis makes no link between Hardy and Lawrence in *D. H. Lawrence: Novelist*, particularly in view of Lawrence's appreciative 'Study of Thomas Hardy'. In Mrs Leavis's words is the reason why: George Eliot was the significant forerunner. Also, she and Lawrence came from the same region of England.

51. Introduction to *Miss Marjoribanks*, p. 15. Mrs Leavis also compares this novel favourably with Disraeli's *Coningsby*, and says of Lucilla, Miss Marjoribanks herself, that she 'has long seemed to me a triumphant intermediary between . . . Emma and Dorothea, and, incidentally, more entertaining, more impressive and more likable than either' (p. 1).

Chapter 5: F. R. Leavis and D. H. Lawrence

1. Lawrence, 'Morality and the Novel', in *D. H. Lawrence: Selected Literary Criticism*, p. 113.

2. Leavis would have liked two reviews of *The Cocktail Party*—'One by Lawrence and one by Albert Schweitzer' (*D. H. Lawrence: Novelist*, p. 323).

3. See *For Continuity*, pp. 114 and 131. Actually, he thought *The Lost Girl* the 'best novel', and interestingly called it 'magnificently Dickensian' (p. 123).

4. Cf. Vincent Buckley's reading of Leavis (*Poetry and Morality*, pp. 186–7):

> The chaotic world of machinery and mechanised people which Dos Passos faces is, after all, not so unlike the mechanical life which Lawrence faces. But Lawrence faces it with all the ethical resources of the human spirit, and obtains an affirmative vision in the face of it; Dos Passos' view fails at the point of spiritual crisis, and never becomes vision.
>
> The same resources of the human spirit which are necessarily engaged in the attempt to *live imaginatively* an answer to human problems are also engaged in the struggle with artistic form. And here again we may note, in parenthesis, that while Dos Passos' Trilogy is formally ingenious, and in a way adequate, it has no formal power capable of aiding him to attain a level of vision.

5. Cf. also: 'A complete wisdom, it perhaps hardly needs arguing, involves greater concern for intelligence and the finer products of civilisation than Lawrence ever manifests' (*For Continuity*, p. 135).

6. Harry T. Moore, *D. H. Lawrence: The Man and his Works* (Toronto, 1969) p. 280.

7. George H. Ford, *Double Measure* (New York, 1965) p. 5.

8. See *After Strange Gods* and Leavis's review of it in *Scrutiny*, III (1934) 184–91.

9. 'T. S. Eliot is distinguished enough, and has had influence enough, for this performance to be given classical status' (*D. H. Lawrence: Novelist*, p. 27). The reference is to Eliot's review of Middleton Murry's *Son of Woman* in the *Criterion*, July 1931, but Leavis doubtless has in mind the other Eliot texts he has been discussing (pp. 21–7).

10. Not only the frigidly 'classical' Eliot but also the intensely 'romantic' Middleton Murry helped Leavis to identify Lawrence's genius. Leavis steered between the two, as Martin Green usefully records in *The von Richthofen Sisters*. Leavis seemed to acknowledge Murry a little more kindly than he did Eliot: 'If then I adduce Murry for disagreement, that is by way not of exhibiting superiority but of making a convenient approach to the peculiar difficulties that Lawrence presents to literary criticism' (*D. H. Lawrence: Novelist*, p. 152). But he could afford to be: Murry had not Eliot's authority (as we may detect from the easy use of 'superiority' here: Leavis would not think of Murry as *his* superior either).

11. Roger Poole, '*The Affirmation Is of Life*: The Later Criticism of F. R. Leavis', *Universities Quarterly*, XXIX (Winter 1974) 64.

12. In a letter written to Mr Humphrey Milford, in 1907, declining the invitation to write a preface to Melville's book, about to be published by the Oxford University Press; repr. in Hershel Parker and Harrison Hayford (eds), '*Moby Dick*' *as Doubloon: Essays and Extracts 1851–1970* (New York, 1970) pp. 122–3.

13. Mark Spilka, Introduction to *D. H. Lawrence: A Collection of Critical Essays* (Englewood Cliffs, NJ, 1963) p. 5. In light of the backstabbing in Lawrence criticism, Spilka's summary of Leavis's achievement is exemplary: all the more generous for his having himself been early in the field of this criticism, and all the more interesting because disinterested. One after another he makes the essential points: the title of Leavis's book 'seems definitive' because Lawrence's novels were his 'chief métier'; his approach through the idea of 'the novel as dramatic poem' was apter than later 'symbolist' approaches, because it 'could keep fidelity with rendered life and avoid excessive symbol-hunting'; he created 'new hierarchies of accepted texts'; his readings illuminated 'meaning and order where previous readers found impenetrable chaos' and so showed an 'integrative intelligence in Lawrence'; he corrected misconceptions about Lawrence and sex, brought out Lawrence's 'neglected powers of characterization' and the 'vitality of wit in his shorter tales'; and, not least, Leavis *did not go overboard* in extravagant eulogy: 'with characteristic firmness, he has judged and discarded works which fail to meet his exacting standards' (pp. 3–5).

Spilka's anthology makes a welcome, and necessary, counterweight to H. Coombes's anthology for Penguin Books—*D. H. Lawrence* (Harmondsworth, 1973)—which is excellent for the Leavis-*cum*-Lawrence enthusiast but combines the virtues and vices of excessive loyalty. Unlike Stephen Wall, editor of the companion volume on Dickens (1970), Coombes keeps his selection fiercely British on the grounds that the American academic mills have travestied Lawrence's art and assimilated him 'into the civilization he condemned' (pp. 55–6). Perhaps so at large; but there are also excellently sensitive readings by Americans which advance 'the common pursuit of true judgment' and which repay a compliment to the author of *Studies in Classic American Literature*. Two appear in Spilka's collection: Marvin Mudrick's 'The Originality of *The Rainbow*' (much superior to his book on Jane Austen) and Mark Schorer's '*Women in Love* and Death'. Neither of these poaches from Leavis.

14. Leavis would write another essay on *Women in Love* twenty years later, by which time he plainly saw the novel in its subtlety of diagnosis of modern civilisation as Lawrence's *Little Dorrit*—*Thought, Words and Creativity: Art and Thought in Lawrence* (1976) p. 68 *et passim*.

15. 'It suggests that the genius of the writer may fairly be described as that of a poetic dramatist, and that, in our preconceptions about "the novel", we may miss, within the field of fictional prose, possibilities of concentration and flexibility in the interpretation of life such as we associate with Shakespearean drama' (*The Great Tradition*, p. 266).

16. This does not cancel, but rather adds interest to George H. Ford's perceptive comment (prophetic of Leavis) that 'such novelists as Joyce and Lawrence anticipated the counter-revolution' in Dickens criticism, and that 'criticism, in devising ways of coping with their narratives, has been aided in coping with those of Dickens'—*Dickens and His Readers* (Princeton, NJ, 1955) p. 254. For Leavis the pattern is Dickens–Lawrence–Dickens.

17. Spilka, *D. H. Lawrence*, p. 4.

18. Cf. what he says of James in *The Great Tradition* (p. 145): 'James's own constant and profound concern with spiritual facts expresses itself not only in what obviously demands to be called symbolism, but in the handling of character, episode, and dialogue, and in the totality of the plot, so that when he seems to offer a novel of manners he gives us more than that, and the "poetry" is major.'

19. Compare the remark that Johnson 'cannot appreciate the life-principle of drama as we have it in the poetic–creative use of language'—*The Common Pursuit*, p. 110.

20. Flexibility is a key concern of Leavis in this book. He wants to emphasise the range and flexibility of Lawrence's art. 'The Ladybird' with its 'boldly poetic–symbolic' mode is discussed expressly for this purpose (*D. H. Lawrence: Novelist*, p. 63ff.) and 'The Captain's Doll', of which he says that 'Flexibility is strikingly illustrated within the tale itself' (ibid., p. 206). And cf. his repeated affirmation of flexibility in Dickens's art in *Little Dorrit* (*Dickens the Novelist*, p. 246ff.).

21. Cf.: 'To call St. Mawr a poetic symbol doesn't help much. To call him a sexual symbol is positively misleading'; rather 'in presenting the drama in which the stallion figures so centrally Lawrence leaves us unable to doubt that his essential—and triumphant—concern is to vindicate "love, joy, delight, hope, true indignant anger, passionate sense of justice and injustice, truth and untruth, honour and dishonour", and the capacity for real belief' (*D. H. Lawrence: Novelist*, pp. 239, 242).

22. 'For it is, surely, a contradiction that Flaubert's case presents classically—all

that would be creative intensity, that intensity of "doing", devoted to expressing attitudes in which distaste, disgust, and boredom have so decisive a part; a
cult of art that amounts to a religion, and the directing spirit of it a rejection of
life' (*D. H. Lawrence: Novelist*, p. 25). Flaubert's art is therefore pseudo-
religious.

23. 'Eliot's Classical Standing' is one of his three contributions to *Lectures in
America* and deals with the early Eliot. The Clark lectures for 1967, reprinted as
English Literature in Our Time and the University, are almost wholly devoted to
Eliot.

24. Cf. Leavis's somewhat similar verdict on Swift back in 1933 (which the
analysis of *Four Quartets* now makes more understandable): 'We have, then, in
his writings probably the most remarkable expression of negative feelings and
attitudes that literature can offer—the spectacle of creative powers (the para-
doxical expression seems right) exhibited constantly in negation and
rejection. . . . A great writer, yes . . . though his greatness is no matter of
moral grandeur or human centrality' (*The Common Pursuit*, p. 86).

25. Also, Eliot can at times reach the highest impersonality, as in the 'Dantesque'
all-clear narrative in 'Little Gidding'. There he confronts his *alter ego*, comes
closest in all his poetry 'to full recognition of the reality of what he is', and '*is*,
and very impressively, a major poet' (*The Living Principle*, p. 256).

26. Buckley, *Poetry and Morality*, p. 210.

27. See especially the critique of *Little Dorrit*, where Leavis takes up the question of
'theologizing students' of Blake, and says of Dickens: 'But . . . to dismiss his
claim to be recognized as a vindicator of the spirit, such as we sorely need, with
the remark that he gives no sign of being concerned—or equipped—to answer
the probing questions that theologically religious critics are moved to put, is
beside the point, and unintelligent. The great artist presents the indispensable
testimony of experience, perception and intuition, he being in respect of these
an adept'—*Dickens the Novelist*, p. 274.

28. Leavis, like Arnold and Eliot, but unlike Lawrence or Dickens, had a classical
education.
      Roger Poole dates Leavis's later criticism from 1962, explaining that the ill-
starred attack on C. P. Snow that year, in *Two Cultures?*, forced Leavis to
clarify anew the criteria necessary for examining the life of a culture (*Universities Quarterly*, XXIX, 66). Perhaps so; but the revision of criteria occurs in
D. H. Lawrence: Novelist. The later criticism adds Dickens and Blake—and so
immeasurable weight—to the critique of 'technologico-Benthamism'.

29. Introduction to Peter Coveney, The Image of Childhood, p. 18.

30. Ibid., pp. 18–19. The earlier Leavis had peremptorily observed, 'Johnson, is
not, like the Romantic poet, the enemy of society'—*The Common Pursuit*,
p. 104.

31. The revaluation of the Romantics has another interesting result. In his Foreword to *Adam Bede* (New York, 1961), Leavis makes much of George Eliot's
indebtedness to Scott. But in *The Great Tradition* he had written that Scott
fathered a 'bad tradition' and that George Eliot had 'no novelist to learn from'
except Jane Austen (pp. 14, 19). In the same Foreword he also links George
Eliot with Hawthorne, benefiting perhaps from Mrs Leavis's account of
Hawthorne ten years earlier.

32. See above, n. 28. Poole's is much the most perceptive account of the later criticism, and I am indebted to it.
33. 'And by "speech" Lawrence means the utterance of thought—thought of the anti-mathematical order' (*'Anna Karenina'*, p. 15).

Chapter 6: The Leavises and Dickens

1. Back in 1948 Leavis wrote, 'I hope to bring out before long in collaboration with Q. D. Leavis a book that deals with the grounds and methods of the critical study of novels'—*Education and the University*, p. 126, n. 3. It never materialised, perhaps because they decided that the best way of doing this is in criticising novels.
2. Mrs Leavis's frequent insertions to the effect 'I have always thought' in the critique of *David Copperfield* (see *Dickens the Novelist*, pp. 61, 70, 102, 107) are more than rhetorical devices to suggest an appreciativeness of longer standing than is actually the case. Besides, even in her most anti-Dickens phase she could refer approvingly to this novel and to *Great Expectations* (see *Fiction and the Reading Public*, p. 158).
3. Not that Mrs Leavis has blinkered herself to the novel. Wherever she can, she links Dickens with poets, too. Thus 'the Pope of the *Moral Epistles*, and particularly of *Epistle IV*, "On the use of Riches" ' counts among the 'more sophisticated influences' in *David Copperfield* and *Bleak House* (*Dickens the Novelist*, p. 144); and in *Bleak House* 'Dickens's view of the nature and function of an aristocracy is . . . remarkably like Yeats's' (ibid., p. 148, n. 1).
4. On Dickens and Smollett see ibid., pp. 30–3; Jane Austen, pp. 144 and 160; Bunyan, p. 320ff.; Joyce, p. 103, n. 1; and Lawrence, p. 83ff.
5. And we may feel, too, that the Leavises were entirely justified in reusing Sylvère Monod's title for their own book, for they charge it with far greater force and meaning. Monod's *Dickens the Novelist* (Norman, Okla, 1968), a revised version in English of his *Dickens Romancier* (Paris, 1953), is a solid work of scholarship, 'a detailed description of the evolution of Dickens's art as a novelist' (p. xiv), which however abjures evaluation: 'No attempt has been made in this book to evaluate Dickens's stature as a novelist' (p. 502).
6. Introduction to *Little Dorrit* in the New Oxford Illustrated Dickens (1953).
   Of course, Trilling wrote first, and the Leavises' silence about his and other excellent Dickens criticism impairs the comparison.
7. It is interesting that Leavis picked on a work with a similar theme for his first detailed illustration of Lawrence's powers as a novelist: see *D. H. Lawrence: Novelist*, ch. 2: 'Lawrence and Class: *The Daughters of the Vicar*'.
8. 'There in the simple *placing*, the simple juxtaposition of the names, is a lot of new work and thinking done. . . . The placing of that unchanged essay ("The World of Bentham") next to "Dickens and Blake", is to make the explicit cultural judgement, to draw up the field differently, to re-empower the chess-pieces by adding new strategic possibilities to them'—Poole, in *Universities Quarterly*, xxix , 78–9. Also, the laudable objections of critics such as Monroe Engel and David Hirsch (see Bibliography) that Leavis had distorted the Dickens canon have now been fully met.
9. George Ford disputes this, rebuking Leavis for hinting that this essay

'single-handedly' pioneered 'a revival of interest in Dickens'—*Nineteenth Century Fiction*, XXVI (1971) 100. But Leavis only says that 'this title and this essay have since been accepted as marking a new approach both to Dickens (and effecting a revolution in Dickens criticism) and to the art of the novel generally' (*Dickens the Novelist*, p. xi). 'Revival of interest' is Ford's interpolation.

For that matter, how can what Leavis actually says be gainsaid? It would require a long enquiry outside the scope of this study to assess the influence of his essay. But such an enquiry might well begin with the examination of Garis's *The Dickens Theatre*—Garis consistently uses Leavis as a sounding-board for his own judgements—and of Robert Morse's critique of *Our Mutual Friend* in *Partisan Review*, XVI (1949) 277—89, and Robert Stange's of *Great Expectations* in *College English*, XVI (1954—5) 9—17. This last has a distinctly Leavis-like beginning: '*Great Expectations* is conceived as a moral fable.'

10. Letter to the *Spectator*, 4 Jan 1963; repr. in *Letters in Criticism*, p. 96.
11. Robert Garis, 'Dickens Criticism', *Victorian Studies*, VII (June 1964) 378—9.
12. Ibid., p. 378. And cf. Georg Lukács: 'Today people repeatedly condemn any serious emphasis on the *what* [of art] as inartistic'—*Writer and Critic*, p. 19.
13. George H. Ford did this with particular efficiency in his review article for *Nineteenth Century Fiction*, XXVI (1971) 95—113, though even he overlooked Leavis's commendatory review of Edmund Wilson's *The Wound and the Bow* in *Scrutiny*, II (1942) 72—3, where Leavis referred to Wilson's essay on Dickens as 'intelligent and illuminating'. How can Leavis have forgotten that he wrote this? Most probably on rereading Dickens he found that Wilson had pursued his psychoanalytic reading of Dickens to the exclusion of the truth that 'the novelist's art is an art of using words', as he phrased it in that review.

   For a sampling of reactions to *Dickens the Novelist*, see, with Ford, K. J. Fielding, *Dickens Studies Newsletter*, II (May 1971) 37—9; Marvin Mudrick, *Hudson Review*, XXIV (Summer 1971) 346—54; W. W. Robson, *Dickensian*, LXVII (May 1971) 99—104.

   Fielding writes with the most equilibrium and common sense: 'It is essential to disregard what its authors say of themselves, as well as of nearly everybody else.' He adds, 'Their greatest achievement in writing on Dickens is still the recognition, as early as the essay on *Hard Times*, that "the final stress may fall on Dickens's command of word, phrase, rhythm, and image: in ease and range there is surely no greater master of English except Shakespeare. This comes back to saying that Dickens is a great poet" [*The Great Tradition*, p. 272]. Although even this observation was not entirely new at the time, it is fair to say that the force and penetration with which it was said did mark a "new approach". What really distinguishes the whole of the present book is its power to express what others have said much more timidly already' (*Dickens Studies Newsletter*, II, 38—9).
14. Introduction to *Towards Standards of Criticism*, pp. 19—20. (See above, p. 8).

   Also see 'How to Teach Reading' (1932), where Leavis follows discussion of 'critical method' with an example of how to read Shakespeare as dramatic poetry, and follows that with 'Prose demands the same approach, but admits it far less readily. . . . With the novel it is so much harder to apply in a critical method the realization that everything that the novelist does is done with words, here, here, and here, and that he is to be judged an artist (if he is one) for the same kind of reason as a poet is. . . . Out of a School that provided the training suggested here might come, not only literary criticism of Shakespeare, but a beginning in the criticism of the novel'—*Education and the University*, pp. 122–6.

15. *Scrutiny*, VI (1938) 437.
16. In a review of Ruth Adam's *I'm Not Complaining*, *Scrutiny*, VII (1938) 85.
17. 'Dostoevsky or Dickens?' (review of William Faulkner, *Light in August*) *Scrutiny*, II (1933) 91–3.
    This review incidentally qualifies Ford's criticism that the Leavises are in their book considerably post-Edmund Wilson in linking Dickens with Dostoevsky, and so very unoriginal. Ford remarks, 'To link Dickens with Dostoevsky, as Wilson did, was an act of real daring at the time his essay was written. To link them again now, thirty years later, as the Leavises do, is a welcome gesture but one no longer calling for a display of nerve'—*Nineteenth Century Fiction*, XXVI, 111. Leavis's review linking them precedes Wilson's essay by six years, even if he does not link them in the way that Wilson does.
18. 'The Americanness of American Literature', *Commentary*, XIV (1952) 466–74; repr. in *'Anna Karenina' and Other Essays*, p. 145. It is of interest to add that Mrs Leavis had published her essay on Hawthorne in the preceding year, as 'Hawthorne as Poet', *Sewanee Review*, LIX, 179–205 and 426–58, and Leavis had been writing his essays on Lawrence's major novels under the head 'The Novel as Dramatic Poem'. In other words, this idea had really taken hold. And in *D. H. Lawrence: Novelist* (p. 18) Leavis added Mark Twain to this list.
19. 'The Critical Writings of George Santayana', *Scrutiny*, IV (1935) 278–95; and 'The Literary Life Respectable', *Scrutiny*, IX (1940) 170–6. And see *The Great Tradition*, pp. 29–31.
20. George Santayana, 'Dickens, 1921', *Soliloquies in England* (1922); repr. in *Selected Critical Writings of George Santayana*, ed. Norman Henfrey (Cambridge, 1968), vol. I, pp. 189, 190 and 192. Compare, for instance, Mrs Leavis's view that the portraits of Sir Leicester Dedlock and Dr Strong are 'the painful guesses of the uninformed and half-educated writing for the uninformed and half-educated'—*Fiction and the Reading Public*, p. 157.
21. 'Charles Dickens', *Inside the Whale* (1940); repr. in Stephen Wall (ed.), *Charles Dickens* (Harmondsworth, 1970) pp. 312–13.
22. *Scrutiny*, XI (1942) 73.
23. Robert Garis, *The Dickens Theatre: A Reassessment of the Novels* (1965) pp. 8, 24 and 39. This is only a Shandean—Joycean Dickens, we might infer.
24. Ibid., p. 53.
25. Ibid.
26. Ibid.
27. Ibid., p. 56. In dealing with *Hard Times*, and with Leavis's critique of that novel, Garis concedes that Dickens is a 'poet of almost Shakespearean calibre', but adds that he lacks Shakespeare's 'regular achievement of complex continuities' (ibid., p. 157).
28. It seems significant that Garis predicates his theory as 'the Dickens problem' (the title to the first section of his study), whereas Leavis talked of 'the challenge of Dickens' (*Letters in Criticism*, p. 96).
29. Garis used the same scene to contrast Dickens's theatrical with Shakespeare's dramatic art (see *The Dickens Theatre*, p. 56). But Mrs Leavis can call Dickens's

'theatrical' when she needs. For instance, in *Our Mutual Friend*, which shows 'very decidedly the breaking-down of Dickens's powers', Mr Boffin is 'a piece of theatrical nonsense resolved with disgusting sentimentality and whimsicality' (*Dickens the Novelist*, p. 116).

30. Robert Giddings, 'The Dickens Forum', *Dickens Studies Newsletter,* VI (June 1975) 47–55. Page references will appear parenthetically after the relevant quotations.

31. In Captain Cuttle we have a good example of *difference* in approach and interest between the Leavises. Leavis finds Cuttle 'boring' (*Dickens the Novelist*, p. 24) and therefore spends little time on him; Mrs Leavis illuminates his part in the meaning of the novel. Similarly, we find Mrs Leavis continually clarifying her account of Dickens by cross-references to minor novelists in whom Leavis has no interest, such as Trollope and Kingsley. Hence she provides a much more satisfying perspective on Dickens as a centre of creativity in the novel than he does, and also evidence of a wider-ranging interest in and knowledge of the novel.

32. Though some readers will remark that the first two belong, according to Mrs Leavis's reading, with folk-tale grotesques, and perhaps even with the Devil of the morality plays; and that Pecksniff is Dickens's version of Tartuffe.

33. The first and last quotations come from 'Why the Novel Matters', and the second from 'Morality and the Novel'; see *D. H. Lawrence: Selected Literary Criticism*, pp. 105 and 110.

34. It is interesting to see how little the word 'moral', and how much the word 'human', occurs in *Dickens the Novelist*. But, if the Leavises have discarded the word, they have not abandoned the concept. Changed circumstances and changed fashions have led them to employ 'human' instead of 'moral'. But by 'human' they mean 'moral'. At least, they signify that it is 'immoral' to be less than human.

35. Lukács, *Writer and Critic*, pp. 18–19.

36. 'He is I think unique, among English and American critics, for trying to establish what we might call a "correspondence theory" of literary truth, as opposed to various aesthetic "coherence theories" of literary truth which have been advanced during the same period, from Eliot through I. A. Richards to the New Criticism and beyond. These latter critics have offered sets of terms in which to think, but these have been sets of terms which bore only on *literary* criteria: Impersonality, Tradition, synaesthesia, irony, paradox, ambiguity, etc. Leavis alone has upheld Realist criticism, struggling to establish a set of terms which intersect with the real world, which "correspond" to life, rather than to accept terms which set up among themselves, very harmoniously no doubt, a merely pleasing "coherence". Leavis, like Lukács, adopts a rigorous fidelity to Reality as an initial stance in which the ethics of the whole critical enterprise consists' (Poole, in *Universities Quarterly*, XXIX, 85).

37. T. S. Eliot, 'The Function of Criticism', *Selected Essays* (1951) p. 25.

38. As Willard Thorp has wittily illustrated in 'The Literary Scholar as Chameleon', in Camden (ed.), *Literary Views*.

39. The essential character of Leavis's criticism closely corresponds to ideals expressed by Leslie Fiedler in 'Toward an Amateur Criticism', *Kenyon Review*, XII (1950) 561–74, and by Douglas Bush in 'The Humanist Critic', ibid., XIII (1951) 81–92. Fiedler believes that 'in *intent*, the good critic addresses the

common reader, not the initiate' because 'the primary act of faith which makes criticism possible compels the critic under any circumstances to speak *as if* to men and not to specialists' (XII, 563); 'the act of evaluation remains . . . the vital center of criticism' (p. 566); instead of 'the sort of jargon most grossly typified in Kenneth Burke, a "treason of the clerks" become diction, anti-humane and autotelic in its implications' (p. 571) the good critic uses 'the language of conversation', in 'his own voice, idiosyncratic, personal', and his vocabulary must be 'humane' (pp. 572—3).

Bush goes further, saying that 'the loss of an active consciousness of our religious, ethical, and cultural tradition is a much worse menace than atomic or hydrogen bombs; and if critics do not labor to preserve and fructify it, who will?'; and that therefore 'the most urgent function of criticism is not to enlarge the learning of the learned, or to refine the perceptions of the refined, but to enlarge the saving remnant' (XIII, 88—9). His critic should set out to create a common reader by 'critical and pedagogical exertion' (p. 91). The relation of these words to Leavis needs no elaboration.

40. As by George Watson in *The Literary Critics: A Study of English Descriptive Criticism* (Harmondsworth, 1973) p. 207.
41. His awareness of mythical levels can be seen in his brief reference to the mythic symbolism of Loerke and Gudrun in *Women in love* (*D. H. Lawrence: Novelist*, p. 176). And see in *Thought, Words and Creativity passim*.
42. See his views on Empson and Richards in *Education and the University*, pp. 71—2.
43. Terry Eagleton, *Marxism and Literary Criticism* (1976) p. 20.
44. MS. letter., 29 Jan 1975.
45. 'There are two reviews of *The Cocktail Party* I should like to see—one by Lawrence and one by Albert Schweitzer'—*D. H. Lawrence: Novelist*, p. 323.

Appendix A

1. 'The Literary Criticism of Frank Raymond Leavis', in Camden (ed.), *Literary Views*, pp. 190—1.

   Cf. also: 'In scholarly terms [Leavis] remains rootedly a British provincial, moved by no perceptible influences except the usual twentyish fixation with France and, in his later years, the nineteenth-century Russian novel. . . . no race of men were ever more exclusively academic than [Leavis and his followers]' (Watson, *The Literary Critics*, p. 207). This bravura performance was well timed by Watson in 1962, the year in which Leavis completed his term as Reader of English at Cambridge—St George of Cambridge debunking the dragon! Not that Watson has much good to say of other critics (see especially his section on Arnold): he himself seems modishly cynical.

2. 'Hawthorne as Poet', *Sewanee Review*, LIX, 179—205 and 426—58; repr. in A. N. Kaul (ed.), *Hawthorne* (Englewood Cliffs, NJ, 1966) pp. 25—63. These quotations are from pp. 26—7.

   Richard Chase interestingly notes that Mrs Leavis's essay is an elaborate restatement of Lawrence's view of Hawthorne in *Studies in Classic American Literature—The American Novel and Its Tradition* (New York, 1957) p. 75. Leavis was in the middle of revaluing Lawrence when she wrote it.

3. See his Introduction to *Pudd'nhead Wilson* (1955). To judge from my own

experience, a whole generation of English readers benefited from this edition by Leavis. It was prescribed reading for my English class at school in 1957.

4. Interestingly, American critics were making a similar plea for *Huckleberry Finn* about the same time: for example, Lauriat Lane, Jr, 'Why *Huckleberry Finn* is a Great World Novel', *College English*, xvii (Oct 1955), 1–5.

5. 'The Americanness of American Literature', *'Anna Karenina'*, p. 146.

6. As for example of James: see *Scrutiny*, xiv (1947) 223–9, and xv (1947) 68–74.

7. 'Melville: The 1853–6 Phase', in F. Pullin (ed.), *New Perspectives on Melville*, (Edinburgh, 1978) pp. 197–228. Page references will appear parenthetically after the relevant quotations.

8. 'Hawthorne as Poet', in Kaul (ed.), *Hawthorne*, p. 25.

9. Dismissing the notion (with a good deal of justice, one must feel) that 'American work in scholarship and criticism has in our time performed the major service to English literature' Leavis adds more controversially, 'The truth is that even the most acclaimed critical work on English authors—Jane Austen, the Brontës, Dickens, George Eliot, D. H. Lawrence—betrays a disqualifying ignorance of the civilisation out of which these authors wrote, and thus an inability to read them. The truth holds from Edmund Wilson downwards'—*English Literature in Our Time*, p. 34. It would help, nevertheless, to know who voiced this opinion and in what context. Leavis does not tell.

10. For an excellent forthright discussion of manners in criticism, see John Fraser, 'Leavis and Winters: Professional Manners', *Cambridge Quarterly*, v (1970) 41–71. Fraser ultimately justifies Leavis's and Winters's brusqueness as a price well worth paying, when criticism is as a whole so timidly and vapidly broad-minded.

11. Significantly, the adjective 'European' crops up again and again when the Leavises mention Dickens (see *Dickens the Novelist*, p. 213; and *English Literature in Our Time*, p. 176). This is new in their criticism and indicates how much their perspectives have expanded. Mrs Leavis's comparison of *Wuthering Heights* with *Jules et Jim* contributes to the expansion.

12. Kingsley Widmer, 'D. H. Lawrence and the Cult of Primitivism', *Journal of Aesthetic and Art Criticism*, xvii (Mar 1959) 353.

13. R. P. Bilan, 'The Basic Concepts and Criteria of F. R. Leavis's Novel Criticism', *Novel: A Forum on Fiction*, ix (Spring 1976) 207–10.

14. Kingsley Widmer, *The Art of Perversity: D. H. Lawrence's Shorter Fictions* (Seattle, 1962).

15. Cf. José Ortega y Gasset's perspective on the importance of art in the modern world in *The Dehumanization of Art* (New York, 1956), where he argues that art in this century has been ridiculing itself and making suicidal gestures merely in order to survive the rampant philistinism, and has consequently become 'a minor issue' (p. 48). The Leavises' *major* achievement has been to keep readers in touch with *major* art.

Select Bibliography

I

Scrutiny, 20 vols (Cambridge: Cambridge University Press, 1963).
A Selection from 'Scrutiny', comp. F. R. Leavis, 2 vols (Cambridge: Cambridge University Press, 1968).
Allum, M., and McKenzie, D. F., *F. R. Leavis: A Check-list, 1924–1964* (London: Chatto and Windus, 1966).

II

Leavis, F. R., 'The Relationship of Journalism to Literature: Studied in the Rise and Earlier Development of the Press in England' (PhD dissertation, Cambridge University, no. 66, 1924). (In Cambridge University Library.)
_____ ,'D. H. Lawrence' (review of D. H. Lawrence, *Nettles*), *Cambridge Review*, 13 June 1930, pp. 493–5.
_____ , *New Bearings in English Poetry: A Study of the Contemporary Situation* (1932; Harmondsworth: Penguin, 1963).
_____ (ed.), *Towards Standards of Criticism* (London: Wishart, 1933).
_____ , and Thompson, Denys, *Culture and Environment: The Training of Critical Awareness* (London: Chatto and Windus, 1933).
_____ , *For Continuity* (Cambridge: Minority Press, 1933).
_____ (ed.), *Determinations: Critical Essays* (London: Chatto and Windus, 1934).
_____ , *Revaluation: Tradition and Development in English Poetry* (1936; Harmondsworth: Penguin, 1964).
_____ , *Education and the University: A Sketch for an 'English School'* (1943; new edn, London: Chatto and Windus, 1948).
_____ , *The Great Tradition: George Eliot, Henry James, Joseph Conrad* (1948; Harmondsworth: Penguin, 1962).

——, *The Common Pursuit* (1952; Harmondsworth: Penguin, 1962).

——, *D. H. Lawrence: Novelist* (1955; Harmondsworth: Penguin, 1964).

——, Introduction to Mark Twain, *Pudd'nhead Wilson* (London: Zodiac, 1955).

——, Foreword to Joseph Conrad, *Nostromo* (New York: New American Library, 1960).

——, Introduction to George Eliot, *Daniel Deronda* (New York: Harper & Row, 1961; London: Panther, 1970).

——, Foreword to George Eliot, *Adam Bede* (New York: New American Library, 1961).

——, *Two Cultures?: The Significance of C. P. Snow* (London: Chatto and Windus, 1962).

——, 'James as Critic', Introduction to *Henry James: Selected Literary Criticism*, ed. Morris Shapira (1963; Harmondsworth: Penguin, 1968).

——, Foreword to Joseph Conrad, *Victory* (Milan: Bompiani, 1964).

——, Afterword to John Bunyan, *The Pilgrim's Progress* (New York: New American Library, 1964).

——, Introduction to George Eliot, *Felix Holt* (London: Everyman's Library, 1967).

——, *'Anna Karenina' and Other Essays* (London: Chatto and Windus, 1967).

——, Introduction to Peter Coveney, *The Image of Childhood* (Harmondsworth: Penguin, 1967).

——, *English Literature in Our Time and the University* (London: Chatto and Windus, 1969).

——, and Leavis, Q. D., *Lectures in America* (London: Chatto and Windus, 1969).

——, and Leavis, Q. D., *Dickens the Novelist* (London: Chatto and Windus, 1970).

——, *Nor Shall My Sword: Discourses on Pluralism, Compassion and Social Hope* (London: Chatto and Windus, 1972).

——, *Letters in Criticism*, ed. John Tasker (London: Chatto and Windus, 1974).

——, *The Living Principle: 'English' as a Discipline of Thought* (London: Chatto and Windus, 1975).

——, *Thought, Words and Creativity: Art and Thought in Lawrence* (London: Chatto and Windus, 1976).

Leavis, Q. D., *Fiction and the Reading Public* (London: Chatto and Windus, 1932).

——, 'Hawthorne as Poet', *Sewanee Review*, 59 (Spring and Summer 1951) 179–205 and 426–58; repr. in A. N. Kaul (ed.), *Hawthorne: A Collection of Critical Essays* (Englewood Cliffs, NJ: Prentice-Hall, 1966).

——, Introduction to Jane Austen, *Mansfield Park* (London: Macdonald, 1957).

——, Introduction to Jane Austen, *Sense and Sensibility* (London: Macdonald, 1958).

——, Introduction to Charlotte Brontë, *Jane Eyre* (Harmondsworth: Penguin, 1966).

——, Introduction to George Eliot, *Silas Marner* (Harmondsworth: Penguin, 1967).

——, Introduction to Margaret Oliphant, *Miss Marjoribanks* (London: Zodiac, 1969).

——, Introduction to *Autobiography and Letters of Mrs Margaret Oliphant*, ed. Mrs Harry Coghill (Leicester: Leicester University Press, 1974).

——, 'Melville: The 1853–6 Phase', in F. Pullin (ed.), *New Perspectives on Melville* (Edinburgh: Edinburgh University Press, 1978) pp. 197–228.

III

Allen, Walter, *The English Novel: A Short Critical History* (1954; Harmondsworth: Penguin, 1958).

Arnold, Matthew, *Essays Literary and Critical* (1906; London: Everyman, 1928).

Austen, Jane, *Selected Letters 1796–1817*, ed. R. W. Chapman (London: Oxford University Press, 1955).

Babb, Howard, *Jane Austen's Novels: The Fabric of Dialogue* (New York: Archon, 1967).

Bentley, Eric (ed.), *The Importance of 'Scrutiny'* (1948; New York: New York University Press, 1964).

Bilan, R. P., 'The Basic Concepts and Criteria of F. R. Leavis's Novel Criticism', *Novel: A Forum on Fiction*, 9 (Spring 1976) 197–216.

Booth, Wayne C., *The Rhetoric of Fiction* (Chicago: University of Chicago Press, 1961).

Bradbrook, M. C., *Joseph Conrad: England's Polish Genius* (Cambridge: Cambridge University Press, 1941).

Buckley, Vincent, *Poetry and Morality: Studies on the Criticism of Matthew Arnold, T. S. Eliot and F. R. Leavis* (London: Chatto and Windus, 1959).

Bush, Douglas, *Jane Austen* (New York: Macmillan, 1975).

——, 'The Humanist Critic', *Kenyon Review*, 13 (Winter 1951) 81–92.

Cecil, Lord David, *Jane Austen* (Cambridge: Cambridge University Press, 1935).

Chapman, R. W., *Jane Austen: Facts and Problems* (London: Oxford University Press, 1948).

Chase, Richard, *The American Novel and Its Tradition* (New York: Doubleday, 1957).

Coombes, H. (ed.), *D. H. Lawrence: A Critical Anthology* (Harmondsworth: Penguin, 1973).

Coveney, Peter, *The Image of Childhood: The Individual and Society—A Study of the Theme in English Literature* (Harmondsworth: Penguin, 1967). Revised edn of *Poor Monkey* (1957).

Crankshaw, Edward, *Joseph Conrad: Some Aspects of the Art of the Novel* (1936; New York: Russell, 1963).

Eagleton, Terry, *Marxism and Literary Criticism* (London: Methuen, 1976):

Eliot, T. S., *Selected Essays* (London: Faber and Faber, 1951).

——, *Selected Prose*, ed. John Hayward (Harmondsworth: Penguin, 1953).

——, *After Strange Gods* (London: Faber and Faber, 1934).

Engel, Monroe, *The Maturity of Dickens* (Cambridge, Mass.: Harvard University Press, 1959).

Fiedler, Leslie, 'Toward an Amateur Criticism', *Kenyon Review*, 12 (1950) 561–74.

Fielding, K. J., review of F. R. and Q. D. Leavis, *Dickens the Novelist*, *Dickens Studies Newsletter*, 2 (May 1971) 37–9.

Ford, George H., *Dickens and his Readers: Aspects of Novel-Criticism since 1836* (Princeton, NJ: Princeton University Press, 1955).

——, *Double Measure: A Study of the Novels and Stories of D. H. Lawrence* (1965; New York: W. W. Norton, 1969).

——, 'Leavises, Levi's and Some Dickensian Priorities', *Nineteenth Century Fiction*, 26 (1971) 95–113.

Forster, E. M., *Aspects of the Novel* (1927; Harmondsworth: Penguin, 1962).

Fraser, John, 'Leavis and Winters: Professional Manners', *Cambridge Quarterly*, 5 (1970) 41–71.

Garis, Robert, 'Dickens Criticism', *Victorian Studies*, 7 (June 1964) 375–86.

———, *The Dickens Theatre: A Reassessment of the Novels* (London: Oxford University Press, 1965).

Giddings, Robert, 'The Dickens Forum', *Dickens Studies Newsletter*, 6 (June 1975) 47–55.

Green, Martin, *The von Richthofen Sisters: The Triumphant and the Tragic Modes of Love* (New York: Basic Books, 1974).

Greenberg, Martin, 'The Influence of Mr Leavis', *Partisan Review*, 16 (Aug 1949) 856–8.

Gross, John, *The Rise and Fall of the Man of Letters* (London: Weidenfeld & Nicolson, 1969).

Gurko, Leo, *Joseph Conrad: Giant in Exile* (New York: Macmillan, 1962).

Harding, D. W., 'Regulated Hatred: An Aspect of the Work of Jane Austen', *Scrutiny*, 8 (1940) 346–62.

Hayman, Ronald, 'Leavis at 80: A Biography', *New Review*, 2 (Oct 1975) 3–24.

———, *Leavis* (London: Heinemann, 1976).

Hicks, Granville, *The Great Tradition: An Interpretation of American Literature since the Civil War* (New York: Macmillan, 1935).

Hirsch, David M., '*Hard Times* and Dr. Leavis', *Criticism*, 6 (Winter 1964) 1–16.

Hyman, Stanley Edgar, *The Armed Vision: A Study in the Methods of Modern Literary Criticism* (1947; rev. edn, New York: Vintage, 1955).

James, Henry, *Selected Literary Criticism*, ed. Morris Shapira (1963; Harmondsworth: Penguin, 1968).

Jarrett-Kerr, Fr Martin, 'The Literary Criticism of F. R. Leavis', *Essays in Criticism*, 2 (1952) 351–68.

———, *D. H. Lawrence and Human Existence* (1951; 2nd edn, London: SCM Press, 1961).

Johnson, Samuel, *'Rasselas', Poems, and Selected Prose*, ed. Bertrand H. Bronson (New York: Holt, Rinehart and Winston, 1958).

Keith, W. J., *Richard Jefferies: A Critical Study* (Toronto: University of Toronto Press, 1965).

Kettle, Arnold, *An Introduction to the English Novel* (1951; New York: Harper & Row, 1968).

———, *Of Books and Humankind* (London: Routledge & Kegan Paul, 1964).

Kilham, John, 'The Use of "Concreteness" as an Evaluative Term in F. R. Leavis's *The Great Tradition*', *British Journal of Aesthetics*, 5 (1965) 14–24.

Klingopulos, G. D., 'The Novel as Dramatic Poem (II): *Wuthering Heights*', *Scrutiny*, 14 (1947) 269–86.

Lane, Lauriat, Jr, 'Why *Huckleberry Finn* is a Great World Novel', *College English*, 17 (Oct 1955) 1–5.

Lascelles, Mary, *Jane Austen and her Art* (1939; London: Oxford University Press, 1968).

Lawrence, D. H., *Selected Literary Criticism*, ed. Anthony Beal (1956; London: Mercury, 1961).

Liddell, Robert, *The Novels of Jane Austen* (London: Longmans, 1965).

Litz, A. W., *Jane Austen: A Study of Her Artistic Development* (New York: Oxford University Press, 1965).

Lodge, David, *The Language of Fiction* (London: Routledge & Kegan Paul, 1966).

Lubbock, Percy, *The Craft of Fiction* (1921; New York: Viking, 1969).

Lukács, Georg, *Writer and Critic* (New York: Grosset and Dunlap, 1970).

Melville, Herman, *Moby Dick*, ed. Harrison Hayford and Hershel Parker (New York: W. W. Norton, 1967).

Miller, J. Hillis, *Charles Dickens: The World of His Novels* (Cambridge, Mass.: Harvard University Press, 1959).

Mizener, Arthur, '*Jude the Obscure* as a Tragedy', *Southern Review*, 6, Thomas Hardy Centennial Issue (Summer 1940) 193–213.

Monod, Sylvère, *Dickens the Novelist* (Norman, Okla.: University of Oklahoma Press, 1968).

Moore, Harry T., *D. H. Lawrence: The Man and his Works* (Toronto: Forum House, 1969).

Morse, Robert, '*Our Mutual Friend*', *Partisan Review*, 16 (1949) 277–89.

Mudrick, Marvin, *Jane Austen: Irony as Defense and Discovery* (Princeton, NJ: Princeton University Press, 1952).

———, 'The Originality of *The Rainbow*', *Spectrum*, 3 (Winter 1959) 3–28; rpt. in Mark Spilka (ed.), *D. H. Lawrence: A Collection of Critical Essays* (Englewood Cliffs, NJ: Prentice-Hall, 1963).

_____, 'Leavis, Dickens, and the Last Days', *Hudson Review*, 24 (Summer 1971) 346–54.

Ortega y Gasset, José, *The Dehumanization of Art* (1948; rpt New York: Doubleday, 1956).

Orwell, George, 'Charles Dickens', *Inside the Whale* (London: Secker and Warburg, 1940).

_____, 'Exclusive Club' (review of F. R. Leavis, *The Great Tradition*), *Observer*, 6 Feb 1949.

Parker, Hershel and Hayford, Harrison (eds), *Moby Dick as Doubloon: Essays and Extracts 1851–1970* (New York: W. W. Norton, 1970).

Phillips, Walter C., *Dickens, Reade, and Collins: Sensation Novelists* (1919; New York: Russell, 1962).

Poole, Roger, '*The Affirmation Is of Life*: The Later Criticism of F. R. Leavis', *Universities Quarterly*, 29 (Winter 1974) 60–90.

Pritchett, V. S., review of F. R. Leavis, *The Great Tradition*, *New Statesman*, 15 Jan 1949.

Richards, I. A., *Principles of Literary Criticism* (1924; London: Routledge & Kegan Paul, 1960).

Robson, W. W., 'The Leavises on Dickens', *Dickensian*, 67 (May 1971) 99–104.

Santayana, George, *Selected Critical Writings*, vol. i, ed. Norman Henfrey (Cambridge: Cambridge University Press, 1968).

Southam, B. C., 'Mrs. Leavis and Miss Austen', *Nineteenth Century Fiction*, 17 (1962) 21–32.

_____, *Jane Austen's Literary MSS* (London: Oxford University Press, 1964).

Spilka, Mark, *The Love Ethic of D. H. Lawrence* (1955; London: Dobson, 1958).

_____(ed.), *D. H. Lawrence: A Collection of Critical Essays* (Englewood Cliffs, NJ: Prentice-Hall, 1963).

Stallman, R. W. (ed.), *The Art of Joseph Conrad: A Critical Symposium* (East Lansing, Mich.: Michigan State University Press, 1960).

Stang, Richard (ed.), *Discussions of George Eliot* (Boston, Mass.: Heath, 1960).

Stange, G. Robert, 'Expectations Well Lost: Dickens' Fable for His Time', *College English*, 16 (1954–5) 9–17.

Steiner, George, *Language and Silence* (London: Faber and Faber, 1967).

Stephen, Leslie, *Hours in a Library*, vol. III (London: Smith-Elder, 1894).

———, *George Eliot* (1902; London: Macmillan, 1926).

Stevick, Philip (ed.), *The Theory of the Novel* (New York: Free Press, 1967).

Thorp, Willard, 'The Literary Scholar as Chameleon', in Carroll Camden (ed.), *Literary Views: Critical and Historical Essays* (Chicago: Chicago University Press, 1964).

Traversi, Derek, 'The Brontë Sisters and *Wuthering Heights*', in *The Pelican Guide to English Literature*, vol. VI, ed. Boris Ford (Harmondsworth: Penguin, 1958).

Trilling, Lionel, *A Gathering of Fugitives* (Boston, Mass.: Beacon Press, 1956).

———, Introduction to Charles Dickens, *Little Dorrit*, New Illustrated Oxford edn (London: Oxford University Press, 1963).

———, 'Jane Austen and *Mansfield Park*', in *The Pelican Guide to English Literature*, vol. V, ed. Boris Ford (Harmondsworth: Penguin, 1957).

Verschoyle, Derek (ed.), *The English Novelists* (London: Chatto and Windus, 1936).

Wall, Stephen (ed.), *Charles Dickens: A Critical Anthology* (Harmondsworth: Penguin, 1970).

Watson, George, *The Literary Critics: A Study of English Descriptive Criticism* (1962; 2nd edn, Harmondsworth: Penguin, 1973).

Wellek, René, 'The Literary Criticism of Frank Raymond Leavis', in Carroll Camden (ed.), *Literary Views: Critical and Historical Essays* (Chicago: Chicago University Press, 1964).

Widmer, Kingsley, *The Art of Perversity: D. H. Lawrence's Shorter Fictions* (Seattle: University of Washington Press, 1962).

———, 'D. H. Lawrence and the Cult of Primitivism', *Journal of Aesthetic and Art Criticism*, 17 (Mar 1959) 344–53.

Wilson, Edmund, *The Wound and the Bow* (1940; New York: Oxford University Press, 1947).

Winters, Yvor, *In Defense of Reason* (New York: Swallow, 1947).

Wright, Andrew, *Jane Austen's Novels: A Study in Structure* (1953; Harmondsworth: Penguin, 1962).

Index